For little blue. You're my safe place. I will always love you!

FINDING FREEDOM AND FORGIVENESS

IN THE LAND OF CANAAN

A Little Girl's Giants

a memoir

FRANCINE WESTGATE

Copyright

Data

Name: Westgate, Francine, 1973—author.
Title: In the Land of Canaan / Francine Westgate
Description: First edition.
LCCN 2024922947
ISBN 979-8-9870340-5-7 (paperback)
ISBN 979-8-9870340-6-4 (eBook)

Editor's Note

Names and details may have been changed to protect the privacy of those mentioned in this publication. This publication is not intended as a substitute for the advice of health care professionals. The publication is based on the author's life experiences. This memoir contains childhood abuse and may contain multiple trauma triggers.

Acknowledgments

I want to thank everyone who encouraged me and helped me along the way.

My husband, William, my sons, Myles, Seth, and Ethan, and my daughter-in-law, Sarah.

My sisters, Charlene Farrington and Pauline Gurske, and my friends, Steven Shelton, Julie Santos, and Tracy Peade, who read the manuscript and provided feedback and encouragement. Selena May Roberts for the photo on the back cover.

My mom and dad for allowing me to share my story without having to candy coat it.

My editors. First, Janice Broyles, who worked with me in the developmental stages. Second, Kathleen M. Kline, who worked with me on the line edits. Third, Kyle Hammersmith, who did the proofreading. Fourth, Erin Sitton, who also edited and proofread the manuscript (twice). And Emily Culver, who answered a million editing questions.

To write this, I went to the deepest depths of my soul, and with a net, I dredged the bottom. These words are what I came up with.

IN THE LAND
OF
CANAAN

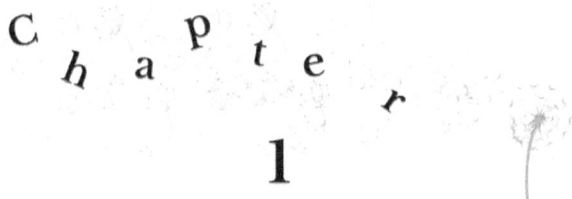

C h a p t e r

1

PANDORA'S BOX

Lynchburg, Virginia: Halloween, 1999

A white car creeps by my house. It turns up the next street and circles back around. It does this several times.

Maybe they're lost. It's too early for trick-or-treaters.

Pushing my curiosity back, I turn away from the window and make my way to the stairwell.

"Boys! Get your feet dressed," I yell. "And don't forget your costumes."

A few minutes later, the sound of gravel crunching outside draws my attention back to the window. The white car comes to a rolling stop in my driveway. I don't recognize the driver or the passenger in the front seat, but when the passenger in the back steps out, *I know her.* Rita is the oldest daughter of a minister at my church, and my newly acquired sister-in-law.

Rita knocks on the kitchen door and asks to use the bathroom. Her clothes reek of pot and cigarettes.

"Who's your friends?" I ask. "I've not seen them before. Does Wayne know you're hanging out with them while he's at work?"

She sweeps a strand of hair behind her ear.

"Leah and Kayne. You know them. They've come to church with me."

"You mean the Kayne who was in jail?"

"They're just friends," she says as she breezes past both me and the boys holding their shoes and firemen costumes.

"Hi," she says, peering over her shoulder at them.

"Hi," they say back.

The bathroom door closes, and the shower turns on. The sound of water spraying the wall and her whispering over the top of it make my brow rise.

I press the small of my back against the kitchen counter and cross my arms. Thirty seconds later, the shower turns off, the toilet flushes, and the door opens. Her tennis shoes squeak across the hardwood floor. A cell phone sticks out of her skirt pocket, and she pulls her T-shirt down to cover it as she makes her way toward me.

"Did Will go to Tennessee for work like he planned?" Rita tilts her head as if curious and pushes her glasses up the bridge of her nose. Then she peers over the thin frames and waits for me to respond.

"*Ayuh*," I say. "He'll be back Friday night. Why?"

"No reason. Call me if you need anything." She takes two steps toward the screen door. Then she stops and turns. "What time are you meeting my mom to decorate the church for the harvest party?"

"Just as soon as the boys get their feet dressed. I've gotta meet the jumpy-house guy at two o'clock. Wanna help?"

Rita raises her hand like a stop sign at me and gives a sarcastic half chuckle. "Have fun with that."

The screen door snaps shut behind her.

The white car backs down the driveway and leaves.

I think nothing more of it until after my husband, Will, returns from Tennessee on Friday night, and two church brothers—Brother Clay and Brother Aaron—come over for their weekly jam session.

Brother Clay and Brother Aaron pass my husband and me in the kitchen on their way to the music room in the basement, where their band name—*39 Stripes*—is painted on the cinder block wall.

"Did someone borrow my equipment?" Brother Clay yells up at us.

Will looks at me, and I shake my head no.

"Why?" my husband calls back with a mouthful of warm brownie he took from the pan.

Footsteps thunder up the stairs. First, Brother Clay, then Brother Aaron appears in the kitchen. Hands spinning like helicopter blades.

"Everything's gone!" Brother Clay says. "My bass and bass amp, his keyboard, your electric guitar, the acoustic guitar."

"You can't be serious," my husband says.

A dry heat sweeps my face as I open the oven door and slide the stuffed shells out.

"Babe, anyone been here while I was gone?"

It's no longer the heat from the oven I feel, but the three sets of eyes boring holes into me like lasers.

"Just Rita," I say.

Just Rita! The one who had served time in jail for stealing a dead woman's checks.

Now Rita's odd behavior makes sense. The white car circling the block, the shower turning on, Rita confirming that my husband had gone out of town, and my plans to go decorate the church for the harvest party. I kick the oven door shut and set the shells on the hotplate in the center of the table.

"It was Rita! She was acting strange."

My husband lets out a strangled yelp. "Call the cops. We've been robbed!"

I throw the oven mitts off, grab the phone from the wall, and make the call.

While waiting for the police to come, my husband calls the pastor. The more Will tells the pastor about the robbery and my suspicion that Rita did it, the louder the pastor's responses become. I can tell by his tone that he's mad—but not at Rita. He's upset at us for calling the police.

We should have notified him first. What were we thinking?

My stomach twists into knots. I gnaw on my fingernails and stare at the steam rising from the stuffed shells.

"What do you mean, come to your house tonight for an emergency meeting?" Will says. "It's nine o'clock. You should be coming over here. It was my house that got robbed, not yours."

He paces the length of the kitchen, all twelve feet of it. The steel-toed boots clomp back and forth over the shiny linoleum, and he grips the phone in anger, making his knuckles turn whiter than a bed full of peonies.

"What do you mean, don't file a police report?" my husband says loudly. "I have to if we want to get our stuff back."

I gulp.

Brother Clay's brow rises like a periscope in enemy waters. Brother Aaron runs his hands up through his hair, keeping them there on top of his head.

My husband inhales and clenches his teeth. When he finally exhales, it sounds like a balloon deflating. His mouth twists with his words.

"But Pastor, why are we being punished? Why are we being made to be the bad guys?"

"Brother Will," the pastor's voice trumpets through the phone. "I forbid you from filing a police report, and if the four of you don't show up for the meeting tonight, you'll be removed from your ministries and sat down for six months."

"But Pastor, how will we get our stuff back?"

"You won't!"

With the pastor's words, I start shaking my head hard and fast.

Please don't say anything else, babe. You know how the pastor is and what will happen if we push back.

I think about Jonah and what I'd been taught in Sunday school about his disobedience. My stomach sinks down, down, down to the bottom of the sea of regret. Regret that we didn't call the pastor first.

Families have been kicked out of the church for less than this. I don't want that to be us. What will our boys do? All their friends go there.

My husband stomps his boot one time, then two, breaking the silence.

"You can't do that. We didn't do anything wrong," he says, squeezing the handset of the phone.

"I can, and I will," the pastor says. "Your wife's vindictive. She's got a grudge against Rita. Rita deserves a second chance."

"Who me?" I say, pointing back at myself.

My husband lets out a gasp.

"You can't be serious. My wife doesn't have a grudge against Rita or anyone. She's one of the kindest people I know. She's given Rita plenty of second chances, and thirds, and fourths. The whole church has. If Rita didn't do it, then she doesn't have anything to worry about...now does she?"

"Brother Will, the ministers will be here within the hour, and if the four of you aren't present, there will be consequences to pay," the voice barks over the phone.

A buzzing sound emanates from the receiver indicating the call ended, and there is a long pause among us in the kitchen, followed by lights. Bright flashing ones shining in the windows.

Two officers step out onto the gravel. One walks around the exterior of the house with a flashlight, and the other approaches the walkway. Another knot forms in my stomach.

My eyes make a silent plea to my husband.

What do I tell them?

My husband motions for a huddle. Brother Clay and Brother Aaron move in closer until their shoulders touch.

"Listen guys, we all know what'll happen if we disobey, so if I can't get your stuff back without having to file a report, I'll give you the cash. It happened at my house. I'm responsible. Deal?"

"Deal," they say as three sharp knocks at the kitchen door send fear surging through my veins.

My hands tremble as I open the door.

"Come in," I say, fixing my dress and my face.

The officer stands in front of the baker's rack with his feet apart. His eyes bounce from us to the stuffed shells to the stack of clean plates with the napkins folded neatly beside them and to our three boys who poke their heads around the corner with wide worried eyes.

I chew my bottom lip and focus on the one brownie missing from the pan. Our Friday night breaking bread together has forever changed.

"Look officer," my husband says, "all we want to know is if we can get our stuff back without filing a police report."

In silence, the officer flips open a small notepad, taps the end of the pen twice. He pauses and looks up.

"Don't you want to put the person in jail who did this?" he asks quizzically.

Put them under the jail would be more like it.

"No, we can't," I say. "You wouldn't understand. Can you just check the pawn shops to see if they have our stuff?"

"It wouldn't do any good. They're not gonna give it back to you without filing a report." His brow disappears beneath the brim of his police ball cap. "Why? You know who did it?"

My eyes drop.

"See! This is what happens," he says. "You don't file a report, and the next time they rob someone they aren't so—"

The kitchen door opens and in rushes my brother-in-law Wayne and Rita.

"Who are you?" the officer asks as his hand moves to his right hip and his gun.

"His little brother," Wayne quickly offers up. "We were on

our way home from the store and saw the lights. Everything okay, Willie?"

"They were robbed," the officer says, his voice flat and deep.

Wayne's long thin neck snaps back in surprise.

I cross my arms and rake my glance past Wayne to Rita.

"Bet you already knew that though, huh?" I say.

She tosses her hands in the air and erupts into tears. "Francine, I can't believe you think I did it. Do you think that too, Will?"

A pause fills the room.

"Willie, how could you, man!" Wayne snatches Rita's hand. "Come on, honey, let's go!"

The door slams.

Red taillights speed up the hill and disappear beyond the graveyard and the poplar trees.

"Maybe we were wrong. Maybe she didn't do it," Brother Clay says.

"If she's guilty, then she deserves an Oscar," my husband replies. "Her performance was, let's just say, believable."

Brother Aaron bobs his head in agreement.

"I know what my gut is telling me," I say. "She did it and now she's gonna get away with it." My eyes water, and I taste the salt of the tears at the back of my throat.

☙❧

THAT NIGHT, I TOSS AND TURN IN MY BED AND CAN'T GET Rita off my mind. I want her to tell the truth. I want the pastor to know I'm a good person. I want my brother-in-law to know I didn't make it up. I want our stuff back and the twelve hundred dollars we gave Brother Clay and Brother Aaron to replace their things.

It's not fair!

I make two fists beneath the blankets and my entire body tenses up like a baby with colic. I haven't felt this kind of anger and injustice since I was a little girl, when all I wanted was for my uncle to tell the truth and for my aunt to believe me.

My eyes water again as I stare at my husband's V-shaped back.

How can he sleep at a time like this?

The pastor's words, the white car, and Rita's suspicious behavior pile up in my thoughts and in my fists, only to empty out with my tears.

I roll over the other way, taking the blankets with me. Snot mixes with tears, and I clench my teeth.

I hate her!

Suddenly, the sound of metal-on-metal sends shivers through my spine and up into my hairline. Red brake lights flash, then stop, flash, then stop.

They're back!

My heart pounds. I try to roll over. To sit up. To move. To call my husband's name—but nothing works, except for my eyeballs. They rotate in their sockets, like when I was a little girl, when night terrors weren't quarantined to sleep, and when monsters, both real and imagined, chased me.

As soon as I am able, I throw the blankets off and zip through the darkness like a field mouse, checking the locks on the windows and doors. When I don't see anything but an old green taxi in the street, I sigh with relief.

I'm not a little girl anymore! I'm a wife! A mom! This reminder comes too little, too late. Pandora's box is open, I can't close it, and from it come all the things I wish to forget.

Back in bed, I pull the blankets around me in hopes that when I wake up, all the fear and anger and injustices will be back in the box where they belong.

I breathe deep and exhale. Breathe deep again and exhale.

I'm fine.

But...am I really? I don't feel fine. I feel like *that* little girl.

My head sinks into the pillow. When I can no longer fight sleep, it yanks me from my bed in Virginia back to the little brown house with the mustard-trimmed door, at night, lying on the top bunk with Patches, our family cat, at my feet and Buster, my stuffed dog, under my arm. The place where fear, anger, and injustice stems. Back to where it all began—back to the land of Canaan, Maine.

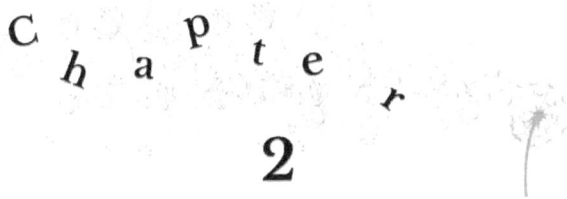

2

THE HOUSE
Canaan, Maine: Blizzard of 1978

My name is Francine, not Frances, Frank, or Fran. Free one—that's what my name means—like the prize inside a Cracker Jack box.

I am five when we move from Florida back to Maine, and it's then I realize three things for sure: My family isn't like everyone else's, giants do exist, and unlike Canaan in the Bible, milk and honey doesn't flow here. It's purchased at the local Shop 'N Save.

This is a land where letters and sounds have their own rules. The *r* sounds like *h* and the *a* sounds like *er*. Soda pop is *soder* pop. Car is *cah*. Dear is *deah*. Polar bear is *polah beah*. And Charlie, my dad, is *Chah*-lie. It's a place where "ah nope" means "no," and the strange word *"ayuh"* with a short-sounding *a* replaces words like "yes" and "okay," and acts as a form of acknowledgment.

Outside the Greyhound bus station, snow falls in sideways spirals. The windshield wipers on my aunt and uncle's red station wagon struggle to move the wet flakes around. Charlene, my twin sister, and Pauline, our older sister by three years, huddle in the back seat with Mum and me, soaking up the warmth of the heater as we listen to "Winter Wonderland" play over the radio.

Aunt Mable's brick-colored hair curls around her stocking cap, her door closes, and she loosens her scarf.

"Wicked good time you picked to move back, Franny," Aunt Mable says to my mum, whose name is Frances, not Francine.

Sensing the tension, I whip my head around to the right to look up at Mum. My brow crinkles.

Are you gonna let her talk to you like that?

But Mum says nothing and stares out the passenger window as if counting snowflakes.

"You girls warm enough?" Aunt Mable asks.

Her upper body shifts again. The scarf lands in her lap. Now she stares into the back seat. Her small beady eyes cling to us three girls like the snow on the windshield wipers.

"Ayuh," Pauline says.

"And the bus ride?" Aunt Mable asks.

Long, I tell myself.

Mum rummages through her pocketbook and pulls out her burgundy cigarette pouch with the gold clasp and torn lighter holder. A click of the gold clasp and out slides a cigarette.

Not another! I shake my head in revolt, remembering the doctor on television saying, "Smoking causes cancer." I'm not sure what cancer is. All I know is that Mum's dad died from it before Pauline was born, and he was a smoker.

The gold clasp clicks shut.

"Oh, fair to middlin' I'd say, Mable. Didn't know you were expectin' a nor'easter." Mum points out the window with the unlit cigarette between her index and middle fingers. "Look, girls, that snowbank is taller than me!" she exclaims, reaching for the lighter.

"That's not sayin' much, Mum. Dad's taller than you standin' on his knees," Pauline says with a giggle.

"Thought you knew everythin'," Aunt Mable breaks in.

I whirl my head the other way to look at Pauline.

Doesn't she? I want to ask her.

"What's-at?" Mum says as if she didn't hear Mable's question.

A beat of silence follows. Then two. The tension thickens like the humidity in Florida on a hot summer day and takes my breath away.

"Helluva storm, ayuh," Uncle Chester pounds out, breaking the tension, and giving me my breath back. The rim of his hunting cap rests on two bushy brows.

Mable gives him a swift whack to the shoulder.

"Keep your eyes on the road, Chester. It's a goddamn greasy mess!" Aunt Mable sputters.

Mum rubs the lighter with her thumb and stares at the snowy pines crawling by.

Aunt Mable's weight shifts in the seat again, and this time she cranes her neck around further to see Mum.

"When's my brother comin' up?" she asks. "Not till after the storm, I hope. Come hell or high water, I ain't comin' back out in this, not even for him. Why if it wasn't for you three girls, I would've—"

"You still pissed, Mable, because I took Pauline to Florida with me? She's my damn daughter, not yours."

Aunt Mable lets out a gasp.

"You could've fooled me, Franny. Why, Chester and I cared for Pollyanna every weekend for three years, while you and my brother drank like fish and acted like hooligans. If it wasn't for us, she'd be an invalid. She was a very sick baby, Franny, or have you forgotten?"

Pollyanna. When did she get that name? I look at Mum with confusion. *Say something! Tell her it isn't true. Tell her you raised Pauline, not her! You did raise her, didn't you?*

But Mum doesn't say anything.

Aunt Mable's eyes move away from Mum to Pauline and give her the once over.

"Lookin' a bit peak-id, hun. Feelin' okay?" Aunt Mable asks. "We still have the spare room set up the way you left it. It's yours whenever you want it. You remember it, don'tcha, Pollyanna?"

Mum lets out a half sigh.

"Charlie and I were different back then," Mum says. "He's gettin' outta' the Navy and finishin' up his discharge papers as we speak. Say, you don't suppose the drive from Florida to Maine will kill 'em, do you, Chester?"

Mum's eyes connect with Uncle Chester's in the rearview mirror and look as if she drinks in his pity.

"Naval Reserves, ayuh?" Uncle Chester says with a soft nod.

"Mmph, that's why we're movin' back. Gonna work on our marriage. Give it another go, you know?"

Mum's words hang in the air. The unlit cigarette bobs between her teeth, and for a moment it's just Bing Crosby I hear, so I hum along.

"Charlie has a mistress!" Mum says, interrupting the radio.

Miss...dress? I sit up straight. *Wait!—Dad has a dress? What's he gonna do with that?*

I peer up at the underneath of Mum's chin and scrunch my nose at her.

"Me and the girls have been livin' in St. Pete while he's been shackin' up in Jacksonville. Say, you don't mind if I smoke, do you, Chester?"

Mum strikes the lighter with a shaky hand and raises it to the cigarette. Her right knee bounces uncontrollably. The orange flame flickers, and she inhales deeply and then deeply some more.

Aunt Mable cranes her neck around further like an owl to eyeball Mum, who sits directly behind her.

"Charlie ain't still drinkin', is he? He damn near killed 'em girls drinkin' and drivin'."

Mum nods in remembrance and purses her lips.

"Does a bear shit in the woods?" Mum responds as she blows smoke and stares straight ahead.

"Oh, that reminds me." Aunt Mable reaches over the seat and touches Pauline's leg. "The pony Chester and I bought you... died. I'm sorry, hun. He's buried in a grave behind Grampy Dodge's garage."

"Flapjack?" Pauline asks. She frowns and pushes a tear aside while staring down at Aunt Mable's hand.

You had a pony? Dad has a dress? I'm startin' to think there's a lot I don't know.

"Dad wears a dress?" I blurt out, unable to squash my curiosity.

"No, ding-ding. Wherever did you get that *idear?*" Mum peers down at me.

"You just said Dad has a dress."

Mum chuckles. "Mis...tress," she annunciates, blowing smoke from her nostrils.

"Oh," I say as if I know what she means now.

The rumble of the engine and warmth of the heater make my eyes heavy. I lay my head on Mum's chest and listen to the chains on the tires rattle.

Suddenly, the little red wagon swerves and tosses me sideways across Charlene's lap and onto Pauline's lap.

"Get off me, dummy," Pauline says with a growl, pushing me up and fixing her eye patch—a square of white gauze and tape.

જ્જ

A HANDFUL OF SONGS LATER, THE WAGON TURNS UP INTO A circular driveway. The tires spin and flick icy clumps of snow in the air.

Mum presses her index finger into the window.

"*Migod*, there it is," Mum says.

My God, there what is? I sit up straight.

"Grammy and Grampy Dodge's house," Mum explains. "Didn't I tell you it was way out in the boondocks? Every Tom, Dick, and Harry this side of the Kennebec knows when you say, 'The House', you mean this one. Need not say more. It's where half of Somerset County comes on Friday and Saturday nights for poker and cribbage."

I look up, way up, at the giant house on the hill. The second story has two long windows spaced apart like eyes, while the first floor has one square window centered below the two long windows. Light from the candlesticks flickers in all three windows and makes a giant jack-o'-lantern face through the snow.

My eyes make their way up to the two narrow chimneys on the roof, and I gulp.

I sure hope Santa can fit.

Above the eave, a metal rooster splits the snowy sky with the letters 'N', 'S', 'E', and 'W'. Black smoke billows from the rooftop and mixes with the white fluff falling from the dark clouds by the bucketful. The scent of birchwood and dried oak drown the smell of Mum's second cigarette smoldering in the built-in metal ashtray on the back of the passenger seat. She pushes the ashtray shut and lights another cigarette.

Out of the corner of my eye, the curtain on the door sashays and a lone face appears.

"You girls ready to see Grammy and Grampy Dodge?" Mum asks, sliding the burgundy cigarette pouch back into her pocketbook.

"Ayuh," we say, wagging our booted-feet and mitten-hands.

"We'll be stayin' here for apiece. Your father's got some work to do on our house before we can move back in."

Our house? Back in? We have a house up here?

I smile with chapped lips and look around for "our house."

Pauline slants her head and points past me.

"That's where we lived before we moved to St. Pete."

In the snowy distance, beyond the garage and tow truck, is a tiny brown house with snow up to the windowsills and two feet of snow on the roof. It's hardly visible, like a flea in a sandstorm.

"Your father built it with his bare hands. Not much to look at, but it's ours," Mum says. "It ain't got runnin' water or a commode, but you twins will get use to the pisspots and the slop buckets. Pauline sure did."

Pauline glances my way with her one eye.

"You don't wanna know," she says low and slow as if to read my mind.

"Could be worse," Mum says. "Beats havin' an apple-knocker, I tell you."

Apple-knocker?

Mum's words make my brow raise.

"An outhouse, ding-ding. Apples fall from the tree and land on the roof. That's where it gets its name. Great-Grampa Hunt had one. Correction, has one."

"It's not like we didn't offer," Aunt Mable says with a huff.

"I'm not touchin' that with a ten-foot oar," Mum says. "Thank you for the ride. C'mon, girls."

Not touching what with a ten-foot oar? And what's an oar anyhow?

Mum throws the strap to her beige pocketbook over her shoulder and steps out into the deep snow. Her red galoshes sink into the white fluff.

"Any deeper and the snow will be up to my wazoo," Mum says with a squeal.

Just then, Uncle Chester's big burly arms swoop down and scoop up Pauline, Charlene, and me from the back seat. He lugs us up the snowy steps to the chipped red door where a woman with badger-streaked hair greets us with a lopsided smile, smoking a cigarette she clenches between her teeth. This is Grammy Dodge. I know this because she introduces herself as such. My dad has the same long nose as hers—an English nose, Mum calls it.

Across the dimly lit kitchen and through a haze of cigarette smoke, a man slouches over a giant oval table with a bottle of beer in his hand and a cigar in a glass ashtray by his elbow. His hair is as white as the flag on a deer.

He takes a sip and sets the bottle down.

"Franny...Girls." He nods.

"Well, don't just stand there. Say hi to Grampy—" Mum says.

"Hi Grampy," we say.

His face isn't familiar.

There's a tall Christmas tree in the corner of the kitchen and a small ceramic one on the counter with tiny colorful lightbulbs. The snap, crackle, and pop of the woodstove draws my attention, and I slowly approach it.

Mum grabs an ashtray from the stack on the tiki-looking bar with a grass hut roof, beside the poker chips and cribbage board.

"Don't touch that, ding-ding. It'll bite," Mum says to me.

I snatch my hand back and eye the flames through the cast iron hole.

A toilet flushes. I stare past the woodstove into the dining room at the door that opens. A scruffy man steps out. Well, he's younger than my dad but way older than me. He's big, like a giant, and dirty. I crinkle my nose. His boots sound heavy, like him. He's coming toward me.

The scruffy man stops in front of me and peers down. His hand gives my pigtails a quick toss.

"I'm Uncle Jerry, your dad's little brother," he says.

"Little my ass," Mum says with a snicker, flicking the ash in the ashtray. "You gotta be a sophomore in high school by now, ain'tcha, Jerry?"

"Ayuh, that is, 'til I quit," he laughs.

Without saying a word, I cast my eyes on Uncle Jerry's grimy boots and work up, over his potbelly to the patch of scruff on his chin and to his beady eyes that resemble Aunt Mable's. Then I take a giant step back from the tickle fingers he makes at me.

"Koochie koochie koo," he says, poking my ribs.

He smells of sweat, stale beer, and motor oil. His rough hands pick me up and cradle me, and then he tickles me more. It makes me uncomfortable, like the blisters on my heels from the boots I wear.

Mum smiles.

"You'll make a wicked good father one day, Jerry, ayuh," she says with the cigarette dangling out of the corner of her lips.

Grammy Dodge reaches for the hard-shell suitcase and Mum grabs the green military bag.

We follow Grammy and Mum up the staircase behind the tiki bar. As I near the top, I almost scream. A headless monster stands on the landing. My heart pounds, and I choke back a yelp. The hairs on my neck raise.

Grammy chuckles and keeps walking.

"It's a sewin' mannequin. It won't bite, dear," Grammy says.

The hallway is long, dark, and spooky. To the left is a windowless cubby with a slanted ceiling and a mattress on the floor. Beside the mattress is a tiny blue lamp with a broken shade.

"This is your Uncle Jerry's room. It used to be a closet, but when you've had *fowah*-teen kids like me, you learn how to improvise." Fourteen—the number of jelly beans in my pocket.

Mum blows a plume of smoke and chases it down with a phlegmy cough.

"Shithead to the rest of us," Mum says. "That's been Jerry's nickname for as long as I can remember. All the way back when your great Uncle Larry would say, 'Show me your pickle and I'll give you a nickel.' Shithead would and your great uncle did."

I'm not sure what Mum is babbling about. I tune her out, stare straight ahead, and focus on the room with the warm glow. The hairs on my neck still stand on end from the headless doohickey.

As we step further down the hall, the wood planks creak and groan.

Passing a small crawl space on the left, I yank the knob and a tiny door opens.

"That's where the ghosts live," Mum says.

I jump back and trip over Pauline's clunky shoe with the one-inch lift for her shorter leg.

"What's wrong?" Pauline asks, cocking her head to get her lazy eye to focus. "Chicken or somethin'?"

"So, what if I am?"

"Oh, hark. You girl's oughtta' be used to ghosts by now," Mum says. "Our house in Florida was haunted, or did you forget that already?" She takes a quick drag and points to the right. "Over there... when your aunts were itty-bitty... they saw glowin' pig eyes lookin' at 'em in that there window."

Charlene's eyes widen, and she gnaws on her fingernails. I grab Mum's hand and squeeze. My palms sweat and my heart pounds out of my chest.

Closer to the room with the warm glow is a second staircase, fancier than the one we climbed at the other end of the house.

In the room with the light, Grammy Dodge sets the suitcase on the bed and kisses us girls on the forehead.

"Good night. See you in the mornin', dears."

"Night, Grammy," we say.

Mum opens the suitcase and pulls out three sets of pajamas with plastic soles.

"Get your jammies on and go to sleep," she orders.

The bedroom is chilly. I slide my feet into the leg holes fast.

From the fancy stairwell, Uncle Jerry's beady eyes peer between two pickets with a look of appraisal that makes me uneasy.

"Take a picture, Shithead, it'll last longer," Mum says without having to turn around, because she's got eyes in the back of her head.

"Night, Franny," Uncle Jerry says.

One... two... three... four... five... six... seven... eight... nine... ten boot steps I count. The creaking of the floorboards stops, and a dim light stretches into the hallway from the little room with the slanted ceiling.

Mum places her cigarette in the ashtray she brought upstairs with her.

"Quick. Under the covers. Santa's on his way. You don't want him to fly over The House and keep goin', do you?" Mum asks.

Forgetting about the ghosts, I shake my head feverishly and throw myself back onto the mattress, my head landing in the center of the daisy pillowcase.

"Does Santa know we moved? Do you think he got the letter

we mailed him? How far away is the North Pole? Do you think he got me the dog I asked for?" I fire off questions one after the other.

Mum tucks the blankets in around me.

"Ayuh...ayuh...ayuh...and ah nope. Now close your eyes, birdbrain, before Santa changes his mind and you get a lump of coal."

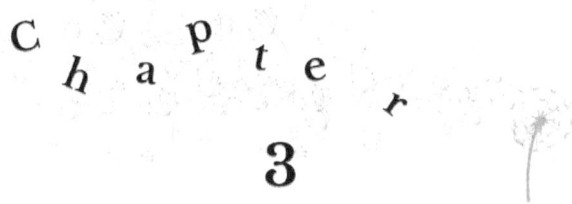

C h a p t e r

3

NAUGHTY OR NICE?

First thing in the morning, I bounce out of bed and down the hallway. I make it past the headless doohickey and descend the staircase. At the bottom, near the coat rack and boot stash, I make a beeline across the gold-colored brick linoleum to the tall Christmas tree in the corner of the kitchen.

To my left, Grammy Dodge sits in her rocking chair with a steamy cup of Red Rose tea in her hand, the tag hanging over the rim.

"Santa ain't come yet, dear," she says.

I frown down at the brick linoleum.

More plastic soles pitter-patter down the stairs and line up beside me. Pauline and Charlene's shoulders collapse like umbrellas upon the sight of the empty tree skirt.

Mum, now downstairs from the room beside the one we girls slept in, yawns and makes her way to the coffee pot with a freshly lit cigarette between her fingers.

"I have it on good mind Santa won't be much longer. His sleigh broke down in New York City. Why don'tcha girls go play on the sunporch," Mum says.

My pajama feet scuff along the linoleum to the sliding glass doors where the sun shimmers through. I map out in my mind which chimney Santa will come down and scrape the frost from the glass with my fingernail to form a peephole.

I peer out the hole at the snow still coming down and give a startling gasp.

"Have you ever?"

"No, I never," Charlene answers, drawing her head back with an even bigger gasp.

"I have," Pauline admits.

My eyes dart around the sunporch.

"Maybe Santa ain't comin'?" Charlene says with a frown.

I put my hand on my hip and slide one pajama foot forward.

"But he's gotta, we've been nice!"

Pauline lets out a low growl.

"Ah nope, dummy! We've been nice, you've been naughty."

"Nah uh," I say.

"Uh huh," she says. Her lazy eye shuffles back and forth. "What 'bout the toothpick?"

Her tongue pushes against her cheek, making a clicking sound as she speaks. Coordination damage, Mum calls it. A combination of Pauline having rheumatic fever as a baby and the hospital giving her too much oxygen at birth.

My plastic sole taps the floor.

"What 'bout it?" I ask.

"Duh, you broke your eardrum and blamed it on Charlene."

"Nah uh."

"Uh huh."

I stick out my tongue and spray spit. "So that doesn't count. I was seein' if it would come out the other side."

"Well, genius, did it?" Pauline asks. The gaze of her good eye pins me to the wall like the tail on the donkey game.

Mum steps onto the sunporch with a bag of cranberries and rattles a jar of popcorn kernels. The sound reminds me of the macaroni maracas that Charlene and I made in kindergarten last month.

Mum's frizzy ponytail springs from the rubber band and frames her face.

"I have a wicked good *idear*," Mum says. "Follow me."

We follow her to the oval table where Grampy sat the night before. Soon the smell of popcorn fills the air. Each of us watches intently as Mum pours the cranberries into one bowl, the popcorn into another, and then she threads a needle.

"You twins sit here, and Pauline, you sit there. Let's string 'em."

String what?

"First a popcorn, then a cranberry, popcorn, cranberry, popcorn, cranberry, popcorn...like this," Mum says, stabbing each of them with the needle.

"Your turn," Mum says, handing me the needle.

I grab two pieces of popcorn. One goes on the string, the other in my mouth. Then two cranberries. One goes on the string, the other in my mouth, and straight back out into the bowl of cranberries.

"Yuck!" I say, wiping my mouth.

Mum smacks me in the ear hole, takes the needle from my hand, and passes it to Pauline, who holds the needle up to her good eye with a piece of popcorn in the other hand. Her good eye stares at the needle, while her lazy eye stares off to the side at me.

Soon popcorn and cranberries fill the string, and Mum ties a knot and cuts the needle loose. Then throws on her red galoshes and fake fur.

"You ding-dings comin' or just gonna stand there like a couple of statues?" Mum asks.

Eagerly, we throw on our coats and boots. We trail behind Mum to the crabapple tree in Grammy's front yard, stepping in her boot prints and sinking as we go.

Mum drapes the edible treat over some branches. Before we can make it back up the snowy hill, a walnut-sized bird discovers it.

"Look, girls," Mum says, "it's a black-capped chickadee. Maine's state bird, unless you count the mosquito, that is."

I turn to see the chickadee pecking at the edible decoration. Soon, other birds join. They hammer the popcorn and cranberries with their itty-bitty beaks, etching patterns in the snow with their tiny twig feet as they compete for a spot on the branch.

Once back inside where it is warm, I kick off my boots. Sitting Indian style on the sunporch, I think about the birds with their cream bibs and black feathery heads.

Out of nowhere, the tinkering of bells catches my ear. I lift my cheeks from my palms. Buzzing with joy, I race from the sunporch to the front door and quickly slide on my boots for a second time.

As I hurry down the snowy steps, doing a jig all the way, a cherry fire truck with silver bells the size of apples on its sides plows up the driveway. The headlights dip and bow, and the tires leave chained hoof-prints in the deep snow.

My spindly fingers reach for the fire truck. I pet it as if it were a real reindeer. The driver's side door opens, and my sapphire eyes ascend to meet the man in the suit.

It's Santa!

I suck in an icy breath.

"I knew you would come!" I exclaim.

Santa's jolly belly bobs beneath his suit. I bat my eyelashes and hope for something more than the lump of coal that Mum and my sisters say I deserve.

An elf in a fireman's hat hands Pauline, Charlene, and me each a gift. I jump up and down and claw at the red and green wrapping paper to find a brown stuffed dog with a black button nose.

"Buster! Your name will be Buster," I say, squeezing my stuffed dog tightly.

As quickly as Santa came, he went, and the echoes of his "ho-ho-hos" disappear into the whiteness of the blustery day.

THE NEXT WEEK DAD ARRIVES FROM FLORIDA. I'M GLAD because I don't like the way Uncle Jerry plays hide-and-seek in the house with me. Or how he tickles me against my will. Or how he jumps out from behind things and scares me. Or how he snaps a wet towel on my bare skin. Or how he pinches me and makes me cry.

In a few more weeks, on move-in day, Mum and Dad march Charlene, Pauline, and me up the snowy footpath past the garage, where Grampy Dodge and Uncle Jerry work on a client's engine. Uncle Jerry holds a wrench, leans his dungaree hip against the bumper, and stares at us as we pass by. How he stares gives me the heebie-jeebies. I hate how he keeps his head down and peers up at the same time. I keep my focus forward until I reach the tar-papered side of the garage and can see the four-foot-tall rusty brown hand pump buried neck-deep in the snow outside of our little brown house. Each window is a different shape and size.

Mum drags the green military bag and blue hard-shell suitcase up the three rickety steps. I tuck Buster under my arm. Pauline and Charlene hold their stuffed animals—the ones the elf gave them.

From the stoop, when facing the mustard-trimmed door, I can see Grammy Dodge's house three telephone poles to the right, and Aunt Mable's trailer one telephone pole to the left. All three properties sit on the same side of Nelson Hill Road. We all use the same footpath to travel back and forth between our three houses.

Mum pushes the door open and steps over the threshold.

"Ta-dah," she says, holding her arms out wide.

I stand on the grimy linoleum and take in the sight. The front section of the house is small and rectangular. The ceiling is covered in splintery sheets of wood—sheets that appear to be a blend of sawdust and wood chips. A kerosene heater sits on the floor in front of the stove and gives off heat. Straight ahead, a plaid blanket hangs over the doorway leading to the back of the house, trapping the heat in the front of the house.

To the right of me is the kitchen area. I know this because of the round table with four chairs. The linoleum peels back like the plastic on a single slice of cheese. An old wringer washer is crammed in the corner beside a teetering stack of what-nots, and the noisy Frigidaire hums like the power lines. Two sets of cabinets hang on the wall—a set of brown wood cupboards and a set of metal ones with peeling white paint. On the counter beside the sink sits two white five-gallon buckets with lids to store water in. Mum opens the rusty doors below the sink so we can see. Under it, two more five-gallon buckets sit to catch the run-off, which empties from the drains.

"These are slop buckets," she explains. "It's where the dishwater empties out. When the buckets get full, we empty 'em in the ditch."

"Oh," I say, staring at the three peas and handful of corn floating on top of the greasy water in the bucket.

To the left of me is the living room. A double-oven stove with six burners takes up space on the carpet beside the armchair with muted-orange flowers. A bulky television rests on a weathered, boxy, blue oak stand with rabbit-ears and a coax cable trailing up to the roof. Mum's charcoal drawings hang on the wall where three different layers of wallpaper are peeling off. A Maine-shaped wood clock, pine shelves lined with trinkets, and a deer tapestry are there too. The tapestry hangs above the musty divan held up by four blocks of wood with matching muted-orange flowers—like the armchair. Beside that, a sad, old, mauve-colored armchair with the bottom falling out. The carpet is a mishmash of free carpet samples Mum had arranged and tacked down.

Because the front of the house is small, Charlene, Pauline, and I only need to take eight steps across the floor to the plaid blanket hanging over the doorframe leading to the back of the house. Mum opens the blanket, and we take one more step up into the hallway with our stuffed animals in tow.

A dimly lit bulb hangs from the ceiling with a long pull string. I cross my arms and shiver from the drop in temperature.

Mum's icy breath mixes with ours and creates a low hanging cloud over our heads.

"No heat back here. Just up front," Mum says. "And that even gets cut off at bedtime. It won't kill you. It'll make your blood thicker."

"I wanna go back to Florida," Charlene says. Her teeth clatter.

"Me, too," I say, "I miss Sunday school and Pastor Craig and climbin' the orange tree."

"You poor abused babies," Mum says.

My eyes adjust to the dim light and the dark paneling lining the narrow hallway, and four doorframes come into view—two on the left and two on the right. Three of them have blankets hanging over them for privacy, and one has a door.

Pauline, Charlene, and I shuffle down the striped carpet past a long metal bookshelf to the first hanging blanket on the right, which is Pauline's bedroom. The walls, floor, shelves, and ceiling are covered in the same wood as the living room ceiling. I reach my hand out and touch the strange wall.

"It's rougher than a cat's tongue." I pull my hand back before getting a splinter.

"It's particle board," Mum says. "Your father put shellac on it and trimmed it with a two-by-four. Whatcha' think?"

I'm not sure, so I shrug, and look past Mum. A small bed sits in the corner on a braided rug that partly covers the particle board floor. A piece of clear plastic hangs over the small window between two sets of shelves.

Across from Pauline's bedroom is the bathroom also made of particle board. A cabinet with a mirror hangs on the wall with no sink or cabinet below it. A checkered curtain hangs over the doorframe, and two five-gallon buckets with lids rest against the particle board wall with a toilet paper holder screwed into the wood between them. *The pisspots*, I assume and plug my nose with my fingers.

The room beside the bathroom belongs to Charlene and me. I stick my head past the hanging blanket into the room and eye the built-in shelves and built-in toy box made from the same combination of wood as the rest of the house. Above the toy box is a window covered in clear plastic. To my right is another window covered in the same plastic and a set of handmade bunk beds built of particle board and two-by-fours. The mattresses come from the yellow foam Dad got from the upholstery shop in Skowhegan. The ceiling is missing a section and a sheet of plastic covers the gaping hole. Wind from the attic beats against the plastic and creates ripple effects across the ceiling.

Pauline hobbles to the window above the built-in toy box and points to Aunt Mable's trailer through the plastic.

"I wanna see Aunt Mable," Pauline says, "I miss her."

Mum sighs loudly. "That's one person I don't wanna see right now."

Pauline peers up at Mum with her one good eye. "Aunt Mable's nice to me. At least she used to be until we moved away."

"Hark the complaints!" Mum says as she takes two steps across the hallway to the only room in the house with a door.

She turns the knob. We lean in to look.

More particle board? I sigh.

"Your father sleeps in the nude, so if you girls know what's good for you, you'll knock first. Lest you get an eye full. You don't want that, now do you?"

"Ew, gross," Pauline says. Her cheeks turn pink with the laughter she holds back. When she can no longer hold it, she grabs her belly and lets out a long, vibrating laugh that sounds like the Woodpecker on Saturday morning cartoons.

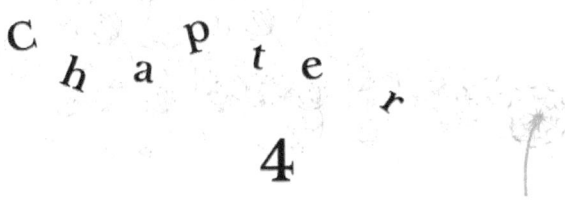

Chapter 4

THREE LITTLE PIGS

On the first day of kindergarten, following Christmas break, I awaken to the sound of Mum's alarm clock erupting through the house. I cover my ears.

Turn that dang thing off!

The blaring stops.

Voices travel through the thin paneled walls.

"Good mornin', babe," I hear Mum say.

"Hmph. Mornin'," I hear Dad say back.

I picture Mum and Dad lying in their bed beneath the electric blanket, warm and cozy, and wish we girls had the same luxury. Squeezing my eyes shut, I pretend to be sunning on a hot sandy beach.

"Smoke?" Mum asks.

"You betcha'," Dad says.

Their box spring squeaks, letting me know that Mum's getting out of bed to wake us up, and Dad's getting out of bed to turn the kerosene heater on at the front of the house.

Another noise almost as loud as the alarm clock erupts. It's the sound of Dad blowing his nose with such force that his brains could have come out.

Mum lets out a series of wet coughs. Allergies or pollen or

something like that, at least that's what she always says. Her slippers shuffle to their bedroom door, it opens, and she crosses the strip of carpet in the hallway to our doorway. The blanket shifts. Mum pops her head in.

"Mornin' sleepy heads—rise and shine."

"I'm wicked cold," Charlene says. Her teeth clatter.

"Ayuh, me too," I say, blowing into my hands to warm the tip of my nose.

"Ain't much I can do 'bout it," Mum says. "There ain't no heat back here. You girls oughtta' know that."

Charlene's frosty puff of breath rises from the bottom bunk and mixes with my frosty puff of breath where I am huddled under the covers on the top bunk with only my face sticking out. Our teeth rattle in unison, like a pair of musical spoons. I wait for Mum's usual response, "You poor abused babies." But she doesn't say it. Not this time.

Mum leans against the doorframe in her flannel nightgown and bathrobe. She takes a drag of her cigarette. The orange glow highlights her face and frizzy lion's mane. Her right index finger tickles her ear hole, and she shakes it fitfully to scratch the itch.

My eyes follow the plume of grey smoke funneling from the cigarette to the hole above my head, where the sheet of loosely hanging plastic separates me from the open attic.

"Your father turned the kerosene heater on up front. Should be warm in apiece. Up and at 'em."

We scramble from beneath the covers and zip, like two field mice down the icy hallway, down the one step pushing aside the thick hanging blanket that separates the back of the house from the front. We make a beeline to the magic flame radiating from the tin box.

Charlene, Pauline, and I huddle on the linoleum in front of the heater in our one-piece pajamas with plastic-sole feet—with the front of the house as cold as the back, we rub our hands together in front of the flame.

"It's colder than a witch's tit in a brass bra," Pauline says as she lets out a giant shiver. The flame licks the white puff of breath coming off her lips.

"Don't let Dad hear you say that," I whisper.

"Why not?" she says sharply, her good eye zeroes in on me. "Uncle Jerry says it."

"Ayuh. He also says the 'C' word, and Mum said nobody should ever say that. Never not ever."

"The four-letter 'C' word?" Charlene asks softly, her eyes growing wide with surprise.

I nod.

When the front of the house is warm and the color in our hands return to normal, Charlene and I throw on our matching outfits and prance around the living room with our strawberry tote bags full of school supplies.

Pauline isn't happy about finishing out the third grade in a new school and moves at the pace of a ninety-eight-year-old box turtle.

"Keep fartin' around, slow-poke," Mum tells Pauline, eyeing the clunky shoes with the lift. "You're gonna miss the bus. Now dress your feet."

Pauline crinkles her nose.

"Not 'em shoes, Mum, puh-lease!"

Mum smashes the Marlboro filter in the ashtray and clicks open her burgundy pouch. Another cigarette slides out.

"Guess you're shit outta' luck, now ain'tcha?" Mum says, raising the cigarette to her lips.

The Bic flicks.

Pauline hobbles from the heater to the flowered armchair with the clunky brown shoes in hand.

"If life's a bowl of cherries, then I'm the pits," she says.

"Poppycock! 'Em shoes ain't gonna kill you. Oh, here. I nearly forgot." Mum dangles Pauline's bracelet in the air with a glint of satisfaction. "Here's your thing-a-ma-jiggy."

Pauline's fingers grab and pull at the medical bracelet. A silver snake wrapped around a stick, and a purple cross in the background can be seen on the charm—the one she got when she nearly died in the hospital from penicillin.

Mum sits Indian style in her sad old chair with her worn nightgown on and no underwear. She taps the cigarette against the ashtray.

"Which one of you twins is first?" she says.

Mum holds a brush and a container of pigtail holders in her lap.

"Not me," Charlene says with her honey-colored hair in a tangle.

"Is that so?" Mum says.

Her gaze forces Charlene to her knees, where she lands unwillingly on the burgundy carpet sample tacked down in front of the sinking mauve chair. Charlene always says her scalp is sensitive and the thought of a brush touching it makes her wince. A handful of tangles later, I take Charlene's spot on the carpet.

Mum is knowledgeable and enjoys educational activities: books, languages, Latin, cultures, PBS, medical dictionary, National Geographics, archeological magazines, Jeopardy, Wheel of Fortune, and crossword puzzles. But one thing she isn't so knowledgeable about is the need to wear underwear. Especially when sitting Indian style in a nightgown. I shake my head.

"What's the matter with you, ding-ding?" Mum asks.

"No underwear," I say.

Mum lets out a whinny of a laugh, and Pauline joins her.

"What?" Mum adds, "I ain't got nothin' you girls ain't got."

The whinnies travel back and forth between them like two horses on a trot.

"That's not the point, Mum," Pauline says with a devilish grin.

Mum tightens the last purple yarn ribbon on my chestnut-colored pigtails.

"Now hurry up," Mum says, looking at Pauline, who's still laughing.

A pause.

"Oh, geesh, almost forgot." Mum reaches for the blue pen beside the gauze and medical tape that lay on the side table with the fisherman wearing a yellow slicker lamp.

Pauline's laughter fades and her cheeks turn from a rosy pink to a flaming red.

"I don't wanna wear the eye patch. The kids will make fun of me," Pauline says as she takes off her glasses with thick lenses.

"Quit bellyachin' and kneel. You wanna go blind?"

Pauline's lips make a straight thin line.

"Ask me if I care," she says as her eyes appear to follow the blue pen back and forth, up and down, left to right that Mum holds up in front of her.

"I feel wicked funny." My hands clutch my tummy.

"Collywobbles," Mum responds. The pen still moving from left to right in front of Pauline's eyes.

"Colly—who?" I ask.

"Just nerves. Classic case of the butterflies. Now get your coat on and stop dilly-dallyin'."

Sixty seconds later, Mum sets the pen back on the side table. She picks up and folds a piece of gauze, and then places four pieces of white tape on the corners. Not wanting to miss the bus, Charlene and I step over Pauline's coat lying in a heap.

"Bye, Mum," I say, swinging open the door, and turning back long enough to give her a mittened wave.

"I didn't raise you in a barn. Close the door," Mum says, shooing Charlene and me with her hand that holds a cigarette between two fingers.

We step out onto the snowy stoop and wait for Pauline. Goosebumps press through my coat, and I listen for the sound of the bus in the distance.

Hercules-sized icicles hang from the eaves and extend into the snowdrift below like glass prison bars. Everything is white, including the topside of the carrot nose on the snowman we made yesterday. The snow buries cars, bushes, and mailboxes. I peer down the white footpath three telephone poles to my left at The House and quickly back, afraid the headless doohickey will appear in the window if I stare too long.

"Did you see it?" Charlene asks.

I turn half a degree and eyeball her.

"The ghost," she says, her lips no longer a soft pink but a silver blue.

I shrug. Facing the road, I glance down the path again. This time, the florescent light over Grammy's kitchen sink flickers. Positive the ghost winked, I turn the opposite direction and face Aunt Mable's trailer, one telephone pole to the right. I white-knuckle my tote bag and wait for Pauline, the more experienced bus rider, to come out.

Minutes later, the door opens and out hobbles poor one-eye.

"What's the matter with you knuckleheads?" Pauline asks. "Think you'd seen a ghost or somethin'," her tongue clicks as she speaks.

"What if we did?"

Her elbow plunges into my rib.

"Hey," she shouts.

"Hey, what?" I shout back, wincing in pain.

"The bus," she points.

The excitement awakens Snoopy, our newly acquired basset hound. He claws at the door and howls to get out. Pauline cracks open the door to say goodbye and before she can close it, the curious and quick Houdini breezes past her bad leg and escapes into the snowy white woods across the road.

The bus races toward our little brown house and slows to a stop. The sound of the brakes scares the crows lining the wires. Thousands of caws sound as one section at a time spread open their wings and darken the skies like a partial solar eclipse.

A stop sign springs from the side and a prism of red lights reflect on the snow-covered road and trees. I climb the steep steps and plop down in the same high-back seat as Charlene and wait for slow-poke to make her debut. The bus should be equipped with a second sign to read, "Pauline Crossing."

As Pauline reaches the top step, laughter erupts, and it leaps like fiery embers from one green seat to the next.

Are they laughing at me? Or at Pauline's pirate-eye and pilgrim shoes?

"Catch that dog!" the bus driver yells. His seatbelt flies off and he jumps to his feet.

Dog? What dog?

No sooner than the thought crosses my mind, something sweeps against my legs and keeps going under the seat. Then it hits me, as it appears to hit Charlene and Pauline by the faces they make.

"Fiddlesticks! What's Snoopy doin' on here?" I say, throwing my palms on my cheeks and looking at both of my sisters.

A firework of laughter erupts.

I lunge into the aisle and snag his back paw, but the quick Houdini slips through my mittens. Charlene crawls under the seat to head him off, and Pauline limps like Tiny Tim down the center aisle. Loud snickers fuel his skittish movements.

Snoopy scampers to the rear of the bus, where two girls stomp their feet to send him back our way, but not in a helpful way.

"Look, it's *The Three Little Pigs*," two girls say, plugging their noses as we chase the dog back and forth, like Mum's blue pen.

The kids bend over the seats with laughter and look as though they'd been sawed in two by some magic trick.

Here comes that little rascal now!

I plant my feet in the aisle and ready myself. And with a giant leap, I lasso Snoopy's plump midsection. Pauline and Charlene land on top of me.

"—pig pile!" the kids shout.

Snoopy wags his tail like a windshield wiper, and his tongue laps my ear hole. I struggle to carry him off the bus to the mailbox where Mum waits in her red galoshes and fake fur coat with the dog's leash in her outstretched hand. The corners of her mouth turn down and makes a fish face from the cigarette she sucks on.

"I swear if it wasn't for bad luck, you wouldn't have any at all," Mum says with a quick eye roll.

"How's this my fault?" I ask, huffing and puffing as I hand him off.

As I get back to the bus and reach the top step, my eyes connect with the driver's. I drink in his pity the same way Mum drank in Uncle Chester's *that* day in the car. Only this time, it's "Not a good start to the day, ayuh?" the bus driver says.

Pauline cocks her head and looks up at the driver with a scowl that could sink a battleship. "Duh, whatcha' think?"

⚜

ON MAIN STREET IN CANAAN, THE SCHOOL BUS PASSES A wooden water wheel, a thirty-five-foot-tall rocket ship, a tin man made from muffler parts, and a giant purple cow statue.

The elementary school sits across the street from Tom's Convenience Store and the purple cow statue. The school is a one-story building with white siding and an American flag hanging from a pole in the front yard.

Inside the school is a wide hallway with black and white checkered tiles. Classrooms line both sides of the hall. In the kindergarten room, the teacher blows up the huggable Letter People and stands them on the shelf below the wall of windows in alphabetical order. Miss A is my favorite of all the Letter People. Miss A wears red shoes and holds her finger under her nose for "Achew," because she's always got to sneeze.

In the corner of the room is a playhouse with a wooden stove, wooden sink, and multiple shelves. One shelf holds plastic pots, pans, and dishes. Another shelf holds the plastic food: eggs, hot dogs, toast, vegetable cans, and tiny condiment containers.

I spend the first part of the morning making breakfast on the stove, pretending to crack the plastic eggs one-handed like Dad does, because he's a chef. Then I force-feed the invisible scrambled eggs to Charlene who clamps her lips tightly in protest.

After nap time, it is snack time. After snack time, the teacher makes the Letter People sing and dance a third time. Then she lets us color and play. And at the end of the day, she helps us into our coats and mittens before she marches us, single file, down the short hallway to the longer hallway and onto the bus.

Despite the rocky start to the day, I sit back in the green high-back seat and smile.

I love kindergarten!

SCRATCH AND SNIFF

F ollowing Labor Day, I start the first-grade. My teacher
introduces herself as Mrs. La Croix. She wears a short-
sleeve dress and her underarms jiggle like fleshy scoops
of Jell-O. As the teacher goes on about the rules, it's only then I
realize that kindergarten doesn't last forever, and this causes my
straight back to melt into the curve of the hard plastic chair.

"No coloring, taking naps, or using the blow-up-people-
letters," the teacher says as she writes on the chalk board.

The chalk "rat-a-tat-tats" and stops. I watch as she returns
only a sliver of chalk to the narrow wood cradle that runs along
the bottom of the board. Her hands sweep up and down in a
vertical motion, sky to tile, tile to sky as she claps away the white
dust on her hands. She clears her throat. I try to clear mine.

After the brief introduction, the class recites the alphabet,
and without the blow-up-letter-people from kindergarten to
assist me, I can't remember if D comes before G, or if Mr. P is
the neighbor of Mr. E, or if X, Y, and Z are something I made
up, so I move my lips and pretend to follow along.

I cross my arms hard over my chest and stick my bottom lip
out at an exaggerated length.

I hate first grade!

❦

DURING THE FIRST FEW WEEKS, I REFER TO MRS. LA CROIX AS
Teacher. "Teacher, I need help—Teacher I need to use the
bathroom—Teacher this and Teacher that—Teacher, Teacher,
Teacher."

"Miss Dodge, my name is not Teacher, it is Mrs. La Croix.
Do not address me as such again."

She holds a yardstick in her hand and eyeballs me.

"Yes, Teacher," I say as I clasp my mouth and suck in my
breath. The whole room narrows to the size of a thimble. "Sorry.
I mean, Mrs. La Croix."

On any given day, Mrs. La Croix holds the yardstick and
paces the tiles of the white walled room. She wears the same
polyester styled dress and cream pumps daily. Her nude knee-
highs crinkle at her ankles like worms withering in the sun, and
she keeps her salt-and-pepper-colored curls short and tight.

Her thick eyebrows move across the top of her cat-eye-
rimmed glasses. They remind me of the black and white
caterpillars I saved from the fire ants in Florida, a rescue that
ended with me breaking out in hives from stem to stern. Today,
she hands out an assignment to complete before recess. The
sight of the math problems on the sheet of paper makes my
insides shriek.

When did she teach us this?

Charlene and the other kids fill in their answers with ease.
Seeing this causes the heat from the caterpillars to return. It
starts at the nape of my neck and spreads to my cheeks.

Noises and frustration swirl in my head like sugar cubes in a
cup of hot tea. I gaze out the window at the swing set beyond
the blacktop for relief from the mental storm about to swallow
me up. I snap back to reality when Mrs. La Croix meets my gaze
with the crack of the yardstick, forcing my thoughts back into
the room with Charlene and the rest of the first-grade class.

After snatching my attention back, Mrs. La Croix waddles to

the wall of towering windows with her nude knee-highs around her ankles and reaches up to hook the tiny plastic loop with her short stubby finger. The cream shades roll down, one after the other, after the other, stamping out the sunlight.

Smooth move! I scold myself.

When Mrs. La Croix steps out of the room to speak to the principal, I lay my head on my desk. My eyelids feel like paper weights.

"You're crazier than Gideon's geese, you know it? Sit up before you get in trouble," Charlene whispers.

I lift my head a small bit.

"Can I help it if I don't know beans?" I whisper back.

❧

DURING READING TIME, THE CLASS BREAKS INTO THREE groups: the good reader, the mediocre reader, and the slow reader. Because I am a slower-than-slow reader, my group isn't with any of the three in the room. We meet behind the school in a detached trailer.

The Title I enrichment program is meant to sharpen the Three R's—Reading, Writing, and Arithmetic. But I wish it stood for Art, Recess, and Rest Time.

Mrs. V, the Title I teacher, comes to get me every day at the same time, when the class is forming their reading circles and all the plastic seats move around the room like musical chairs. In the trailer behind the school is where I go. Depending on the day, we play games, practice cue cards, or read books aloud.

Today, Mrs. V hands me a book to read to her. I move my index finger slowly across the page.

"Jane said, 'Oh look! See it go. See it go up.' 'Up, up', said Sally. 'Go up, up, up,'" I read aloud.

Mrs. V smiles and turns the page, so I keep reading.

At the end of the session, before she takes me back to class, Mrs. V takes out a roll of scratch-and-sniff stickers.

47

"Strawberry or grape?" she asks.

"Grape," I say with a beamy wide smile, sticking it to the top of my hand. The sticker makes me feel smart.

When I'm back in the room with Charlene and the rest of the first graders, the teacher hands out a piece of paper with an empty grid on it.

"Fill in the numbers from one to one hundred," Mrs. La Croix instructs.

I put my elbows on the desk and watch as everyone scribbles away on the sheets. The grape sticker is powerless outside of the reading trailer.

When did she teach us this? I ask myself for the umpteenth time, peeling off the sticker and crumpling it into a ball.

Mrs. La Croix taps the clock face above the chalkboard with her yardstick.

"Five more minutes," she announces.

Swallowing the cotton seemingly in my throat, I glance down at the empty sheet in front of me. My heart skips like a tire going downhill with me in it.

If I don't finish, she'll make me miss the class kickball game again. I can't let her do that!

I bite my lip and scan the desk beside me where Michael the Brainiac sits. His answers pop off the page at me, so I stop chewing my lip, grab my gnawed-on pencil, and start to write.

"You're gonna get caught," Charlene says. Her eyes wide with worry.

Mrs. La Croix paces the room with a slow waddle. Her knee-highs crinkle around her thick ankles, and she stoops to pull them up. They stretch and stretch and stretch and snap. She stands upright and smooths the front of her lavender dress with cream-colored diamonds on it.

The teacher lifts her eyes to the clock and counts backward.

"Ten, nine, eight, seven—"

I scribble as fast as I can with my tongue sticking out of the corner of my mouth.

"—four, three, two, one. Time's up. Turn your papers over."

I flip mine over, place my pencil on my desk, and smile with pleasure. I think I may have figured out how to make it through first grade.

❦

THAT AFTERNOON, MUM AND DAD TAKE US TO AN AMWAY meeting in Clinton, the next town over. While the adults discuss health and wellness products over coffee, we girls play upstairs. The teenage daughter of the Amway consultant offers to give me a ride down the stairwell on her shoulders to get a drink of Kool-Aid from the kitchen. She crouches, and I climb on.

How bad can it be? Saves me the walk.

From my perch, I gaze down the fifteen steps to the bottom, and put a choke hold on her.

"Don't trip," I say, regretting my "yes."

"Trust me," she says, making my thoughts go straight to Kaa from the *Jungle Book.*

She wraps her hands around my ankles and takes the first step down.

On the second step, her foot slips. Every hair on my body screams timber as I fall tail over teakettle down the flight of hardwood steps and collide with the horsehair plaster wall at the bottom.

There's a body-sized indentation in the wall and I'm deafened by the sound of my own scream. I draw my leg up and cradle it.

The Amway consultant reaches me first.

"Where's it hurt, hun?" she asks.

Where doesn't it hurt? would be a better question.

A sharp pain shoots through my leg with an agony so awful no words come out. I hold my breath and clench my teeth tighter than the bark on a tree.

The Amway consultant bends my leg and straightens it. Then she does it again.

"Good news," she says, "it's not broken. If it was, you wouldn't be movin' it."

As she bends it a third time, I release the breath I held, and let out a second hair raising scream.

"She ain't movin' it, dipshit, you are," Dad yells. "Now get the hell outta' the way before I move you."

❧

THAT NIGHT, AFTER LEAVING THE EMERGENCY ROOM IN OUR cobalt-blue station wagon, nicknamed *The Titanic* by my cousin Steve because as he says, "the wagon's so big that it floats into the driveway," we arrive home, and I see my cousins playing next-door. It's Friday night poker night, when all the kinfolk and townsfolk near and far gather at The House to drink, smoke, and play cards. The kids, mostly cousins, do whatever it is they want as long as whatever it is doesn't include blood.

I swing my casted leg out the car door and into the gravel.

"Can I go? Pretty please with a cherry on top? I won't play. I'll just sit in the grass and watch. Pinky swear," I say, extending my pinky toward Mum.

Mum holds my crutches and eyeballs me with a half smirk.

"Don't be a dingbat," she says.

"But all the cousins—"

"The answer is still no," Mum says.

With tears in my eyes, I place the crutches under my armpits, hobble up the rickety steps and through the door to the divan, with its dull orange flowers.

The sound of my cousins racing up and down the footpath between the three properties makes my eyes well. Their bare feet slap against the beaten path that runs in front of our house. I absorb the vibrations of their steps through the flowery conductor my ear lays on.

The words "Tag, you're it!" taper off into the distance. I press my ear harder into the cushioned armrest and wait for the sound of their feet to return.

There's a soft knock at the front door.

"It's open," Mum says as she arranges a stack of pillows under my casted leg.

Richard, my favorite cousin, enters with his mum, Aunt Jenny, my dad's older sister. As always, she's wearing a long dress. Her nose and cheeks are red and blotchy with *rosacea*.

"A little birdie told me you broke your leg," Aunt Jenny says with enough blue in her eyes to make a dutchman a pair of pants. This is something Mum always says when she looks into my eyes.

Richard holds one hand behind his back.

"Hope this makes you feel better," he says, bringing his hand forward.

My eyes light up, and I tear open the package to find a Play Dough farm set.

I empty the contents of the box in my lap. A plastic mat. A pig. A cow. A chicken. A horse. And four cans of clay: red, green, yellow, and white to go with the farm-animal-shaped cookie cutters.

"A real humdinger you've got there," Richard says, touching my cast. "Can I be the first to sign it?"

He takes a marker from Aunt Jenny's pocketbook and shields the words as he writes. When he's done, he reads aloud, "To the best cousin on the planet. Get well soon."

Without warning, Richard's older brother, Steve, and his three sisters burst through the door. The three girls wear long dresses like Aunt Jenny, because, as their preacher man says, "Girls shouldn't wear pants or they'll go to hell." Although I wear pants, I love it when my cousins come to get me and my sisters for Sunday school. They feed us Twinkies and clam-flavored potato chips on the way home.

Steve's upset, which draws my attention briefly away from

my new Play Dough set. Aunt Jenny leans forward and sweeps Steve's bangs back.

"What is it, hun?" Aunt Jenny asks.

"He got whooped—" the girls say frowning up at Aunt Jenny.

"How come?" Aunt Jenny asks.

"Uncle Jerry said I cussed, but I didn't," Steve says. "Dad whooped me for no good reason."

Their family is what others call *Holy Rollers*, and although they visit Grammy and Grampy Dodge's house occasionally on a poker night, they don't participate in the drinking, smoking, cussing, or gambling.

Aunt Jenny wipes Steve's cheek.

"He must've thought you did. Your uncle Jerry wouldn't make a thing like that up."

"Yes, he would. He does it all the time!" Steve says. "I knew you wouldn't believe me. No one ever does!"

Steve looks to the divan where I lay.

"Uncle Jerry's a wicked meanie," I say, punching out a pig with the Play Dough cutter.

Pauline tilts her head and peers over her book at me. "Mean is too nice a word. Brutal is more like it," she says.

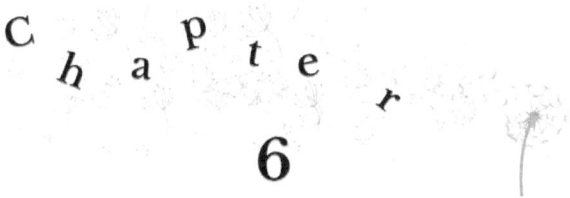

CORNSTALK-VERTIGO

With June inching into July, the doctor cuts the dingy cast off my leg. The leg is now skinnier and paler than the other. The skin wrinkles like a prune and smells like a combination of apple cider vinegar and wet dog hair.

When we get home, I retire the crutches to the back of the hall, Mum heads to the bedroom for a quick nap before putting supper on, and Dad, who is also in the bedroom, prices flea market and Amway items for the upcoming weekend. My parents' need to hoard anything and everything fills the house with tittering boxes of what-nots.

While Dad works in the bedroom, I quietly take Mum's stepladder from between the peeling wallpaper and the wringer washer to aid me in sneaking two blueberry Puffed Pies from the top of the Frigidaire. The Puffed Pies cost nothing and come with the monthly government-cheese-box. The box contains the standard: dried milk, dried peas, dried beans, flour, butter, four large blocks of cheddar cheese, rice, and the most amazing strawberry and blueberry Puffed Pies. I don't know which I like better.

Dad uses a stainless-steel cheese slicer and slices one block of cheese for sandwiches, and the other three blocks he keeps for lasagna, scalloped potatoes, macaroni and cheese, and cheesy shepherd's pie. The blocks of government cheese last a month, while the boxes of Puffed Pies last a week.

I peer down at Charlene from on top of the stool and drop two Puffed Pies into the tote bag.

"Want a soder pop?"

"What kinda' soder pop?" she asks.

"Dad's Moxie," I say.

"No way, Jose. You're gonna get us in trouble."

"Not if you don't tell." I narrow my eyes and glare at her.

Charlene looks down at her big toe with the scab covering the tip and says nothing else.

I heave on the silver handle and grab two of Dad's cherished Moxie's from the Frigidaire. Besides fresh blueberry pie and Hershey's chocolate ice cream, Mum and Dad keep 'his' and 'her' stashes around the house: Snicker bars for Mum, butterscotch Life Savers for Dad. Peppermint Patties for Mum, black licorice for Dad. Dr. Pepper for Mum, Moxie soda for Dad. If we girls know what is good for us, we don't touch their stuff—and as long as Charlene doesn't tattle—I normally get away with sneaking a treat or two.

After filling the tote bag with picnic items, I swipe Pauline's lucky rabbit's foot from the hook where the car keys hang by the front door and put it in my pocket for good luck, then head outside with Charlene to explore.

To the right of us, Aunt Mable sets her grass on fire and hoses it down.

"Makes the grass come in greener," she says.

The smile on her face tells me that she's in a better mood than yesterday, when she and Mum got into it, because Aunt Mable said I stove her girl's toy all to hell after the head fell off.

I didn't wreck it. The head fell off in my hands. How's that my fault?

Mum says she likes to blame things on me because I'm the

scapegoat for Lottie and Dottie's reckless treatment of their toys.

Although I can't be sure what goats and horses have to do with me staving up toys and a doll's head falling off, the argument ended with Aunt Mable's famous line, "Put that in your horse pipe and smoke it."

We zip down the footpath past the garage where Grampy and Uncle Jerry hammer a dent out of a hood, past Grammy Dodge's white geese, Lulu and Larry, past the harem of chickens clucking around Rex the rooster in the dirt of the driveway, and past the shaggy hedge of rose bushes. When we reach the sliding glass doors of Grammy's sunporch, we slow to a crawl, keeping our eyes on the blue exterior door overlooking Nelson Hill Road. As we pass the living room window of the used portion of Grammy's house, the hair on my neck raises. We approach the blue door of the unused portion of The House and take off in a sprint. So not to be captured by the ghost that haunts the unused portion, we slow down only when we reach the sumac trees, where we cross Grammy's property line and enter Mr. Peabody's cornfield. It's there, in the sea of corn, that Charlene and I pretend to be ants in the elevated stalks of our grassland.

While concealing ourselves in the golden corn, we come across a dried up bear print in the mud. The manure that Mr. Peabody uses contains dead chicken parts, which the animals, including Snoopy, love to dig in to retrieve mangled beaks and chicken feet. It smells worse than the pit we empty our pisspots in.

As we merge deeper into the corn stalks, I open the tote bag and haul out the two blueberry Puffed Pies. As I'm about to take a bite, a cluster of stalks begins to rustle and whatever is moving them lets out a shriek. Fear surges through my veins and I drop my blueberry Puffed Pie. The thick and lofty plants surrounding us make it impossible to determine the source of the ruckus.

A dog?

A fox?

A deer?

A moose?

A bear?

Charlene's lips tremble.

My mind flashes to the bear print we shrugged off when we entered the cornfield. Then another culprit comes to mind. One who pinches us and makes us cry, who likes to snap wet towels at our bare skin and who likes to give us tittie twisters. The one who, on any given day can be seen spying on us kids from almost anywhere on the property—Uncle Jerry. Two games he likes to play for sure: Mr. Tickle and hide-and-seek. I hate it when his fingers touch me and where they touch me. It doesn't feel right.

The beastly shrieks come closer, and my bare feet sink into the topsoil mixed with smelly chicken parts.

Charlene's eyes water, and she chews on her cuticles.

Row after row, the tall stalks splinter and fall. The ground vibrates and rumbles. My knees knock together.

It's big. Real big.

Charlene hugs me tightly.

We stand stock-still with our arms around each other's necks, hoping whatever it is will veer off. When it doesn't, I drop the tote bag, grab her hand and hightail it in the opposite direction through the cornfield until the thundering footsteps stop. Until it's nothing but the sound of my own heart pounding that I hear.

She peers up at me. Her body twitches with fear.

"I can't see the road," she says.

I stand on my tippy toes. The cornstalk-vertigo turns my internal compass topsy-turvy, and I pull the stalks down to peek over the tops. Across the way, I spy Mr. Peabody's maple grove, where starting in late February and early March pairs of white buckets hang like pearl earrings on the trunks to drain the trees of their sap.

To the right, I spy our special playhouse hidden amongst the sumac trees that separates Mr. Peabody's cornfield from Grammy's property. The branches of the sumac touch the ground in a big sweeping circle and create the perfect hide-a-way.

With Charlene's hand in mine, we traipse hard and fast toward the sumac trees. The sound of Mr. Peabody's tractor sputtering up Nelson Hill Road toward the muddy main entrance, not far from where we came in, sets off another round of alarm.

"What if Mr. P catches us?" Charlene asks as we forge our way through the last rows. "He doesn't like us kids playin' in his corn."

"Stop bein' a little Miss Goody Two Shoes," I say. "Have I ever gotten us into trouble before?"

"Is that a trick question?" she asks.

Before we realize it, Mr. Peabody is upon us, and he stares down from his green tractor that is older than Methuselah's goat.

Charlene lets go of my hand, skips ahead down the muddy main entrance and out onto Nelson Hill Road, while I stay behind to smooth things over with Mr. Peabody. I cross my ankles and clasp my hands together. The stance makes me recall Pauline's words: 'You have two horns holding up a halo.'

I glance up sheepishly.

"Hi Mr. P," I say.

He flicks his suspenders and tips his hat forward.

"You behavin' Dodge?"

"Ayuh, Mr. P. Of course."

"That'd be a first," he says, "now wouldn't it?"

"Whatever gives you that *idear*, Mr. P?"

"Dodge, you know darn good and well," he says. "Now scat! Don't let me catch you in my fields again."

"Yessir. Sorry, Mr. P." I skedaddle down the road before he can say another word.

A telephone pole away, Charlene clutches her foot in pain and leaps in circles on one leg in the middle of the dirt road.

"How bad is it?" I ask.

She squeezes her bloody toe and grimaces.

"Lemme see." I peel her fingers back from her toes she holds. "You stubbed it wicked good this time. Took the scab right off. If you keep it up, pretty soon you won't have any big toes left."

"Don't tell Mum, please," Charlene says.

"I won't. Pinky swear," I say, holding my pinky out to latch around hers.

I know how much she dreads hearing the "dingdong," "dim-wit," "nim-rod," "nincompoop," and "pick your feet up" remarks Mum will say if I tell.

As we make our way past Grammy Dodge's mailbox and toward our own with tiger lilies growing around the milk-can-base, I spot a cluster of stinking Benjamin's in the woods to the left. The deep, crimson-colored flowers draw my attention away from Charlene's bloody toe.

I leap over a shiny bed of poison ivy and wade through a five-foot-tall patch of ostrich ferns, up a slight incline to the cluster of beautiful red flowers. The stinking Benjamin's give off a strong unpleasant odor of three-day old roadkill, but in my mind their beautiful color makes up for the smell. I pluck a handful to put in a vase.

"Whatcha' doin' with 'em there flowers?" Charlene asks.

"None ya."

"What's none ya?"

"None your business," I inform her.

From the eave of our little brown house, the seashell wind chimes tinkle, and I open the door with the flowers behind my back. Mum lowers the book in her hand and leans forward in her sad old chair. She sticks her nose out and sniffs the air like Snoopy our basset hound.

"What's-at smell?" Mum says.

"For you." I bring the bouquet around to the front.

"Not by the hair of my chinny, chin, chin," she says. "Get 'em damn flowers outta' this house. You oughtta' know better than that, ding-ding."

"But—"

Dad rises from the divan and charges at me like he's a matador and the red flowers are his cape.

"But, but nothin'! Did your mother stutter?" he yells.

My shoulders slouch and I take slow strides backward out the door, down the rickety stoop, to where Charlene stands with her bleeding big toe. She gives me the *see-I-told-you-so* brow in the clouds look. I toss the flowers in the grass and give a quick nod for her to follow me.

She hobbles a short way down the path behind me, beyond the garage to the crabapple tree in Grammy's front yard. We sit on the hill and watch the cousins play angels and demons, much like the game of cops and robbers.

Without warning, I'm catapulted like a rag doll into the air and land with a thud on Uncle Jerry's shoulders. I squeeze his neck and hold on for dear life. He trots past the tire swing, up the circular driveway, prancing, jogging, and galloping playfully.

Jud, a much older cousin, grabs Charlene and throws her on his back.

Charlene and I laugh as they prance us around the yard, back and forth, up and down the grassy hill.

"Giddy up." I cheer my horse on.

My horse breaks into a sprint and chases Charlene's horse down the dirt road to the junkyard, beyond the four apple trees and the empty hog pen. The horses halt at a two-toned mafia-styled car, blue and cream, buried in the puckerbrush with vibrantly colored Indian paintbrushes and Queens Anne's lace sprouting up around it.

Jud slides Charlene off his back.

"You sure we won't get caught?" Jud asks.

"Ayuh, I'm friggin' positive," Uncle Jerry says as he lowers me onto the pale-blue seat in the front, where the sun-dried leather is as rough as a lizard's skin to the touch.

The jagged rip in the leather pinches my skin and a horsefly repeatedly pings the cracked windshield looking for a way out.

My knee bumps the steering wheel, and in the back seat, Charlene pleads for Jud to open the door and let her out.

I sit up on my knees and peek over the seat. Charlene wipes tears away with her hands. Uncle Jerry jerks me backward and forces me to lay flat on my back. His whiskers rub against my neck and his hands slide up my shirt.

"Koochie koochie koo," he says, poking my breastbone.

Uncle Jerry sits up on his knees and unzips his pants. His head tilts awkwardly against the cloth ceiling.

Stop! What are you doing? I want to say, but the words slide back down my throat before they can escape.

He extends his hands. The two tie strings around my neck come loose and my halter top flops forward. My stomach fills with collywobbles. Like the horsefly that pecks at the windshield, my eyes look for a way to escape. My six year old mind wishes to be somewhere else. I allow my mind to take me back to the crabapple tree where the cousins play.

Three sharp knocks on the passenger window jars my thoughts back into the mafia-styled car. Two of my dad's sisters, Nina and Bernice, peer at us with their mouths wide open as barn doors. Bernice tries to get a better look by pressing her double-chin and nose against the glass.

"Shit, shit, shit," Uncle Jerry says under his breath.

"Shit is right," Jud responds.

The sound of dungarees and zippers going up fills my ears.

Thank goodness, I cheer in my head.

But lucky for the boys, our aunts' attention isn't on them. It's on us. Nina and Bernice fling the two-toned doors open. They haul Charlene and me out into the prickly grass and the puckerbrush where I struggle to find my footing and to hold my halter top up.

The boys escape out the opposite doors and take off on foot down into the junkyard.

Our aunts' grab our shoulders and shake us. Our heads bobble back and forth.

"Whatcha' doin' with 'em boys?" one asks.

"You twins got a hankerin' for some trouble," the other says.

One ties the halter top strings back around my neck, while the other fastens the buttons on Charlene's shirt. They steer us toward The House at a fast clip, gripping our forearms tightly as we walk.

Did I do something wrong?

I taste the salt at the back of my throat where my tears collect. *I don't understand. Why are we being blamed?*

"The next time we catch you girls alone with 'em boys, we're tellin' Grammy Dodge," one says.

"Ayuh," is all I could muster.

They release their grips on us. Feeling weird and dirty, I run hard and fast until I'm all alone and far away.

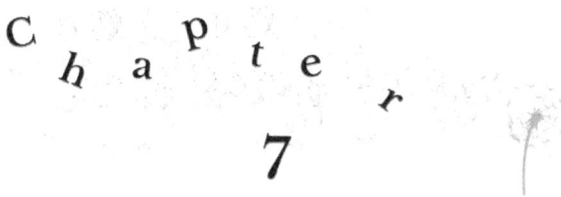

7

MINT CHOCOLATE CHIP

Today, instead of setting up at the flea market, Mum
and Dad plan a trip to Winslow to visit Grandma
Foley, Mum's mother.

The tea kettle erupts like the train whistle. Mum pours the
water into the yellow plastic basin on the kitchen table and
mixes a dipper of cold water with it.

"Hurry up girls, scrub-a-dub-dub. Your grandma's expectin'
us in an hour," Mum says, wetting the washcloth and rubbing a
bar of green soap on it.

Charlene and I leap off the divan with the Cabbage Patch
dolls that Grandma Foley made us when she purchased a pattern
and three doll heads at the local craft store with the authenticity
certificates included.

"Which one of you twins is first?" Mum asks.

"M-M-M-Me," Charlene says.

She sets her Cabbage Patch on the kitchen chair beside her
and takes the cloth.

Charlene wets the bed and speaks with a stutter now. Mum
says it's because the wires in her brain got crossed somehow. But
none of this started until Jud pushed her into the back seat of

the mafia-styled car. Not that I can tell Mum about it. She probably won't believe me anyhow.

The pink jumper Mum gave me earlier puckers around my thighs and the elastic bands cut into my legs. I put on my Jelly shoes, grab my doll, and head for the door.

"Not so fast, Dingy," Mum says. "You haven't scrubbed yet."

"But Dad's beepin' the horn," I say. "You know how he gets."

"Your father can wait." Mum grabs me by the ear and walks me back two steps to the table.

"Your neck is black." She licks her finger and rubs my neck with it.

"Ew, stop. Gross!" I jerk my head away.

"If I didn't know any better, I'd say you twins were a couple of sparrows, since you like rollin' around in the dirt so much." She sips her coffee.

"Sparrows?"

"Ayuh. They take dirt baths like you birdbrains." Mum giggles and crosses her legs so not to pee on herself.

"My teeth are floatin'." Mum bounces in place. "I better go whiz before it's my eyeballs."

She sets the coffee cup down and makes a mad dash for the hanging blanket, then disappears down the hall.

Charlene washes her face and neck, and then sticks her foot —the one with a scab the size of Texas on the big toe—in the chair.

"Hurry up," Pauline mutters. She drums her fingernails on the table.

"I-I-I am," Charlene says.

The hanging blanket moves, and Mum steps down into the sunken front room with a lit cigarette in her mouth.

"You got peanut butter in your ears, girl?" She smacks Charlene on the ear and snatches the washcloth away. "How many times do I haveta' tell you to let your sister's wash their faces before you wash your goddamn filthy feet?"

"I f-f-forgot," Charlene says with a frown, before erupting into tears.

Mum rinses the cloth, and the water rocks back and forth in the basin. A gritty layer of soap scum and dirt collects on the insides of the plastic tub.

She wrings the cloth out. Her red lipstick paints her front teeth as she clutches a cigarette between them and pushes my head down. "When's the last time you washed the back of your neck?"

"You just asked me that."

Mum rubs the cloth back and forth over my neck like a dull sheet of sandpaper.

"That wasn't so bad, now was it?" she lets go of my head.

"Do you want me to lie?"

"Keep it up, smart ass, and you'll stay home." Mum pushes the basin across the table to Pauline.

Pauline's naked except for a worn-out pair of underwear and her eye patch. The size C bra with the underwire hangs over the back of the kitchen chair, and her nipples hang down—way down, the way an orchid does. According to the doctor, Pauline is overweight—more than twice the normal size of a nine-and-a-half-year-old.

Pauline lifts each breast and washes under it. As she does, I stare at the long bubbly scar below her belly button where she had kidney surgery.

"Whatcha' gawkin' at?" Pauline lets go of the breast she holds up and puts her clothes on.

"Nothin'," I say.

I cast my eyes down and wait for the basin to make a second pass around the table so I can wash my feet.

As Charlene washes her other foot, curiosity causes me to pick up Mum's black coffee and take a sip.

"That'll put hair on your chest," Mum says matter-of-factly.

Maybe that's how Pauline got her beard. I spit the coffee out.

"Congratulations!" Mum says. "You've managed to get coffee all over the damn place."

Outside, the car horn blares.

"How long do you expect me to sit in the car?" Dad yells from the dooryard.

Mum opens the house door.

"Hold your horses, babe. We're comin'."

Dad presses the gas. The engine revs loudly.

"Get your asses out here or I'll leave the lot of you."

Grey smoke from the tailpipe billows up the steps and crashes like a four-foot wave into the grey smoke streaming from Mum's nostrils.

"Dress your feet girls, before your father blows a gasket."

"But I haven't washed 'em—" I start to say.

"Take the cloth with you," Mum says. "You can wash 'em in the car."

She slides the cigarette pouch in the pocket of her housedress and tosses the suds-less water out the door into the grass.

"I call door." I grab my Jelly shoes and my doll, then I race outside.

I slam the car door and push the lock down.

Pauline knocks on the window.

"Unlock it." Her lazy eye rattles back and forth.

"Go around."

"Unlock." She clenches her teeth.

"No."

"Yes."

"No."

"Dad," Pauline says with a whine.

I stick my tongue out. My spit sprays the window with the Marvin the Martian sticker stuck to it.

Dad opens his driver side door and plants his boot in the gravel.

"If I've told you once, I've told you a thousand times," he

says, "unlock the damn door before I give you somethin' Ajax won't take off."

I pull the lock up and move my knees for her to climb over them into the middle, between Charlene and me and our dolls.

"You wreck everythin'," Pauline says, her shoulders in a heap.

"Nuh uh."

"Uh huh."

"At least I don't have one eye," I say.

"Say it again, and they'll be three hits," she says with a low sounding growl. "Me hittin' you. You hittin' the floor. And the ambulance hittin' the road."

"One eye," I whisper.

Dad's nostrils pulse as he eyeballs Pauline and me in the rearview mirror.

Pauline gives Dad the *Don't look at me, look her* finger point.

"What'd I do?" I ask, crossing my arms over my chest.

Mum cranes her neck and blows smoke over the headrest. "You heard your father. No more shenanigans, Francine."

I poke my bottom lip out. "Not fair."

"Life never is," Mum adds, turning back around to face the front.

⊙⅗⅋

WE PULL UP TO GRANDMA FOLEY'S AT CLAYTON'S TRAILER Park in Winslow. From the window next door, Wally, the African parrot squawks, "Hello. Hello. Hello."

"Polly, want a cracker?" I say as I step toward the window with my index finger raised to pet the bird in the cage.

The parrot bobs its head. Its feet pitter-patter happily on the wooden perch.

"Wouldn't do that if I were you," Mum says. "Liable to pull back a stub."

Grandma Foley opens the screen door and steps down onto the iron stoop. Charlene and I run up the four steps to kiss her before disappearing into the park to find an unlocked display trailer to play in.

Charlene and I scout around until we find a *For Sale* sign in the window of a new trailer. We enter through the unlocked door. The living room carpet is all the same—a plush hunter green—rather than a mixture of carpet squares like in our living room. We feel the soft green threads with our fingers and toes, and then we sit in the middle of the floor with our dolls.

"I wish we lived here," I say.

"M-Me too," she says.

I leap to my feet and drag my doll across the carpet to the smooth linoleum in the kitchen. The linoleum is shiny and not peeling. I stand on my tippy-toes and touch the hot and cold knobs on the sink, feeling the shiny gooseneck faucet last.

"I wish we had runnin' water." I picture our chipped ceramic sink with the three empty holes.

Charlene gets up off the carpet and we carry our dolls down the hall to the first bedroom. The small bedroom has a door that locks, a closet not made of particle board, and a nice window— not one held shut by a rusty, bent nail.

Charlene follows me farther down the hall to the large bedroom at the end. It has a fancy bathroom with an oval tub. We climb into it and pretend it's a swimming pool.

The sound of keys rattling from the other end of the trailer interrupts our fun.

We climb out of the tub and sneak into the hallway, where we see the park's custodian in the living room.

"Stop," he yells.

I grab Charlene's hand, throw open the back door, jump, and land with a thud.

We sneak around the trailer park like burglars, jetting from trailer to trailer until the station wagon is within sight. When we sprint past Wally the African parrot, he squawks at us from the neighbor's window. Charlene and I jet up the iron steps into Grandma Foley's trailer. Then we run down the thin paneled hallway to the spare room where we find Pauline lounging on the bed watching *Psycho* with her eye-patch on the nightstand and her hand in a bowl of popcorn wedged between her lap and her boobs.

"Want some?" she asks.

Popcorn falls from her fingertips like Yahtzee dice and lands on the bed spread.

My heart pounds from all the running, and I collapse on the bedspread beside Pauline.

Midway through the movie Dad hollers down the hall.

"Girls! Move it or lose it! I've got *pa*-ghetti to fix," he says.

Mum says Dad has a speech impediment which is why he also says *Jimba*, instead of Jimmy, and *Spacific* Ocean.

Dad is a chef at a restaurant in Skowhegan and cooks in fives. Five meaning bulk and number. When he makes spaghetti at home, he uses a five-gallon pot to mix the sauce and adds five-pounds of bacon and five cans of sweet peas. In a separate five-gallon pot, he cooks five pounds of pasta, enough to last five nights. If we were Jewish like my friend Oliver, five might mean Dad is full of grace, but we are not, and he is not.

When I gripe about the peas in the sauce, Mum scolds me.

"There's children in third world countries who'd gladly eat spaghetti every night of the week, like Roberto," she says. His picture hangs on our Frigidaire beside the check Mum mails each month to Feed the Children.

But for now, we ignore Dad's command to "Move it or lose it!" and relax in the guest bedroom.

My muscles tense when the chain fixed to Dad's wallet starts to clank as his bootsteps thump down the hallway at breakneck speed. The door bangs open, and Dad removes the cigarette from between his lips.

"Move your asses!"

He points down the hall as smoke streams from his nostrils like a fire breathing dragon. Dad hates to repeat himself. Wit and conversation rarely happen without Budweiser, and—since quitting cold turkey—he speaks in single-lined-sentences ending mostly with exclamation points.

We spring up and bolt past Dad down the hallway. Grandma Foley follows us outside to the blue station wagon for hugs and kisses. Her round glasses squeeze her small nose. Her dry lips absorb the cherry lipstick she put on.

"You twins be thinkin' 'bout whatcha' want for your birthdays." Grandma Foley kisses each of us on the forehead.

"I want the Smurf watch from the Sears catalog," I say. "The one with the blue band."

"M-M-Me too!" Charlene sits up straight in the seat with the traces of Grandma's red lips tattooed between her eyes.

The Titanic shifts into drive. Mum places her hand in its usual travel position—up high and between Dad's legs, and she sings the song "Sneaky Snake" by Tom T. Hall. For some reason, although I'm not sure why, the song Mum sings about a sneaky snake dancing in the grass in her baritone smoker's voice brings a smile to Dad's mostly straight face.

Dad gives Mum a quick side-eye glance, before the smile on his face is sucked back in and returns to the thin straight line below his mustache. We three girls turn around in the seat to wave goodbye to Grandma Foley, who Mum says is legally a midget because she's only four-foot-nine inches tall. Dad's a giant. This I know because his head towers over the top of the Frigidaire.

The Titanic rumbles down the road and takes an unexpected right turn. I prop myself up and peer out the dirt-streaked window with the Marvin the Martian sticker stuck to it. It's Smiley's Ice Cream parlor.

Hot diggidy dog!

I do a jig and sprint to the counter to study the menu board. Mum orders chocolate, Dad orders butterscotch, Pauline and Charlene order strawberry. I can't make up my mind.

Dad licks his butterscotch ice cream. "Time ain't gettin' any slower. Hurry up damn-it, or I'll choose for you."

Hmmm...Strawberry or mint chocolate chip?

My finger ticks back and forth like a pendulum to the tune "Eeny, Meeny, Miny, Moe."

Dad sighs loudly.

I peer up at him.

He frowns down at me. He stomps his boot and raises his palm as if to slap me.

Mum sits on the front seat of the car with her legs hanging out the car door. She smokes a cigarette and eats her ice cream. "Hurry up, slowpoke! I've got laundry to get in."

"Mint chocolate chip," I say, before Dad picks a flavor I don't want or lets his hand make contact with the back of my head.

Pauline and Charlene have finished their cones by the time I hop in back with mine. As the Titanic presses for home, the wind funnels in all four windows whipping my hair around. The loud rumble of the muffler—rigged up by a coat hanger—is accompanied by Mum singing a song about a bullfrog named Jeremiah.

I slowly lick my ice cream, unlike Charlene and Pauline, who must have devoured theirs' whole. Now they lie on top of each other, asleep in the back seat.

As Mum sings, I lean against the door for comfort. The door swings open, and I tumble out on the pavement with my face landing in my ice cream.

Mint chocolate chip drips from my eyelashes, down my chin, and onto my shirt. But it's the sheer pain I feel first. Blood drips from some places and gushes from others. A jagged piece of skin hangs from my elbow. I peel myself off the road and look up to see the heads of my family shrink in size as the Titanic barrels into the sunset.

Covered with sandpapery-scrapes, I hop up and down and flag my arms. "Come back!"

On the roadside, worry and pain collide with my ability to think. *Did they know I fell out? Did they pretend not to notice?*

As I stumble along the yellow line, I imagine Mum, in her

usual way, saying, "I dunno' officer. She simply disappeared. Alien abduction. Eighth wonder of the world. Beats the hell outta' me."

I think how the family would be happier and better without me. My sisters rarely fight, but I can ignite an argument faster than my parents can light a cigarette.

In a painful side-swagger, I walk toward Smiley's Ice Cream Parlor. With each step I take, episodes of mischief and name-calling flood my head. A river of guilt flows along with my nose. I blame myself for Charlene's fear of spiders because I pranked her by putting a handful of dead ones in her bed. Another devilish act floods my mind—the whooping Charlene got when I stuck a toothpick in my ear while she was asleep, broke my eardrum, and blamed her for it.

Alone, and with a wide range of confessions, I stop in middle of the road and raise my right hand like on *The People's Court*.

"I solemnly swear to tell the truth, the whole truth, and nothin' but the truth, so help me God."

I wait for a long-haired man in sandals and a tan robe to appear. When he doesn't, I pray harder and louder.

"I won't lie—or call names—or play any more pranks on my sisters. I promise."

I pause for divine intervention, like a giant fish or clapping thunder or a loud muffler.

Nothing.

"Pretty please with a cherry on top. I'll do the dishes for a week." I look up into the canopy of trees beside the road.

Still nothing.

"Alright, I'll do dishes for a month, and I won't sneak any more Snickers bars or Moxie soda from Mum and Dad's stashes."

I stumble down the road and picture my face on a missing poster.

"Hello? God? Deal, or no deal?"

Suddenly, the rough rumble of the muffler pulls alongside me, and with it, a talking mustache coated in butterscotch ice cream.

"Still in one piece, I see," Dad says.

"My ice cream." I chase those words with a guttural sob. Green goop drips down my face and makes my lashes stick.

Dad's hand extends out the driver's side window to hand me his half-eaten butterscotch ice cream cone.

"You owe me a butterscotch," he says with a serious tone.

"Is she d-d-dead?" Charlene asks.

"Use your noodle, girl," Dad says. "Does she look dead to you?"

Charlene shrugs and stares down at her Cabbage Patch doll in her lap.

"Where's it hurt?" Mum climbs out of the car and runs her fingers over my head for knots.

"Everywhere," I say.

"Gormy little thing, ain'tcha?" Mum says. "It's a wicked good thing you're so hardheaded. Now get in the car before I wrap you in bubble wrap."

Pauline's face is red with laughter. She squints out tears.

"It ain't funny," I say as Dad drives in the direction of the hospital.

"It ain't?" Pauline wipes her eyes. She catches her breath and peers up at me with her wobbly eye. "You spend more time at the hospital than the doctors do. I got an *idear*. How 'bout they put'cha on the pay roll?"

"Shut up, fatso." My promises to God are long-gone.

Chapter 8

ROYAL FLUSH

The sun descends behind the line of towering pines, leaving a pink and peach light in the slow swirling clouds. A chorus of mosquitos dance around our heads, and from the mustard-trimmed door, Pauline and I watch the cousins gathering at The House for Friday night poker night. Their joyful sound harmonizes with the mosquitos and the pond frogs croaking in the cattails.

"You comin'?" I ask.

"Hell naw. What do I look like—a fool?" she says. Her head bobs awkwardly up and down at an angle as she speaks. Another thing she does that Mum says is from the coordination damage.

"What's-at?" I say.

"I'd rather be dead." Pauline cradles Peter Rabbit in one arm as she pushes herself up from the stoop with the other.

The sound of her thump-step-thump makes its way over the threshold into the house and across the peeling linoleum.

I trail behind her as she walks down the hallway.

"Why not?" I say. "It's Friday night poker night. You gotta go. All the cousins will be there."

"Ask me if I care," she says. "Now beat it!"

I ignore the quiver at the corner of her lip and Peter Rabbit who nibbles at her blonde hair like a piece of straw.

"But you're gonna miss all the fun."

"Take a long walk off a short bridge, will you?" Her voice is angry.

She sets Peter on the pillow beside her, then curls up on top of her blankets with a sketch book and a pencil. The page is open to her latest drawing, a fairy with sad eyes. She scribbles "Pauline Lillian May Dodge, July, 1980" on the bottom before flipping to a fresh page.

"Fine. Have it your way."

I drop the corner of her privacy blanket and scurry down the hall, stopping long enough to grab my Raggedy Ann doll. A moment later I rush out the door to catch up with Mum, Dad, and Charlene on the footpath near the garage. Mosquitos mix with the bondo-dust floating through the air.

The pockets on Mum's sad, old housedress clank with quarters. Dad carries the sacred cigar box filled with poker chips.

I drag Raggedy Ann behind me on the path through the clovers and purple pig's weed. When I near Grampy's tow truck, I count the cousins who arrive—Lottie and Dottie, who live in the trailer right next door. *Two.* Tamara, Laurel, and their brother Tyler, who show up on their heels and who live just up the road. *Five.* Richard, the one who gave me the Play Dough set when I broke my leg, his brother, Steve, and their three dress-wearing sisters. *Ten.* There's Tonya with the chipped front teeth, whose top two teeth form an upside-down heart shape when she smiles, her siblings, and a handful of others, not including Charlene and me.

Total of twenty-one.

I smile and put my counting finger away.

Richard and two other cousins hide in the rhubarb bushes and pop out with a roar.

"Put'cha hands behind your head, or I'll shoot!" Richard

demands. He walks behind me and jabs me in the back with his stick pistol.

"Never—" I say.

I dash barefooted through the tall grass with Raggedy Ann bouncing behind me. When I come to the chicken coop, I kneel in the grass and hide.

The sound of my rapidly beating heart fills my ears. I crouch low to the ground and spot a delicate puffball in the dirt beneath the corner of the coop—an old, round, brown mushroom that, if squeezed, deflates and releases a cloud of dust spores. I pick it up, careful not to squish it.

"Stick 'em up," a voice behind me says.

"Don't shoot," I say, standing up slowly and turning around to face Richard.

"What's-at?" he says.

"A puffball. Wicked cunnin', ayuh?"

His pistol hits the ground and turns back into a stick. We march through the tall grass to the freshly mowed field by the garage, over to where the older cousins assign teams for hide-and-seek.

"Count me in," Uncle Jerry says. "I pick Francine."

No. Please. Pick somebody else. I don't like the extra attention he gives me. I don't like how he touches me. I don't like where he touches me.

The florescent light flickers as he scrolls the dented garage door down. The undersized wheels squeal on their tracks.

He walks toward me, wiping the grease from his hands on a small towel. I look up, way up, past his beer belly to his three-day old whiskers.

It's me, David, and him, Goliath.

I'm immediately dizzy. My hands feel clammy and knees shake. My belly fills with collywobbles.

His rough mechanic hands sweep me up, and I'm jolted into the air. Raggedy Ann and I—along with the puffball in my hand—land on his back with a thud. He "neighs" and rakes his boot through the grass as if it's a hoof, and he trots excitedly around the tow truck with Dodge's Auto Salvage painted on both sides. Uncle Jerry races past the twenty-one cousins lined up against the tar-papered garage—half of them shoeless, the other half shirtless—waiting on hide-and-seek to begin.

"Francine's Uncle Jerry's pet!" the cousins' chant.

I'm not his pet!

"One Mississippi, two Mississippi, three Mississippi..." Richard counts.

The horse neighs and rakes its hoof through the grass one more time. It takes off like it's the Kentucky Derby, galloping past the trail of parked cars, and halting behind the unused portion of The House.

No longer the horse, Uncle Jerry lays me down beside the forsaken septic mound and pushes me backward, squishing my prized puffball. Slivers of slate and sharp pebbles pierce my elbows and tailbone.

"That hurts!" I say.

"Sh-h. Uncle Jerry loves you," he says. "Not a peep."

His sandpaper hand holds my face down and covers my mouth and nose.

I can't breathe, the same way I couldn't when a cinnamon FireBall lodged in my throat, before Mum freed the hard candy with her finger.

"Don't think 'bout tellin' anyone, not even Richard. I'll kill you. This is our secret," he says. His head signifies what my answer should be.

In the distance, Richard continues to count. "Ninety-seven Mississippi, ninety-eight Mississippi, ninety-nine Mississippi, one-hundred. Ready or not, here I come!"

Uncle Jerry shushes my cries and removes his hand. A feather-like touch sweeps across my belly button. The sound of my zipper breaks the silence and with a second feather-like brush my shorts slide off. He yanks my white underwear with the pink flowers down.

"We don't tell secrets. Ayuh?" His voice is as hard as steel.

I shake my head.

Yes.

No.

I don't know.

My muscles stiffen and lungs slow. *Am I breathing?*

My mind commands me to move—to get up—to run, but I can't.

He yanks my tube-top up and rubs his scruffy face on my breastbone, like he did in the mafia-styled car. The weight of his chest crushes me.

My pinky won't budge to squash the tiny insects with the siphons buzzing around my head. I roll my eyes to spin over. But I'm stuck. His body lays across me like the lid on a coffin. The stench of sweat, motor oil, and beer burn my nostrils. He kisses my lips but I seal them tightly together.

I yell words in my head, but fear blocks their passage to my mouth.

A second and third mosquito sup.

Why can't I move?

Tangled in fear, tears seep from my eyes and fill my ear holes.

He sits up on his knees.

I silently celebrate and wait for him to leave. Instead, his hips wiggle until his mechanic pants hug his kneecaps. He places his hand back over my mouth and his hips jerk forward. The shock is so deep and painful my insides twist and turn like a murmuration of black birds.

This isn't Mr. Tickle anymore.

A scream erupts in my throat but can't escape with his hand locking it in. The pain rips through me—I'd rather suffer a thousand broken legs than one more minute of this.

More tears spill from my eyes and ripple down my cheeks. Moans and gargles escape his mouth.

A stick snaps nearby.

"Come out, come out, wherever you are," fills the night air.

Again, Uncle Jerry presses his hand to my mouth.

"Friggin'-A. You say a word, I'll kill you," he says, low and slow.

The footsteps draw closer.

"Come out, come out, wherever you are," Richard says a little louder.

Uncle Jerry squeezes my lips forcing them into a fish face and he narrows his eyes.

"Don't make a sound," he whispers.

The Man in the Moon reflects in the sweat of his forehead. A bead of salty water splashes my skin as Richard's footsteps taper away.

Wait! Come back! I want to yell.

My lips sting from his scaly hand baring down on them.

"Uncle Jerry loves you. Ayuh?"

I blink twice.

He lets go and pats my head before reaching into his pocket.

"This is for being a good little girl." He drops two dimes and a nickel in my hand.

Drunken laughter roars from the oval poker table.

"Royal flush!" Grampy shouts.

The clanging of the chips comforts me. I picture Grampy in his blue mechanic shirt with Dodge's Auto Salvage embroidered above the pocket and a pack of smokes in it. He sips a beer with a tri-union of cancer-sticks by his elbow—a cigar, a pipe, and a smoldering cigarette.

But now I'm back and gravel digs into my tailbone. Uncle Jerry zips his zipper and hurries away. I place my ear against the ground and monitor the vibrations of his footsteps as he runs.

The hinges on the screen door creak.

"Deal you in, Shithead?" I hear Grampy say.

"Ah nope, Pop, I have an engine to finish. I'm just gettin' a brewsky," Uncle Jerry says.

The hinges creak a second time, and I lay stock-still until the florescent light from the tar-papered garage glows. Relief from the light pacifies me and I exhale the breath I did not know I held. A shadowy image flashes by the curtainless windows and I shield my eyes from the ghost that haunts The House. I'm fearful the headless doohickey or the glowing pig's eyes my aunts saw when they were little will appear.

I quickly slide my shorts back on, stuff my underwear in my pocket, and then sweep the ground for Raggedy Ann but I can't find her. Sticky goo trickles down the insides of my legs. With slow, small steps I enter The House. I thread my way through the fog of cigarette smoke and drunken laughter, past the tiki bar with the grass-hut roof, by the oval poker table with the two oak leaves to accommodate as many players as possible, through the dimly lit dining room, and into the bathroom.

I shut the door behind me and turn the light on.

There's so much blood.

I'm going to die. I need help. I can't tell.

I pull my underwear out of my pocket and use them to wipe between my legs and then wrap the bloody underwear in toilet paper before shoving them to the bottom of the wastebasket.

With the small of my back against the wall, I slide into a seated position on the floor between the toilet and wicker-wastebasket. I cover my mouth with both hands and scream, but all that comes out is a silent squeal.

Minutes later, someone knocks on the door.

"You okay?"

It's Richard.

"Go away." I pull myself up and twist the faucet handle.

The full blast of water drowns my sobs.

"That was a wicked good hidin' spot you and Uncle Jerry had," Richard says through the door.

"Leave . . . me . . . be." I smear snot and tears up through my hair.

When I'm sure Richard is gone, I edge the bathroom door open and peer out. Cutting through the fog of cigarette smoke with my eyes, I scan the drunken faces, and when I don't see

Uncle Jerry, I dash to the living room and curl up tighter than a pill bug on Grammy's mustard-colored divan and wait for poker night to end.

As I lay half asleep, fear parades in my head and drums up the image of a werewolf-like man chasing me. Its fangs drip with blood and it wears a pair of men's pants and work boots. The fingernails are black with grime. Its breath smells like stale beer and it runs on all fours.

My eyes spring open. Grammy's television makes white static noise, and I glance at the clock to see it's 3:00 a.m. Poker chips clank on the oval table.

My cousins, along with Charlene, lay like a clowder of cats throughout the living room. Charlene shares the divan with me. Tamara and Laurel huddle together in the oversized chair. Tonya and her siblings stretch out under the coffee table. Others lay in front of the television, in corners, under end tables, or wherever else cats find to sleep.

The chips clank, drunken laughter ripples from the poker table, and the sound of work boots clomp toward me. I close my eyes and peer up through two thin slits. Uncle Jerry steps over Tonya and her siblings to tower over me with Raggedy Ann in his hands and a murderous grin on his face.

"Don't think 'bout tellin'," he says as he leans over and whispers in my ear with a voice two octaves lower than normal.

I take a long, shuttering breath and let out a thimble of a yelp. His smelly breath touches me, tickles me, terrifies me. My heart beats faster than a double-bass pedal, and I hold my breath.

"They've yet to believe that church boy, Steve. Don't think for a second anyone will believe a pissant like you."

He takes the greasy hand towel from his shoulder and twists it into the perfect rat's tail.

My eyes water.

"Please, I'll be a good girl." I suck air through my teeth and shield my legs as the twisted towel slices through the air, stinging my bare skin.

"Do you understand?" he says with a thin ribbon of teeth showing.

I blink my answer and watch him walk away.

Despite my sleeping cousins all around me and Charlene at my feet, I feel alone. A silent wail escapes my lips, and I bring my legs back into the fetal position.

I stare at my flattened puffball and the sweaty two dimes and a nickel in my hand.

"Girls—" Dad bellows from the poker table. "Wake your asses up. It's time to go!"

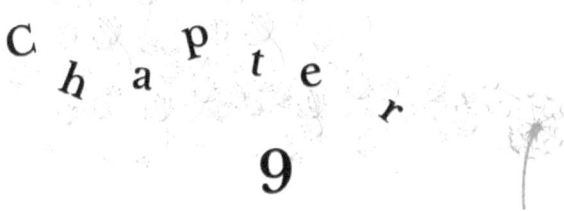

9

VOLCANO MABLE

My birthday, August 18, 1980, comes and goes, and even though just a month ago, my life as I knew it changed, I am now gratefully and happily seven years old. I wear my blue Smurf watch and stare with glee at Clumsy's arms which rotate around the face to tell me the time.

I set the table for a late supper. As I stir the Kool-Aid in the pitcher, it dawns on me that I haven't seen Pauline all day.

Leaving the spoon to swirl in the purple water, I race to her bedroom and throw open the privacy blanket. The covers on her bed lay in a heap, and her sketches lay on the floor. In the past few months, she's hardly left her room except to catch the school bus or eat supper. Like bears, frogs, and bees, she hibernates.

In my parents' bedroom, Dad works at his desk stuffing sports cards in plastic sleeves. I pop my head in the doorway.

"I can't find Pauline," I say.

I don't know why I'm worried, but I am. Maybe because this wouldn't be the first time she's taken off. She's not that much older than me and Charlene, and when I think of ghosts in windows or monsters in heavy boots, my belly feels sick.

Dad's elbow knocks the pricing gun over as he gets up and hurries down the striped carpet to the front of the house. He steps onto the stoop and calls for her.

"Pauline, suppertime!" His powerful voice fills the air.

The neighborhood dogs and cats react under the sway of his voice, but not Pauline, not this time.

Charlene dashes next door to Aunt Mable's to see if she's there. I hustle the three telephone pole lengths to The House, past Lulu and Larry, Grammy's white geese, honking and snaking their necks.

The chipped red door is open. I burst through the front door and into the kitchen.

"Hi Grammy! Have you seen Pauline?"

Grammy Dodge has a flyswatter in her right hand, a bottle of Coca-Cola in her left, and a cigarette between her teeth. She's a professional fly killer, with the blood-and-guts on the swatter and ceiling to prove it.

"Ah nope, dear. Why?"

She peers out the window, looking over the field toward the garage light.

Without saying anything else, I zip back down the footpath past the honking and snaking geese, past the rusty brown hand pump to Mum's sad old chair, where Charlene shakes her head, I shake mine, and Mum unpacks a worried look.

As she sets down the box of dried prunes, Mum's eyes water. Then it hits me: *Pauline's run away—again.*

Within twenty-minutes, the surrounding woods, junkyard, and cornfields crawl with relatives and poker friends. Grampy's clients, aunts, uncles, and cousins call Pauline's name. With flashlights in hand, Dad sends them out to search every crevasse, junk car, cornfield, and wooded area within one square mile. But there is one who isn't looking for her: Uncle Jerry. He's in the garage working.

Brightly shining stars etch out Aquarius and Capricorn and eighty-six other constellations, which Mum points out on clear nights, just not tonight. The stars sparkle in the heavens and mirror the lightening bugs on the ground. The heavenly flares light the sky along with the moon as Mum waits on the stoop for news of Pauline's where-a-bouts. Mum hot-boxes—a newly opened pack—and her hands tremble the way Dad's voice did when he yelled for Pauline and she didn't come.

Mum flicks the embers and then the filters in the grass, one filter after another. The smoldering arrangement creates a new constellation of fleeting red lights.

I stand beside the stoop in the grass, smashing the smoldering butts like Smoky the Bear would want me to do.

Mum's hair springs wildly from the rubber band, and she strikes a match to light another cigarette.

"Why I oughtta'..."

The voice echoing from across the yard makes the hair on my neck raise. Aunt Mable barrels toward us over the grass in the dim light of the moon.

My eyes widen.

She's gonna blow!

Aunt Mable paces toward Mum and me with her fists bunched. My cousin Steve nicknamed her *Volcano Mable*, a befitting name as she blows up frequently. One time she blew up at Tamara and Laurel's mum during a poker game. The fight ended with my Uncle Ray threatening to shoot Aunt Mable with the shotgun he grabbed from behind the tiki bar. It's the only time I'd ever seen Aunt Mable back down from a fight.

In a few quick strides, Aunt Mable reaches the stoop where Mum sits. Looming over her, Volcano Mable pokes Mum in the shoulder angrily with her index finger.

"This wouldn't've happened if you'd let me raise her," Aunt Mable says. "Pollyanna wouldn't've run away. She could be dead for all you know."

"I love my girls." Mum's voice shakes.

"You sure have a funny way of showin' it, Franny."

"Don't talk to my mum like that!" I stomp my foot in the grass, one time, then two.

Aunt Mable cranes her neck around.

"Why, you little shit. I'll say whatever the hell I please. The apple doesn't fall far from the tree, now does it? Why don'tcha put that in your pipe and smoke it?"

"Go on, go look for Pauline," Mum says to me. "Search the cornfields like I told you."

"I have—twice already." I sigh.

"Do it again, damn-it!" Mum rocks on the stoop and holds her knees the way I wish she would hold me sometimes. "How many times do I haveta' tell you, Mable? Pauline's *my* daughter, not *yours*."

"You sure didn't mind me and Chester keepin' her while you and my brother drank yourselves into a stupor. We took good care of Pollyanna. Now look at her—"

"Blame it on me, why don'tcha, Mable? What's new? And we didn't take her from you. We moved to Florida, or did you forget?"

Aunt Mable wags her finger at Mum. "I wanted you to take the twins and leave Pollyanna with me. She had so many ailments. If it wasn't for me and Chester, she...she—"

"If it wasn't for you and Chester, what? She'd be an invalid. How can I forget? You constantly remind me."

"It broke Pollyanna's heart when you moved away and left her pony for me and Chester to tend."

"Which I told you not to buy. What'd you expect? That we take a pony cross country? I told you she was too young to have it. And yes, we were shitty parents, but who the hell isn't?"

Aunt Mable taps her flip-flop in the gravel. "I offered to pay for a septic system to be put in, but you and Charlie refused. The girls are filthy all the time and look like ragamuffins. Not to mention, Franny, this isn't the first time Pollyanna's run away, but who's countin'?"

Aunt Mable's neck muscles flinch.

"Aggravatin' cuss, ain'tcha?" Mum flicks a barely smoked cigarette on the ground.

"Well, don't say we didn't try—"

"Why don'tcha walk a mile in my moccasins before you go judgin' me? We do the best we can with what we have."

"You do the best you can? I know where all your money goes, and it ain't on 'em girls."

Mum raises her brow. "What we do with our money isn't your business."

"It *is* my business. You and Charlie make it my business when you borrow money from us. If Charlie didn't spend all of his paychecks on flea market junk, you'd have some money, now, wouldn't you?"

"You're just jealous."

Aunt Mable clenches her fists. Her body tenses up and shakes wildly as if daring Mum to say it.

"You don't have kids, so you raise everybody else's," Mum says it, taking the dare. "Instead of havin' your claws in Pauline, now you've got 'em in Lottie and Dottie. You've somehow convinced your own brother to let you raise his kids."

"Watch it, Franny," Mable warns. "You're treadin' on thin ice now. I had a baby once and she died, or have you forgotten? And for your information, Chester and I adopted Lottie and Dottie. They're our girls now."

Mable rears her hand back like to slap Mum. Then she pauses.

"Hit a nerve...did I?" Mum hisses and rubs her wool-lined moccasin over the smoldering cigarette in front of her.

Aunt Mable glares at Mum.

"Well, Franny, at least my girls don't piss in buckets. Put that in your pipe and smoke it!"

"I don't recall 'em complainin'." Mum strikes a match and holds it to another cigarette between her fingers.

"Of course not. They don't know any better."

Mum sets the cigarette pouch on the stoop.

"You're too thick-headed to talk any sense to. Now I'd appreciate it if you'd go home," Mum says.

Dad comes around the corner. "What the hell do you want?" he says, sharply.

Aunt Mable throws her hands in the air and storms the one-telephone pole distance back to her trailer. Her words trail behind her like the tails on a tuxedo.

"Don't worry, babe," Dad says. "We'll find her."

"What 'bout the quicksand pit? Or the ghost town? Or Walker Hill? Or . . . or . . ." Mum weeps, dropping her head into her hands.

"We'll find her, babe." Dad takes a drag from Mum's cigarette, the orange glow highlighting his mustache.

Having had enough outside, I go into the house, where the television blares and Pauline's dinner sits on the table with aluminum foil wrapped over it. I march down the hallway and open the hanging blanket to her bedroom. She rarely allows anyone behind it and would be furious if she caught me. The only creature with the rite of passage is Peter, our rabbit.

Pauline's bedroom has clothes, books, papers, and our parents' bowling trophies here, there, and everywhere. It's difficult to know where to begin—worse than mine. But I'm sure she's left a note somewhere. She always does.

Due to a laundry list of ailments, a teal typewriter with a bell-return sits on Pauline's particle board desk. She types her homework, mainly to strengthen her wrists and hands until she can hold a pencil properly like the doctor said. She uses a typewriter at school, too, where she spends most of her day in a utility-sized closet.

Pauline is masterfully sarcastic. But, underneath the layers of sarcasm, she's paper-doll thin. She turned ten years old in November. Mum and Dad pay to have bras special-made to fit her, because as Mum says, "She's well endowed." Pauline hates to be called "Dolly Parton," and her "coming of age" brings oily hair, periods, over-active sweat glands, oozing acne, weight gain, facial hair, and unwanted attention from boys who treat her breasts like a petting zoo.

I find an envelope on her pillow. It reads:

TO: SHITHEAD,

I hope you die, so I can spit on your grave.
Pauline

SHE HATES HIM JUST AS I DO. HE'S THE REASON WHY SHE RAN away. Or maybe it's me. I hang my head and rub the splint on my hand, where Pauline broke three of my fingers last week when she punched me, because when she was struggling to put on her shoes, I said something maybe I shouldn't have.

"What's wrong, Dolly Parton? Can't see your feet over your big knockers?" I remembered saying.

Pauline growled and threw a punch at my face. I blocked it with my hand, snapping three fingers on my right hand like string beans.

"Here she comes!" says a voice from outside Pauline's bedroom window.

The sound of Pauline's name brings me back to the present, and I race outside to see my sister hobbling up the driveway.

Dad wears a T-shirt that reads, I belong to HER with an arrow pointing to the left, and Mum wears a T-shirt that reads, I belong to HIM with an arrow pointing to the right, T-shirts they bought at the flea market.

"Your father and I've been worried sick." Mum's lips tremble.

"I didn't go far," Pauline says, "I was hidin' in that there tree."

She points to the oak across the road from Grammy Dodge's house.

"Migod," Mum says, placing her palms on her cheeks.

"You're grounded," Dad says.

Pauline limps up the three steps and through the front of the house. I follow her inside.

Hungry, I fix a fluffernutter sandwich for myself. While I spread the fluff on one slice, Pauline's words in the note to Uncle Jerry, "I ran away," stick with me like a mental Post-It note. Within seconds, I'm covered in notes with different words.

A werewolf.

Mr. Tickle.

Pauline's letter.

The puffball.

The mafia-styled car.

The six-legged octopus.

Pauline's letter.

The marshmallow squishes between the slices, and I lick the excess with my tongue. *Wonder how many cousins hate Uncle Jerry, too?*

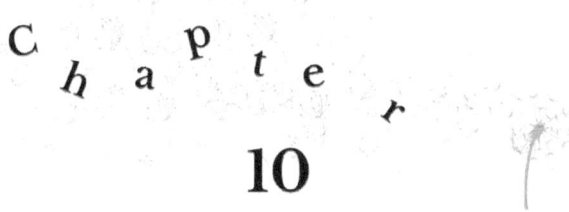

10

THE GREEN SCHOOL BUS

There are three lunch groups: full pay, reduced, and free. Some of the kids hold baggies with coins to give to the lunch lady.

I must be free because she never asks for any money.

I take my tray and scurry across the gymnasium to sit with Charlene. We both eat Salisbury steak and mashed potatoes with gravy.

After lunch, I head back to the classroom to complete my math assignment, while the rest of the class heads outside for recess.

My desk is near the hand sink in the back of the room by the fishbowl. The row of towering windows provides enough light for me to work and highlights the hot pink polka dots from the Barbie lipstick I dotted all over my body earlier in a foiled attempt to fake the chicken pox.

I scribble furiously with my polka-dotted hand to complete the math assignment in hopes to pet the baby moose that visits the playground during recess and whose picture was featured in the *Canaan Gazette*.

Jacob, a chubby-cheeked third grader with freckles, pops into the classroom to put his lunchbox away. He's one of the cool kids, which means he's a walker—who lives in a fancy house near by—not a bus rider.

Jacob reaches up, puts his lunchbox on the top shelf, then turns on his heel to face me.

"Wanna' see somethin'?" he asks.

"Ayuh," I say with surprise since he normally doesn't speak to me.

He takes ten steps across the checkered tile floor, and when he nears my desk, he undoes his snap and pulls down his pants.

I pause a beat.

"Is that your wiener?" I say with a gasp. My mind trying to make sense of it.

Are all boys like Uncle Jerry? Maybe Jacob knows my secret. But how? No. That can't be. I haven't told anyone.

I push my chair back, give a high-pitched shriek, and bolt out of the room and down the hallway with my polka-dotted arms flailing wildly in the air. My saddle shoes click-clack-clucking on the checkered tile all the way to the principal's office.

"Jacob showed me his wiener." I huff and puff and suck in air.

Five days later, when Jacob returns to school after being suspended, he stands on the wooden contraption above me and calls my name.

"Whatcha' want?" I plant both saddle shoes in the mulch and gaze up at him.

Jacob takes a deep breath and hocks a loogie from way back in his throat. With my mouth wide open and a ray of sunshine in my eyes, he spits. The slimy torpedo lands in my mouth and slides down my throat.

"Ptooey. Ptooey. Ptooey," I spit, gagging and heaving and clawing at my tongue.

"Pay back—" Jacob says with a hint of satisfaction.

THE FOLLOWING SATURDAY, I STAND ON A WOODEN CHAIR AT the kitchen sink and squeeze toothpaste onto my toothbrush. When the bristles touch the back of my tongue, I gag and spit and remember the loogie.

I lower the metal dipper into the five-gallon bucket of water beside me and bring it to my lips, swoosh the water around a bit in my mouth, and spit it out. It empties into the drain and makes a tribal drum sound in the empty slop bucket below.

Mum sits at the table sorting the floaters from the sinkers to make Boston baked beans with Boston Brown Bread for supper. She prepares three bean pots, and from experience, no matter how many scoops I feed to Snoopy under the table or how many helpings I throw in the rubbish, the three pots of beans have the uncanny ability to stretch four nights like magic beans.

Mum loves baked beans, but they don't agree with her, neither does cabbage or dried prunes, which is why we nicknamed her *Pepe Le Pew*. I like baked beans, but not three pots worth. Come the second night, the front of the house wreaks of silent-deadly-fumes. Furthermore, Dad and Pauline compete for the "Loudest Belcher" award.

I jump down from the kitchen chair, put on my blue windbreaker—to protect against the chilly spring afternoon—grab Holly Hobby and Raggedy Ann, then skip down the grassy footpath to play with Charlene and my cousins at The House.

When I reach the corner of the garage, I turn left toward the green school bus surrounded by a tangle of wildflowers: Queen Anne's lace, black-eyed Susan's, red and orange Indian paint-brushes, and purple morning glories. The morning glories climb the sides of the bus and cover its roof. It's no longer a school bus, but an engineless camper—complete with a kitchenette, a bathroom, and a bedroom in the far back.

I push the bi-fold door open and motion for Lottie, Dottie, Tonya, and Charlene to follow me up the steps.

"We're not supposed to," Lottie says.

"Grampy ain't gonna know," I say. "You're just a bunch of

chickens, that's all." I wedge my hands under my armpits and wiggle my shoulders around. "Brawk, braaawk, brawk, braaawk, brawk."

Tonya pushes out her bottom lip. "I'm no chicken," she says.

"Ayuh?" I say, "then prove it."

I push past the lot of them and make my way down the aisle, where I crouch behind the arm of the bolted-down divan with Raggedy Ann in one hand and Holly Hobby in the other.

After a long minute, I peek the painted eyes of my Holly Hobby doll around the edge of the divan.

Where'd everyone go?

The scent of motor oil and sweat hits me like a wall of rain. Before I can see the grungy ball cap hiking up the steps, my stomach sinks at the thought of Uncle Jerry. Now I'm the one bolted to the floor.

The bi-fold door glides shut. Uncle Jerry fumbles to latch the eye hook, shutting us in and keeping everyone else out. Then he totters back and forth as he moves toward me with a beer in his hand. It splashes on his boots and flows down the metal grate—wetting the heel of my shoe and Holly Hobby's patchwork dress.

The beer bottle rises to his lips. He tosses his head back and takes a swig.

I hide my face behind Holly Hobby's blue bonnet.

"How's my little girl? New haircut, ayuh. Looks wicked pretty." His words slur. "You look like a woman. How old are you now?"

"Eight," I whisper.

He sweeps the flowery panels shut, leaving a crack to make room for the sunlight. His inky black fingers wrestle with his belt buckle. I squeeze my eyes shut and hear the swoosh of his pants as they fall. Then hear the swoosh of mine.

I swallow hard.

"Please Uncle Jerry, I'll be a good girl," I say, swatting at my tears like a fly.

His hand muzzles my mouth and forces the words back in.

"Look at me."

My eyes flutter open in obedience.

"Hark the ruckus before we get caught." He lets go of my mouth and raises my chin with his finger. His armpits reek worse than a thousand stinking Benjamins.

"I love you," he says.

Teardrops fall from my eyes and wet his sandpapery hand.

"I know you do." I force the lie out through the fish face he makes with my cheeks.

Soon, the jolly sounds of Charlene and my cousins return. They bang on the bi-fold door. The sound of their knocking is magnified by the scream that is caught in my throat.

"Open up or we'll tell," they say as they march around the green bus like Jericho, one time, two times, three times, then seven.

I close my eyes and picture Aunt Jenny in Sunday school with the Joshua finger puppet she made from felt and replay in my head how Joshua won the battle of Jericho. And in that moment, I am determined, I will do the same—I will keep silent.

Charlene and the others bang on the sides of the bus like a drum set.

"Get lost you little pissants." Uncle Jerry clenches his teeth.

"Francine's Uncle Jerry's pet," the cousins chant, ignoring him.

Stop calling me that! I'm not his pet!

"Scram!" Uncle Jerry says angrily. He bangs the window with his fist. The cords in his neck stick out like the pages of a pop-up story book.

The playful chatter disperses in the direction of the crabapple tree. He turns his attention back to me and lets go of my lips. His eyes stab me.

"I love you," he says again as he runs his fingers through my curls. "Do you love me?"

Tears spout from my eyes. *I hate you! I wish you were dead!* I swallow the words I wish to say.

"You know I do," I reply, forcing a smile on my face to reassure him that I'm okay—we're okay—it's okay. Afraid of what will happen if I don't, all the while wiping away the snot that drips from my nose.

Several agonizing minutes later, he yanks his pants up and opens the flowery panels. A ray of sunshine beams against my cheek.

"If you tell, I'll kill you," he says.

You're a monster.

My lips close around the words I want to say.

He buckles his belt and pats my head.

"You're my good little girl. You don't want anythin' to happen to us...like jail...do you?"

My eyes widen.

"That's what will happen if you tell."

I don't want to go to jail. My hammering heart pounds. I hug my dolls to my chest.

"Now pull your pants up and dress your feet." He reaches into his pocket and drops two dimes and a nickel in my palm.

They clank together and I close my hand around them.

Sweat drips down his forehead from his ball cap. He grabs the beer off the tiny counter and totters off the bus. I shake my head to free my thoughts. Too sore to tie my shoes, I curl up in a ball on the bolted-down divan with my dolls.

God, it's me, Francine, I begin. *For once, can you take the peanut butter out of your ears and listen to me?*

Since Uncle Jerry started doing bad things to me, I had taken up praying just like Aunt Jenny showed me in Sunday school, but I must be doing it all wrong. If God can do anything like Aunt Jenny said, then why won't He stop Uncle Jerry from hurting me?

I look up at the metal ceiling. *You must not love me.*

Tears fill my ear holes.

"Fran—cine!" Dad calls, in the distance, in two long syllables. His powerful voice fills the air.

"Comin'," I call back with a voice smaller than a mouse.

I tuck Raggedy Ann and Holly Hobby under my arm still in my blue windbreaker. Descending the stairs, listening to the clunking sound my untied saddle shoes make, feeling them rubbing the back of my heel with every step.

My knees jitter as I approach the footpath near the garage. Light from the welding torch flickers, then stops, flickers again, then stops. Uncle Jerry's blackened image appears in the doorway. A mare's nest of debris bunches up in my thoughts along with a tumbleweed of fear in my belly.

He slides the welding shield up and locks eyes with me. "How's my little girl?"

"Fine," I say with a hiccupy cry.

I clutch my belly and drop my dolls in the inky oil spot at my feet.

He takes a few quick steps. Picks the dolls up for me. Pats the grass off them.

"You sure you're fine?" He looks over his shoulder at Grampy, who is on the phone in the garage.

"My belly hurts, that's all."

"We don't tell secrets," Uncle Jerry says under his breath.

I smile on queue.

"You better get down the path apiece before my brother comes lookin' for you. We wouldn't want him suspectin' anythin' now, would we?" Uncle Jerry asks, sliding the welding mask down, then popping it right back up.

Wordless as my dolls, I twirl the tips of my hair around my finger and stare down at my loose shoestrings. I rock back on my heels and give a slow head shake.

"That's my good girl! If anyone asks where you got the bruise between your legs, you tell 'em you fell ridin' your bike. You did fall ridin' your bike, right?"

I give a hard nod.

"Good girl." He reaches into his pocket and pulls out two more dimes and a nickel.

Grampy hangs up the phone in the garage and grabs the keys to the tow truck.

"Let's go Shithead," Grampy says. "Got a car broken down on Route 2."

Grampy walks right by and doesn't acknowledge me. *He never does.*

The driver's door of the tow truck opens and Grampy climbs into the cab. He lets out a wicked cough, and before closing the door, spits on the ground.

It's red!

Then I remember Grammy trying to make him go see a doctor and calling him an "aggravating cuss" because he refused.

"Comin' Pops," Uncle Jerry says as he turns around and steers me by my shoulders onto the worn path with a nudge toward home.

As I near the backside of the garage where the rhubarb plants grow wild, instead of following my normal routine of examining the plants for the ripest and pinkest stalk to dip in sugar, I scamper by without stopping.

With each step, the blaring television gets louder. The rickety stoop creaks. I fling open the mustard-trimmed door. The dolls and the loose change hit the linoleum. Making a beeline for the bathroom, I remove a lid and swat green bottle flies away from the pisspots.

Toilet paper and feces fill both five-gallon buckets, but I sit down anyways. The soiled paper touches my bare skin and the fumes from the bucket irritates my already sore parts. My belly lets out a rumble and diarrhea spills out.

Mum charges through the pink and white privacy curtains with two chewable aspirins. "You're lookin' a bit peak-id. Runnin' a fever, I see."

"Babe—" Mum says as she calls to Dad. "I thought I told you to empty the pisspots."

"Hold your horses," Dad calls back from the living room,

where moments earlier he was thumbing through a catalog, checking off items to order for the flea market.

Mum gives a sharp sigh.

"Never mind," she mutters, "I'll do it myself. Like everythin' else."

She pauses and looks down.

"Helluva bruise you got there, String-bean," the name she calls me when I'm sick.

She opens my legs and pushes my thighs apart.

"I haven't seen bruises like these since Moses wore knee-pants. Where'd you get 'em?"

I can't tell you. He'll kill me!

It's Uncle Jerry, I practice saying in my head, but the words don't make it to my mouth.

"I banged it on the banana-seat while ridin' my bike. I told you 'bout that yesterday."

"Poppycock!" Mum says.

The skin between her eyes wrinkles. She retreats to her bedroom and calls for me to join her.

I hold my stomach with both hands and slump over as I make my way from the pots, through the pink and white checkered drapes, and out into the hallway, where I pass Dad on the striped carpet. He takes a left into the bathroom, spitting and sputtering like old man Peabody's tractor.

"Pull your skivvies down and lie back." Mum points to her bed.

"What? No! Mum, please. You can't be serious."

"As a heart attack," she says.

"Why not on the other side of the bed? Why this side?" I look out into the hallway to see where Dad is, not wanting him to see me naked from the waist down.

On the verge of waterworks, I drop my underwear and climb up on Mum's bed and lay with my legs dangling over the side.

If she suspects something... I'm dead!

Doctor Mom stoops to examine me.

"Anyone touch you down here?" she asks, poking and prodding.

I shake my head hard and fast.

She removes the shade on the lamp for better lighting. When the lighting doesn't do it, she grabs the flashlight off Dad's desk.

"No. Why?" My heart pounds and my palms sweat.

Her left brow makes a peak.

"Are you sure?"

The inspection makes me uncomfortable.

She's too close. It's taking too long. I don't like it.

"I'm wicked sure," I say.

But am I really?

I pick my head up and see Dad coming out of the bathroom with the two five-gallon pisspots. He spins sideways with his back to me, so not to see me, eases by the teetering stacks of what-nots in the hall, and out the back door to the pit in the woods where the grass is neon green and a spring of water bubbles up from the ground.

"Your peach is red and swollen. When's the last time you washed down here?"

"I dunno'."

"You haveta' keep your girl parts clean," she says, turning the flashlight off.

"I will. Now can I get dressed?"

"Not so fast," Mum says. She thumbs through her worn medical dictionary, until she finds the page she is looking for.

"It could be the start of a UTI. Hard tellin' not knowin'," she says, before disappearing out of the room.

The soles of her wool-lined moccasins scuff down the striped carpet in the hall. The refrigerator opens, then slams, and seconds later, she returns with a cup of juice.

"Drink this," she says.

My mouth puckers at the taste of the cranberries.

When I'm done forcing it down, I place the plastic cup on

Mum's nightstand. After shimmying my underwear back up, I climb under the covers of her bed.

Pauline and Charlene climb up into the bed beside me and get cozy. Mum takes the record player down from the closet and puts on our favorite Disney record, *Jack and the Beanstalk*.

The heels of Dad's boots clomp down the hall from the direction of the back exit. This time he holds two empty buckets.

"Babe, don't forget to swoosh a cap full of Pine-Sol in each bucket before puttin' the lids back on," Mum says as Dad walks by the open door and into the bathroom.

Charlene's cheeks pucker with the laughter she holds back.

"Pine-Sol? That's like puttin' lipstick on a pig," she manages to say between chuckles.

I cover my mouth with the blanket and giggle.

"Must be somethin' to it," Pauline says. Her lazy eye shuffles back and forth between us. "Because Mum's been doin' it for as long as I can remember."

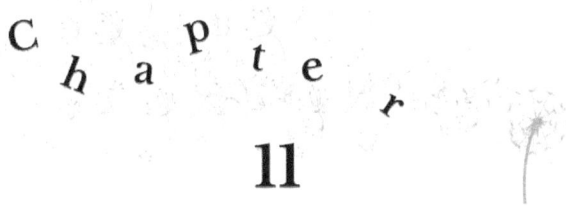

11

THE DRESS WEARING SAVIOR

Mum smashes a filter in the ashtray and tosses me a pink flowery dress with a sash.

"Put this on," she says.

"No way, Jose. Dresses are for girls!" I cross my arms over my chest and let the dress fall to the floor.

"It's family picture day at Olan Mills. I don't hear your sisters' complainin'," Mum says.

The springs on the divan creak, and in a flash, Dad stands over me in his baby blue dress suit. He taps his freshly polished Navy shoe on the carpet and holds his hands on his hips.

"Do it, damn-it!" He points at the dress on the floor.

Grey smoke streams from his nostrils and we lock eyes like two bucks locking horns.

"Okay, geesh," I say after a beat, breaking the stare.

I wiggle the dress over my head and plop down in front of Mum's sad old chair so she can fix my hair.

Mum ties a bow on top of my head with a puffy purple ribbon. Before I can get to my feet, she yanks me back down and jerks my ear forward.

"When's the last time you scrubbed back here?"

"You always say that."

I bristle at the sound she makes while licking her thumb. I bristle more at her scrubbing behind my ear with it, and even more at the coffee and stale cigarette combo smell her spittle leaves on my skin.

"Let's get to gettin' it," Dad says, "I wanna check on Pop's before we leave for Olan Mills."

Pauline, Charlene, and I grab our matching sweaters, then line up behind Mum and Dad. We follow them down the path to The House.

In the kitchen, adults and kids lean against walls and sit wherever they can find a seat: on the kindlin box, in the rocking chair, on the counter. Because Grampy is weak, he hasn't been out of bed since the day he spit blood on the ground. Uncle Jerry sits at the oval table in Grampy's head chair.

Mule, a neighbor, stands by the stove. He wears a pair of dungaree overalls and no shirt. His ears stick out along with his belly, and he is daring in a scary kind of way. Last week, Mule doused his car with gasoline and set it on fire in middle of the bog road. The explosion sounded like a rocket ship blasting into space. This morning, he stands at the stove unflinching with his hand over the dancing blue flame.

I follow Mum and Dad into the room off the kitchen, behind the tiki bar, where Grampy rests. I can't help but stare at the extra skin on his jowls collecting in fleshy scoops. To the left of the bed sits his worn mechanic shirt and mechanic pants neatly folded with his rectangular glasses on top of them.

I study the room where he lays and everyone crammed into it —a stream of endless hugs and sad eyes, the scent of talcum powder and mouthwash mixed with cigarettes and booze, an empty tissue box, shimmering cobwebs, and a Maytag dryer.

"Cancer sucks," Pauline says. Her nose prickles and she burst into tears, wetting her eye patch.

What's cancer? And how long is eternity? It sounds like a long time. Longer than the wait between birthdays.

Grammy sits on the edge of Grampy's bed and leans over him with her left foot planted on the floor. Her back arches like a half-moon protractor. He coughs up blood and phlegm as she dabs his mouth with a clean tissue and weeps.

"I dunno' what I'll do without'cha, old man," Grammy says.

She squeezes his hand and then, without warning, wilts into his lap.

Mum clears her throat. "It's the death rattle. Only a matter of time now."

Shrills fill the room. Shivers run up my spine and into my hairline.

"Is he good enough? Did he do enough?" Grammy asks, lifting her head.

Of course, Grampy's a good person. Why is she asking this?

I frown up at Mum who chokes on emotion.

"Grammy's askin' if Grampy's goin' to heaven."

Well, isn't he?!

My mouth hangs open.

"Pop's is a wicked good man, Ma," Mum says. "He'd give the shirt off his back. I've seen him do it. If you ask me, that alone will get him in. Saint Peter will be there to welcome him, and Ole' Gabrielle, why he'll even blow the trumpet."

"Ayuh, I think you're right, Franny." Grammy continues to dab his mouth.

Mum wipes her eyes and reaches over me for an ash tray. A dusting of ash roosts on my shoulder.

I sweep the grey flakes off my sweater and catch Charlene giving me a head nod. She tiptoes out of the room toward the chipped red door. I follow her.

Outside, Rex the rooster and his harem of clucking chickens scratch for bugs. I toss them a handful of dried corn from the barrel. Their clucking intensifies, and from the coop flaps Lulu and Larry—Grammy's two white geese. They fly toward us, honking and snaking their necks.

Around the corner appears Aunt Jenny, the dress-wearing savior.

"Shoo, shoo," she yells as she whacks two sticks together.

I'm glad about it. Earlier on the way up to The House, Mum told Dad to "Guard his family jewels." She said this after our uncle nearly lost his when Grammy's goose, Larry, bit him.

But I don't know what jewels Mum means. Dad only wears two—a watch and a wedding band.

The honking geese swerve right. Charlene and I swerve left, and run in our matching dresses and saddle shoes to the meadow across the road. We scour the ground covered in tall grass for arrowheads left behind by our Black Foot and Wabanaki ancestors and pick tiny yellow buttercups to test our ticklish levels.

We romp through the colorful Indian paintbrushes, black-eyed Susan's, and Queen Anne's lace, spinning and twirling in our matching dresses. The two of us delight that the bottoms of the dresses rise and fall like the parachute game in gym class.

After a short break, we scale a knee-high stone wall and stroll along the top of the rocks carefully so not to "lose a foot in a fisher hole" as Mum says. We walk to an unfamiliar patch of woods, where vibrant green fiddleheads spring from the moist soil like the wiry tentacles on shrimp, perfect for harvesting.

Charlene stabs her finger at the clearing through the triune of trees—white birch, balsam fir, and sugar maple—to the giant teepee covered in deer skins.

"Have you ever?" she says with a gasp.

"No, I never," I say with an even bigger one.

"M-M-Mum's right! Gypsies do live in these woods. Last one there's a rotten egg." Charlene takes off in a sprint through the thicket toward the clearing.

In the field, by the teepee, sits a rusty rotisserie rack, a fire pit, a broken lantern, corroded pots, a big ball of purple wax, a few miniature spoons, and a scarf with holes in it.

I turn toward Charlene. "I got an *idear*. You know the book Pauline's readin', right?"

She eyes me with suspicion.

"We can play *Hunchback* and pretend to be gypsies. You be Frollo."

"No way, I'm Esmeralda. Y-Y-You be Frollo."

I put my hands on my hips. "You're crazier than Gideon's geese. It was my *idear*."

"Why am I always the baby or the boy?" she asks.

"Because, stupid, babies wet the bed."

She shrugs as if to say, *Point well taken.*

In a flash, our youthful imaginations whisk us away to a medieval village with cathedrals, villains, and unlikely heroes.

Charlene, being Frollo, chases me around the teepee and toward the trees, where I collapse on a jack-in-the-pulpit flower, crushing its green and purple tubular bloom.

"Koochie koochie koo," she says, standing over me with tickle fingers.

Her words "koochie koochie koo" yank me back to the mafia-styled car, then yank me back further to the first time I met Uncle Jerry at Grammy's house, when he reached for me with his tickle fingers.

Within seconds, it's no longer Charlene's face I see pretending to be Frollo, but Uncle Jerry's face. Then I sink into the bed of leaves and pine needles and screw my eyes shut, curling into a ball.

I'm not afraid, I'm not afraid, I'm not afraid, I will myself.

"What's w-w-wrong," Charlene asks, drawing me back with her soft stutter.

My eyes open. I stare up at the clouds that serve as the ceiling above me while trying to forget what just happened. I'm no longer The Beautiful Esmerelda but a girl-shaped robot who operates on two dimes and a nickel.

"I'm fine," I say, but, *am I really?*

"Let's go check on Grampy." I jump up like nothing happened, and grab the purple ball of wax left behind by the gypsies to give to Mum.

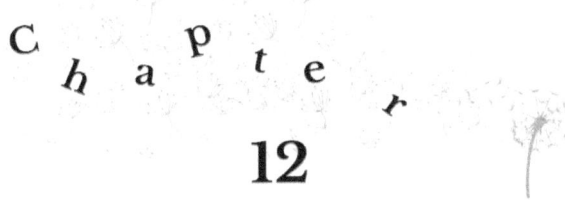

12

IMPS AND A JALOPY

In May of 1982, the fourth-grade class takes a trip to Margaret Chase Smith Elementary School in Skowhegan to listen to the first woman senator of Maine speak. On the bus ride over, I rest my head against the window. The vibration of the bus makes me sleepy and soon I'm dreaming or maybe I'm remembering—I don't know. The images that haunt me in my bed at night now parade in my head like a tutu-wearing circus dog—

Grampy's fleshy scoops.

A six-legged octopus.

And a werewolf in a mechanic suit.

A green school bus.

Twenty minutes into the ride, Charlene nudges me. I shake my head free from the dream. My heart beats rapidly. The secrets I keep only make the monsters more real.

We shuffle into the auditorium where fourth graders from all of the Somerset County schools gather to hear the Senator speak. My mind struggles—*why does the octopus in my dreams only ever have six legs?*

"Senator Smith is known as 'The Mother of the Wave' and

she condemns bigotry and injustice. Ladies and gentlemen, I give you, Margaret Chase Smith," the principal announces.

The Senator is old, slow, short, and as she wobbles to the microphone, I notice she has a hunch on her back. A white tuft of hair moves every now and again and pokes up above the wooden podium. I observe with my chin in my palms. Not sure what she is babbling about, I notice my belly is grumbling. I try not to think about it.

۝

BEFORE SCHOOL LETS OUT FOR THE YEAR, CHARLENE AND I take a walk around the block. A five-mile route from our house on Nelson Hill Road to Salisbury Road to Hill Road, and back onto Nelson Hill Road. Today, we wheel the red Radio Flyer Ryder wagon down the road in hopes of finding discarded bottles and cans to cash in at the local recycling center for the Scholastic Book Fair. At the recycling center we get ten cents a bottle and five cents a can. I have my heart set on a set of Care Bear erasers with matching stickers. Charlene has hers set on a Judy Bloom book.

We stroll past Grammy's house and past Mr. Peabody's cornfield toward the stop sign where Nelson Hill Road and Salisbury meet. The little wheels on the wagon squeal loudly behind us.

Two telephone pole lengths from the end of Salisbury Road, where Hill Road joins it, we spot what looks like a bottle glistening in the sun. As Charlene digs in the leaves, I drop the handle to the wagon and reach deep into my pocket for the matches and cigarette I took from Mum.

"What's-at?" Charlene asks, returning with the bottle.

"What's it look like? Mum ain't gonna miss one cigarette."

"Nine-year-old's d-d-on't smoke," Charlene says, "and besides we'll get caught."

"Not if you don't tell."

With the stick teetering between my lips, I strike the small red head of the match against the sandpaper strip and raise the orange flame to my mouth. I peer down my nose at the cigarette that bobs up and down. My eyes cross while I'm trying to light it. When lit, I breathe in and before I can exhale, I'm struck with an aggravating cough. Black smoke streams from my nostrils and burns the inside of my nose like fire. The taste of charcoaled skin settles at the back of my throat.

"Your turn," I choke out.

"No way, Jose." Charlene turns her head away in protest.

"You wanna be cool, don'tcha?"

The words "Boys, come back!" cause us to whip around to see two Doberman pinschers pounding the pavement toward us with their teeth and their lips raised up in a snarl.

"Run!" I yell.

The cigarette tumbles from my fingers and onto the pavement.

Charlene steps one way and I step sharply the other. Our foreheads collide causing us to topple over like Dominos in middle of the road.

The Dobermans stand over us and wag their nub tails, panting, drooling, and licking the dirt streaks from our cheeks.

Mrs. Cleo hightails it toward us wearing a black pirate patch over the eyeball which she lost in a work accident. She pulls the dogs off us.

"You twins, okay? Their bark's worse than their bite."

Not worse than their drool, I want to say but instead answer, "Like an apple pie order, ma'am," while wiping their slobber from my cheek.

"Whatcha' doin' in this neck of the woods?" Mrs. Cleo angles her head and looks down suspiciously.

"Collectin' bottles and cans," I say, placing my heel over the smoking cigarette in the road to hide it.

"Alright, I'll leave you twins to it," she says.

As soon as Mrs. Cleo is out of sight, Charlene whirls her head around to me. "This wouldn't've happened if—"

"Don't blame me," I interrupt her. "You wanted to be cool too."

Charlne crosses her arms over her chest and pokes her bottom lip out. "If cool's Skowhegan then I'm C-C-Cincinnati."

"Oh, hark your bellyachin'. Let's go before the dogs break loose again and we ain't so lucky next time."

At the top of the hill, by the cornfield, we see every Canaanite this side of the Kennebec River entering The House for Friday night poker. Uncle Jerry is standing outside keeping watch over the kids, a task which he voluntarily does. "A kind gesture on his part," some say. "Isn't that cunnin," others say. And "A wicked good father you'll make one day," everyone else says.

Charlene and I park the wagon under the oak tree and observe Uncle Jerry hauling the cousins around on his makeshift sled—the hood of an old truck—chained to the back bumper of a beat up, old car.

Uncle Jerry drives the beat up car around the yard with Jud in the front seat and Clint in the back. Pauline calls these two friends "Jerry's imps" along with four other of his friends: Stan, Ruben, Joey, and Trent, who live up the road apiece. On any given day, these friends can be seen helping Jerry keep an eye on us.

"Last call," Uncle Jerry says.

He pokes his head out of the driver's side window and points at Tonya with the chipped front teeth.

"Tonya's Uncle Jerry's pet," the cousins chant.

Charlene and I watch from the tire swing by the oak tree as Tonya lies belly down on the hood and grabs hold of the metal edges.

The sled rambles down the driveway and out onto the road, streaming up the shaggy hedge of roses near where we stand, past the green school bus, past the apple orchard, and past the mafia-styled car, before disappearing into the junkyard.

A memory swarms before me of when I rode on the hood and what happened to me in the junkyard before he and his imps brought me back. I am happy it's not me or my sisters this time, but I'm sad for Tonya. I swat the memory away and join the rest of the cousins in a game of cops and robbers.

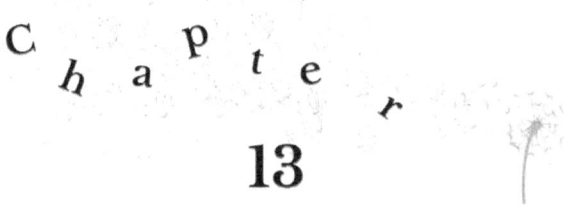

THE SIX-LEGGED OCTOPUS

Mum stands at the stove frying donuts in a pan. The purple pocket on her housedress droops like the lady slipper orchids she uprooted from the bog road.

"I've got a school project due tomorrow," Pauline says as she walks in the door from getting off the school bus.

"Sounds like a personal problem to me," Mum says.

"I'm serious! I gotta write a paper on fashion and bring somethin' for show-and-tell." Pauline pauses and stares at Mum over her glasses. Then adds, "Do I look like somebody who knows anythin' 'bout fashion to you?"

"Ah nope," I say, dropping my schoolbooks on the divan.

"Nobody asked you," she says with a growl.

I give a shrug and hopscotch over the mishmash of carpet samples. Mum has them arranged, first burgundy, then gold, then both green and gold, and finally brown. I stick the landing on the peeling linoleum and throw my hands in the air like an Olympic gymnast signaling the completion of a performance.

"Perfect score," I say, before snatching a donut from the wax paper.

Mum blows cigarette smoke out of the side of her mouth and eyes me. "Smart ass! You're gonna spoil your appetite."

She removes four donuts from the hot grease and places them on the cooling rack in front of Pauline.

"Go ask Grammy Dodge," Mum says. "Maybe she'll have an old hat or somethin'."

Pauline picks up the mesh strainer full of sugar and taps it. The gentle tap causes confectionary powder to fall like snow over the donuts.

"Wicked good *idear*, Mum. Why didn't I think of that?"

My brows stand up like meringue peaks.

I know why.

With a mouthful of donut, I hopscotch back over the mishmash of carpets to the armchair. My attention is drawn to the fly that buzzes around the newest addition to Mum's mail-order plant family—a Venus flytrap, which sits beside the coy tickle-me-plant on the boxy, blue oak stand.

"That fly's fixin' to bite the dust," Pauline says with a grin.

Mum shuffles across the living room in her wool-lined moccasins to the Venus flytrap.

"Watch this, girls. It's gotta touch two hairs," she says.

"What's gotta touch two hairs?" I lean forward, closing the distance between me and the flytrap.

Mum tosses the hand towel over her shoulder and points.

"See those? The fly has to touch two hairs within twenty seconds for the trap to spring shut."

"That fly ain't got a snowballs chance in you know what," Pauline says with a chuckle. Her cheeks turn a warm rouge before sounding her signature Woody the Woodpecker laugh.

Mum exhales a plume of smoke. The cloud settles over the rosette of tiny leaves in front of me.

"Watch. You'll see. It lures its prey in by its nectar," Mum says. Her r sounds like h as if saying, *nectah*.

My brow lifts, and the skin between my eyes wrinkles.

"What's nectar?" I look over at Mum

"It's its sweetness, ding-ding," she says.

The trap snaps shut and the fly attempts to squeeze through the stiff grassy-fangs acting as prison bars to keep it in.

"And what's those?" I point.

"Those long thick hairs are *cilia*. In layman's term, it means 'The fly's shit outta' luck'." Mum laughs and crosses her legs so not to whiz herself.

"Keep an eye on the donuts, will you, Pauline? My eyeballs are floatin'," Mum says. She rushes to the hanging blanket, pushes it aside, and disappears into the back of the house.

Pauline's lazy eye stares off to the side at me. But she's no longer laughing.

"Come with me?" she whispers, forcing the words out through the gaps in her teeth.

I know why she's asking and why she is hesitant. We learned a long time ago on *Mutual of Omaha's Wild Kingdom* to stay with the pack to avoid a lion attack. At the very least, stay in pairs: Lottie and Dottie, Tamara and Laurel, and today Pauline and me.

If I dare.

Ever since I'd found Pauline's letter about her hating Uncle Jerry, I felt a little more of a connection with her than before. I'd never asked her, but I do wonder, every now and then, if she has nightmares about monsters like I do. Does she dream about the six-legged octopus, too?

"Where's Uncle Jerry?" I whisper.

"He left a few minutes ago with his friends. I saw them drive by." She lowers her voice and tilts her head at an angle. "You don't think I'm dumb 'nough to go while he's home, do you?" Her head dabs as she speaks.

Once again, we study each other as if waiting for a secret to pop out. But I don't say anything more and neither does she.

Mum returns to the kitchen and reaches for the metal dipper on the counter. She dips it into the five-gallon bucket of spring water on the kitchen counter and rinses her hands.

"What's all the whisperin'?" Mum asks.

"Oh just somethin' or rather," I say, jumping up from the armchair. "Ready?" I ask.

"Ready as I'll ever be," Pauline says, arming herself with her lucky rabbit's foot.

The door closes behind us and I stand on the stoop with Pauline in front of me. Her protective arm stretched out behind her to keep me safe. We peer down the path of three telephone poles to the left, and scan our eyes all the way back, then peer down the path one telephone pole to the right and scan our eyes all the way back. Just to be certain, we remain still as we listen for movement, any movement, sticks snapping, leaves crunching, or rocks and apples being thrown our way before we step down off the stoop.

We do this, because every green square inch between Mr. Peabody's two cornfields, the smaller cornfield to the right of Aunt Mable's, and the larger one to the left of Grammy's, is under the patrol of Uncle Jerry.

With the coast clear, we book it down the path past the hand pump and broken-down Omni with four flat tires, past the burdock bushes and rhubarb plants, past Rex the rooster and his harem of chickens, and through the chipped red door, where a chocolate cake cools on the counter. The center of cake sunken the way Grampy Dodge used to like it.

I miss him.

Pauline thump-steps-thumps across the gold-colored linoleum toward Grammy, who fries liver and onions.

"Hi, Grammy," Pauline says, her tongue thrushes in her cheek as if trying to pick food from her teeth.

Grammy smiles.

"Well, Pollyanna, I ain't seen you in a month of Sundays. To what do I owe the honor?"

"I'm gettin' kinda old to be runnin' around with the kids, if you catch my drift?" Pauline says, glancing down at her own chest and then back up at Grammy's cat's eye-rimmed glasses. "Would it be okay if I borrow an old hat or somethin' for a school project tomorrow?"

Grammy sets the long-pronged fork down and picks up the flyswatter. She circles the kitchen with it looking for the next fly to kill, and when she spots it, she sneaks up on it. The flyswatter moves at lightning speed through the air and smashes the buzzy thing. Its black guts add another spot to the already fly-and-gut speckled ceiling. The plastic weapon is covered with wings, legs, and tiny heads.

"Of course, dear," she says, closing in on another fly. "Check the trunk upstairs in the bedroom over the livin' room."

Upstairs? I gulp.

Pauline elbows me. "C'mon chicken. We don't have all day."

We hurry past the double-leaf oval table, where a bowl of cucumbers and vinegar sits, past the high-back rocking chair in the corner of the kitchen, past the wooden record player console in the dining room, past the mustard-colored divan in the living room to the interior door which opens into the unused portion of The House.

"I hope a ghost don't get us," I say as I take small steps toward the fancy stairwell, sweeping the area with my eyes and looking for floating faces, rapidly growing mold, and words written in blood across the mirror in the foyer before stepping up onto the first oak tread.

Pauline looks down at me from the top step. "Hurry up before Uncle Jerry gets back. Did I tell you, I think he's possessed?"

"Like on *The Exorcist?*"

"Ayuh."

"Makes perfect sense to me," I say, climbing the stairs.

At the top landing, I see the full-sized bed where I lay when I was five, when Mum told Uncle Jerry to take a picture because "IT'LL LAST LONGER." Swatting yet another memory away, I enter the nook to the left with the slanted ceiling and beat back cobwebs with my bare hands.

A twin-sized headboard leans against the shiplap, Grampy's cherished painting of the dog's playing poker leans against the dresser on the floor. A large empty frame balances between two stacks of what-nots and the Dodge family Bible lays open on a chest of drawers. The page is open to a picture of Paul and Silas. I know it's them because an angel opens the prison door.

Why doesn't an angel do that for me? What prayer did they pray that I haven't? I must be doing it all wrong because nothing ever comes of my prayers.

Then it hits me, *Maybe God doesn't know my real name? Instead of "God, it's me, Francine," I should be praying, "God, it's me, Ding-ding," or "God, it's me, Nimrod," or "It's me, Numbskull" or "Nincompoop," or "Idget," or "Pissant," or better yet, "Girl." Maybe God doesn't have peanut butter in His ears like I thought. Maybe He just doesn't know my born name.* And so I tell Him in my head as I run my finger over the page, *It's me, Francine Marie Dodge. And that's Dodge like the car.*

As Pauline slides a box out of the way, the empty picture frame topples to the floor kicking up dust.

"Hark up the ruckus," Grammy shouts, banging on the ceiling with something—probably the broom handle.

"Wicked sorry, Grammy," we say in unison.

Pauline slides another box out of the way and spots the trunk with the leather straps and metal latches. She opens it.

At first glance, there's a round hat box, a wooden music box with a tiny ballerina dancer, a pair of glittery heels, and an old black and white photograph.

Pauline holds the photograph up to her good eye and studies the faces, and then points to one.

"I've not seen him before," she says. "This must be Grammy's son, Jimmy, who died when he was nine. Mum says Dad won't talk 'bout Jimmy because it makes him too sad."

"What's-at?" I say, looking up from the trunk.

"This must be Jimmy," she says, again. "He died when he was nine."

"I'm nine," I say.

My voice rises along with the black hat and its short veil in my hands until it makes its way onto my head and squishes my curls.

"Did you hear what I just said? He died." A tear collects in the corner of Pauline's eye.

"Do I look like Mae West to you?" I ask as if not hearing her, positioning my head at an angle with my nose pointing up at the sunlight. The veil hangs over my eyes.

A laugh swells at the back of her throat. Like a gurgle.

"Do I need to answer that?" She peers over her glasses at me.

"It's possible. We're cousins, ain't we?" I say.

"Fifth cousin, dummy." Her lazy eye shuffles in its socket.

"So, then there's a chance." I smile.

"I wouldn't go that far." She sucks air through the gaps in her front teeth and exhales a laugh. Then she puts on the glittery heels and pokes her legs straight out. "How do these look?"

"Do I need to answer that?" I eye the scars on her ankles left from the fatty tumors the doctor removed when she was little. They wrap around both ankles like thorn-bush tattoos.

Her smile disappears, and her greasy hair falls forward.

"It's a joke. I'm jokin'," I say.

She stares at her clunky medical shoes discarded on the floor.

"I wish I could wear real shoes like you. I'm tired of bein' made fun of. I'm tired of wearin' an eye patch. I'm tired of walkin' with a limp. I'm tired of bein' called a Cyclops and Quasimodo and bein' the butt of everyone's joke."

"Pay no mind to 'em Cooley sisters. They're nothin' but a bunch of aggravatin' cusses."

"I know. It's not just 'em. It's—"

"Who?" I interrupt. "Lyle and Eddie. Don't worry 'bout 'em bunch of cusses either. They don't know beans."

"Yeah, I guess," Pauline says as she pulls a black dress from the trunk, and then tosses it at me. "Here. Put this on."

Granules of dust flutter through the air.

"Dresses are for girls." I cough out.

"You are a girl, dummy," she says low and slow.

I cross my arms hard over my chest. "I'm not a girl. I'm a tomboy. You put it on."

Her good eye bores a hole in me.

"Duh, whatcha' think a tomboy is?"

I shrug. "A girl who don't wear dresses," I say, tossing it back to her like a game of hot potato.

Outside, gravel crunches and tires spin up the driveway toward the chipped red door. Fear closes in on me like the *cilia* prison bars.

They're back!

The vehicle skids to a halt. The muffler hums, and the car outside idles unhappily because the engine knocks like my heart against my rib cage. I count the doors on the car as they slam shut.

One, two, three doors. Which three are they? Uncle Jerry, Jud, and Clint. Or maybe it's Uncle Jerry, Stan, and Jud. Or could it be Uncle Jerry, Clint, and Stan? Joey and Trent? I don't know.

Their voices float on the air to my ears. My stomach twists in knots and wrings the tears from my eyes.

Pauline grabs my hand. The mood ring Dad bought her at the flea market changes from a soft blue to a dark grey.

"I hate Uncle Jerry and his imps," she says, "I hate 'em all!"

Their drunken banter rises upward through the thin cracked panes and snakes toward us. The door in the kitchen bangs open and slams shut. Glass bottles clank together. Beer bottles I assume, as it's the only drink Uncle Jerry fancies, and boots, so many boots, vibrate the wooden steps as they ascend the staircase behind the tiki bar. Although I am relieved they are at the other end of the house, shivers run through me like cold streams in ice-out season.

"Sh-h! Did you hear somethin'?" Uncle Jerry says. He lowers his voice, then adds after a beat, "Must be Missy, Ma's dumb mutt. Last week she got in a fight with a porcupine. The porcupine won."

Laughter fills their end of the hallway.

I suck in my breath where I sit and bring my legs to my chest to hug my knees.

Quietly, Pauline slips the sparkly heels off and grabs her clunky medical shoes. When she is sure Uncle Jerry and his imps are no longer in the hallway, she holds her index finger up to her mouth. "Follow me and be quiet."

"No way." My sniffles turn to soft sobs, and my body convulses.

"Don't cry. They'll hear you," she says as she pulls me by the hand down the steps.

At the bottom of the staircase, Pauline opens the blue exterior door facing Nelson Hill Road.

"When I say go, you run hard and fast. Don't look back no matter what," she instructs.

"No matter what?" I ask. My voice shakes along with my legs.

"No matter what," she says.

"But what 'bout you?"

"I'll be right behind you. Now go." With her hand on my shoulder, she pushes me out the door.

As I run, leaves crunch under my feet, and when I reach the oak tree with the tire swing, ignoring her instruction, I peer over my shoulder for my sister's whereabouts.

As she passes the corner of the sunporch and steps off the grassy hill into the circular driveway, Uncle Jerry pops his head out of the upstairs window.

"Friggin-A! Boys, it's our lucky day. There goes 'em little pissants now."

Their thunderous bootsteps rumble down the stairwell behind the tiki bar and out the door in the kitchen.

"You haveta' run faster. You haveta' try harder. Get the lead out," I shout at Pauline.

My heart pounds.

When Pauline catches up, she grabs my elbow and runs in lopsided strides beside me.

I glance back a second time to see six dungaree legs in boots chasing us and recall the dream of the six-legged octopus.

Pauline releases my elbow and slows down.

"I can't run anymore. Go without me." Her hand shoos me on.

A trill fills my lungs and creeps into my throat.

"You haveta'," I say, "they'll get you."

She huffs and puffs and grabs her rib cage.

"Better me than you," she says, bending over to catch her breath.

I tug on her arm, then her shirt, whatever I can grab a hold of until she starts to run again.

Uncle Jerry rounds the corner near the garage and points to his imps, directing them which way they should go.

Pauline's stiff uneven strides slow us down. We zigzag through the obstacle course of dented fenders and pile of broken windshields toward the apple orchard by the mafia-styled car.

"Hide there." She points, coming to a full stop.

"Hide where?" I look around.

"In the woods over there. Behind the beam." Her finger stabs the air in the direction of the trees where a charred beam lay against a boulder.

"That's my hidin' place. You'll be safe. I'll distract 'em."

"I'm not leavin' you," I say.

"Go, before they catch us both." Her voice is forceful.

I hate myself for not staying, but I leave her and sprint toward the beam. Every step is haunted by guilt for leaving her to face the monsters alone. I got the "Get out of Jail Free card." But it's not fair. Life never is.

Through the thicket, I see them closing in on her.

Leave her alone. You're scaring her. Stop crying, Pauline. They'll hear you, Pauline.

She curls into a ball amongst the snake berries and milkweeds, between two boulders.

Jud zeros in on her, and his long weightless hair blows sideways in the breeze.

"I found the little pissant," Jud announces from the boulder where he stands above her.

Oh, no, please! I screw my eyes shut and pray.

It's me, Pissant. The other one. Are you there, God?

Pauline squeals and I force myself to look at her.

Her patchless eye ascends like a dreary black bird—up, and up, and up some more.

The sunlight breaks through the trees and speckles Jud's face with yellow leopard spots. He stands over her with a scary smile. The image draws me back to the day he placed Charlene in the back seat of the mafia-styled car. The day she began to stutter. And the same day she started wetting the bed.

Clint and Uncle Jerry wind their way through the brush toward Pauline to where Jud stands. All six dungaree legs close in on her like the grassy fangs on a Venus flytrap.

"Mother f-er! Where's your sister?" Uncle Jerry asks.

"I dunno,' but if I did, I wouldn't tell you," Pauline says. Her body shakes like a newborn deer.

Uncle Jerry leans down. "If you don't want me to hunt Francine down and drag her out here to join you, you'll do as I say, ayuh?"

"Leave my sister outta' this. I'll do whatever you want."

"Say, Pollywog, what ever happened to your precious rabbit?" Uncle Jerry asks.

Pauline lets out a growl. "His name was Peter, asshole, and he died!"

A grin stretches across Uncle Jerry's face.

"Ayuh. I know. But don'tcha wanna know how?"

"Why should I care? He's dead, ain't he?"

The familiar combination of Peter's name being called and Pauline sobbing yanks me back to the day when she held Peter Rabbit on her lap in the living room, and for no reason other than to be mean, I said, "Get that friggin' rabbit outta' this house before we all catch lice!" I made her cry. Then Dad made me cry when he reached his hand around the door jamb and slapped me in the ear hole.

Three days later, our cat dragged Peter's bloody ears into the living room and dropped them beside the armchair with muted orange flowers, where Pauline ate a banana wrapped in a slice of cheese and watched television. I can still hear her scream.

The bloody image of Peter fades, and the three men come back into focus.

"Damn right he's dead!" Uncle Jerry says with a sneer.

"Mum said I left the cage open, but I didn't—I locked it. I'm sure of it."

Pauline cries.

Uncle Jerry presses his lips together and hunches over her.

"I killed 'em! I scalped Peter!"

He grins, but not just any grin. It's a grin that stretches all the way to China, a scary one even from him.

"You did what?" Pauline asks, sweeping back tears like feathery bangs.

"I scalped him. I have the knife to prove it." He reaches into his pocket and pulls it out.

Pauline narrows her eyes.

"I hate you! You're a monster!"

"He is a monster," I let those words roll off my tongue in a whisper.

Uncle Jerry flips open the jackknife and rubs the blade against his open palm.

"You think I'm kiddin'? I'll kill you and your pissant little sister. I don't give two shits 'bout you or her, nor does anyone else!"

He starts to twirl the knife between his fingers.

"You should've heard Peter squeal. He cried like a little girl."

"Keep Peter's name outta' your mouth," Pauline tells him.

Tears stream down my arm and pool in my lap. I grab my mouth in shock and hold in the scream.

He'll kill her. Me. Us. I know it.

Uncle Jerry signals for Jud and Clint.

"You know what to do boys," he says.

They step forward, smiling like two hyenas, and drag her from between the milkweeds and onto the private dirt drive leading to the junkyard. Her clunky shoes drop like stars onto the road, and they walk in circles around her, taunting her, touching her, tapping her like an adult game of Duck, Duck, Goose.

Nickels and dimes clank on the ground.

Her face is red and blotchy. She rakes her fingers through the dirt, scoops up the change and throws it back at them.

"Keep your filthy loot," she says. Her voice crackles.

With one nod from Uncle Jerry, Jud and Clint grab her by the feet and hands. They haul her oversized eleven year old body, soon to be twelve, down into the junkyard out of sight. I lean against the beam and wait for her to return.

The leaves move beside me and make a noise.

It must be a garter snake or a chipmunk.

I sweep the leaves away to find a cobalt blue bottle with an eagle imbedded on it. It's pretty. Prettier than the sparkly heels from the trunk.

The bottle wobbles. I rub a thumbprint sized window in the dirt on the glass to reveal a tiny mouse trapped inside. I tap the bottle and plug my eyeball over the hole.

"Whatcha' doin' in there, huh?"

I set the bottle on the ground and pick up a small rock. Then tap the glass until it breaks and watch as the weary mouse staggers out.

The tiny, sweaty creature looks at me as if I'm the angel from the picture in the family Bible and the bottle was its prison bars.

I wish I could be free like you. Now go on...get. I nudge the mouse with my index finger.

Sometime later, three silhouettes emerge from the junkyard. My heart sinks when Pauline is nowhere in sight.

Did they kill her? Did they bury her in a hole?

I duck low to the ground and watch them from behind the beam. Their chatter fills the air. Jud high-fives Clint and Jerry high-fives them both.

"Did you see the fear on her face when I held her down?" Jud asks with a chilling laugh.

"If looks could kill, you'd be dead," Uncle Jerry says. He wipes the sweat on his forehead with his shirt. "Wicked good work, boys! Who needs a brewsky?"

"You betcha'," Clint says. "I worked up a helluva sweat. Gotta give it to her. That chick's feisty."

"Count me in," Jud says.

When the chipped red door closes, I exhale the breath I didn't know I held and grab Pauline's clunky medical shoes. I comb the junkyard calling her name, looking inside each vehicle as carefully as the school nurse searched my head for lice —eliminating one vehicle at a time just as the nurse eliminated one strand of hair at a time. When Pauline doesn't respond, I burst through the mustard-trimmed door and race past Dad eating one of the chocolate donuts Mum made earlier.

"Shut the damn door," Dad yells from the divan.

Not listening, I reach Pauline's room and yank the hanging blanket aside to find her shaking body beneath the covers.

"Go away!" Pauline's voice trembles.

The springs on the divan creak, then stop. Dad's boots pound down the hallway behind me and the chain hooked to his wallet clanks. Within seconds, he's towering over me, chef shirt unbuttoned and bare belly hanging out.

"You got peanut butter in your ears, girl? Go close the damn door like I said." He presses his finger into my nose.

I drop the corner of the blanket and make a beeline to the

living room, where Mum sits crisscross apple sauce in her sad old chair wearing her purple housedress with no underwear.

"You'd think we'd raised you in a barn or somethin'," Mum says, tipping her head back and lowering a sardine into her mouth until it reaches the tail fin like a magic sword trick.

I close the front door, then turn and stare at the blanket covering the doorway that leads into the back of the house and sink into despair.

Chapter 14

CALAMITY JANE

In December of 1983, a cluster of black-capped chickadees huddle on the snowy boughs of the blue spruce tree in the front yard. They perch on needles that smell like cat urine and peck the snow, etching delicate patterns with their tiny twig-feet. I toss fruitcake in the snow and watch as the birds gobble it up. I love the winter whiteness. The snow, like my tears, has a unique cleansing power. It is nature's whiteboard, where everything bad is wiped clean until the spring, when the foot-chases start back up.

Pauline, Charlene, and I gather on the striped carpet in the hallway to help Mum, in her red one-piece long johns, get the Christmas decorations down from the attic. My white-fog breath mixes with their foggy breath. Our teeth clatter in chorus. I close my eyes to imagine warmth and heat. When that fails, I throw on the sweater and the yarn socks Grandma Foley knitted me last year for Christmas, before returning to the shelf-cloud of breath in the hallway.

Happily, I yank the rope dangling from the ceiling. The staircase unfolds, pummeling Mum in the forehead, knocking her backward into a stack of what-nots and then into the paneled wall.

"You tryin' to kill me?" Mum asks with words as wobbly as her footing. She rubs the knot forming over her brow.

"Sorry, I forgot the springs were broke," I say.

"That's not all you forgot. You'd forget your damn head if it wasn't attached." A puff of white breath rolls off her lips. The corner of her mouth turns up. "I see birds . . . tweet . . . tweet . . . tweet," she says with a slight chuckle.

Pauline's belly bobs with laughter. Her cheeks turn a warm rouge to match the color of Mum's one-piece long johns with a flap in the back.

Mum's slippered feet march across the hall to her antique three-way mirror where she leans in and examines the lump on her forehead.

"Darn that smarted girl. If it wasn't for bad luck, you wouldn't have any luck at all." Mum eyeballs me out of the corner of her eye.

"It was an accident," I say, turning a quarter of the way around and elbowing Pauline. "Stop laughin' fatso. It ain't funny."

"It ain't?" she says. Her head bobs like an apple.

Mum returns to the dropdown staircase rubbing her forehead. "Let's get these decorations down before you accidentally kill someone."

A loud knock fills the house.

"Somebody get the damn door," Dad yells from the stoop.

The tree!

I smile as I dash to the front of the house. An icy blast of arctic air whips my hair back as the door swings open.

Dad's mustache is white with ice. He shakes the long-needled pine over the stoop to remove the excess snow, then drags it over the curled linoleum and mishmash of carpet samples.

I dodge the snowy prints his boots leave and make my way to the five-gallon bucket with rocks and wooden wedges beside it.

Dad stands the tree in the bucket and holds it while I stack the rocks and wedges around the trunk.

Afterward, he sits on the divan and lights a cigarette.

Mum steps through the hanging blanket and into the front of the house with a box of ornaments in her hands and a lump the size of a Robin's egg between her eyes. She sets the box on the coffee table in front of Dad and rubs her forehead in dramatic fashion.

"What's the matter with you?" Dad asks. He blows a thin line of smoke in Mum's direction.

"Your damn daughter. That's what."

Dad's neck rotates my way.

My neck snaps back. "What makes you think it was me? I'm not your only daughter," I say.

"Do I look stupid to you? Now go help your mother like I said."

"Whatcha' think I was doin'?" I say with a sigh.

Pauline shoves a box of ornaments my way.

"Sort these, will you?" she says quickly.

The look she gives me tells me to zip my lips and not spoil the holiday mood. I heed her warning and sift through the box. Some ornaments need repair while others need the rubbish can. I separate the gold stars from the wreaths and the Santa heads— salt dough ornaments Mum handbaked and painted with meticulous detail using a fine brush—while Charlene sorts the wooden ornaments we girls painted.

Mum is artistic and resourceful and at times volunteers on art day at school to help the art teacher. Once for Valentine's Day, Mum hand-drew and colored cards for all our classmates. She wrote greetings inside bubbles that said: "Be my Valentine" and "You're the best, Valentine."

From the sad old chair, Mum untangles the strings of lights and replaces the blown bulbs with working ones. When she's done wrapping the tree with the lights and hanging the garland, she pillages through the box to find her favorite ornament to place on the branch, a battery-operated sparrow. She pushes the button and the sparrow chirps loudly and sharply.

Mum crawls under the tree in her rouge one-piece long johns with the sagging flap in the back and spreads the white sparkly tree skirt out before arranging her prized light up Kincaid village around the tree stand. She snaps together the set of black train tracks, then places the train on it.

"All done," she says, plugging in the village and the lights on the tree.

As she backs out from under the tree, her frizzy hair snags a branch. She laughs at her hair getting caught, then laughs some more at the peep show the sagging flap provides.

"The star... I almost forgot the star," Mum says.

The movie *Miracle on 34th Street* plays on the television, and a cigarette hangs from Mum's lips. She holds the star and reaches up standing on her tippy toes. She stretches hard as if it were possible for her to reach without a step ladder.

She stretches again and again with no luck. The cigarette recedes, and the grey ash breaks like shale rock dusting the branches.

"Try, try again, my ass," Mum says. "My arms are too damn short like the rest of me."

Dad's thin lips make a straight line. "I could've told you that. Now give it here before you hurt yourself."

With the hand that holds his own cigarette, Dad places the star on the tree. His face radiates with joy—a sight as rare as an ivory billed woodpecker.

Dad makes his way to the rusty wall cabinet in the kitchen. He opens one door and pulls out a jar of molasses. He opens another door and pulls out a baking tin.

He tosses the tin at me. I catch it midair like a frisbee.

"What's this for?"

First he nods, then he grunts.

I shrug in confusion.

"Snow, nimrod," Dad finally says.

His beamy wide smile is gone.

I still don't get it. I look at the pan in my hand, while rolling over the words: SNOW, NIMROD.

"Did I stutter? Go and fill it." His voice rises.

"I'm not a mind reader," I say.

"Keep it up, wiseass. You're this close." He holds up his index finger and thumb a hair apart from each other.

Mum settles in her sad old chair with a box of dried prunes and pulls out a sticky cluster. The grin she gives tells me that she remembers what happened the last time she ate dried prunes and has me already wanting to plug my nose.

"No yellow snow," she says, sucking her teeth to remove the sticky dried fruit from between them.

"I'm not stupid," I say.

"You're not?" Pauline says. "Could've fooled me."

I shoot her a look.

Mum closes the box of prunes and sets it on the end table by the fisherman in the yellow slicker lamp.

"Don't forget, girls, we have twenty-five wreaths to make tonight." She sucks the stickiness from her fingertips, one by one.

"How could we?" I eye the heap of pine boughs on the floor between the wringer washer and the peeling wallpaper.

"Move it," Dad says, shoving me out the door and into the snow drift.

Within seconds, I'm back inside swatting white fluff from my clothes and watching Dad drizzle molasses over the snow in the pan. When the jar is empty, he grabs three wooden salad bowls from the cabinet behind him.

"Who wants some?" he asks with the sparkle of a chef in his eyes.

"Me." I shoot both hands straight up in the air. Then Charlene and Pauline stick their hands up.

Mum wiggles free from her sad old chair and makes her way to the kitchen to the pile of pine boughs.

"Girls," she calls, bending over to sort the boughs, removing the scraggily ones.

The flap on the back of her long johns sags like a sack of beans, but she knows this because she crosses her legs so not to whiz herself and lets out a seemingly endless chortle.

I wish you'd wear underwear, I want to tell her, but instead ask, "Do we haveta'?"

"A little hard work ain't never killed anyone," she says.

"That you know of," I add.

"Quit bellyachin'. You want Christmas, don'tcha? This is how your father and I afford it. If you girls make six wreaths each, and I make seven, we'll be done faster than you can say Jack Robinson."

Mum sets her cigarette in the Maine shaped ash tray on the counter.

"In the mornin' we'll drop these off at the factory in Skowhegan and pick up supplies enough to make twenty-five more," she says.

"Lucky for us," I say, grabbing a wire hoop from the stack.

I snip a bough to size, then hold it against the hoop and wrap wire around it, tugging hard on the wire to secure it, then grab another bough, snip, and wrap.

"Why can't Dad help?" I mumble.

"Ewwww. Who dealt it?" Pauline puckers her nose and releases her Woody the Woodpecker laugh.

My forehead scrunches up. My nose follows.

We all swivel toward Mum, who has tears squirting from her eyes.

"What? Can I help it if prunes don't agree with me?" she says with a snicker as she crosses her legs and shakes with laughter.

THE NEXT DAY, AFTER DROPPING THE WREATHS OFF IN Skowhegan, Charlene and I throw on our snowsuits with rips and holes and stuffing hanging out of them. The snowsuits, though high waters, keep us warm. To compensate for the short length, we slide Wonder Bread bags over our socks and secure them as high up our calves as we can with rubber bands. We top it all off with the accessories Grandma Foley knitted us: leg warmers, hats, scarfs, and mittens.

Charlene and I make our way up the path, stopping every few feet to stamp out a new snow angel. We enjoy leaving imprints along the way, like watermarks on white paper backgrounds. When we reach the hill where the cousins' sled, Charlene and I squeeze onto the toboggan behind Lottie and Dottie. To gain momentum, we rock back and forth and wait for Tonya, at the bottom of the hill, to signal us when we can go. The hill leads into the road and Grammy Dodge has us take extra precautions.

When Tonya flags her arms over her head in an 'X' formation, we push off down the hill toward the road.

The arctic wind blasts my face and causes my eyes to water. The tears freeze instantly to my cheeks.

When the toboggan nears the road, we dive off into the snowbank like synchronized swimmers. Over and over, we trek up the hill and sled down, each time becoming slower and stiffer.

Ice-balls and burdocks cling to my mittens and weigh them down. My thighs burn. I can no longer feel my fingers or my toes.

"I'm headed inside before I catch frost bite," I say.

My cheeks feel numb and tight. The cold makes it difficult to talk. My ears tingle painfully.

"Ayuh," the cousins say without fuss, following me up the hill like penguins toward The House, where we migrate to get warm.

On the top step, I stand the toboggan in the snowbank and make my way inside to the woodstove.

I sit on the kindling box and tug at the brown spheres on my mittens. The burdocks stick like Velcro, making them merely impossible to pull off. As I yank on the burdocks, a car horn blares and mixes with a hair-raising scream.

Aunt Mable crosses the kitchen in three long strides and peers out the square window above the sink.

"It's Pollyanna!" she yelps like a wounded puppy. "She's been run over by a car!"

Her words don't make sense.

Pauline hates snow and sleds! She was helping Mum make blueberry pies when I left.

Choking back tears, I drop the burdocks and zip to the sliding glass doors to see for myself.

A blonde spree of hair sticks out from underneath the neighbor's front bumper. I slide the glass door open and sprint through the snow to her.

"I couldn't stop. I didn't mean to. It was an accident," Mrs. Jane says, looking down at my sister's lifeless body.

I drop to my knees and squeeze Pauline's hand.

"Can you hear me?" My tears crystalize and fall like itty-bitty ice pellets, bouncing off her cold cheek.

"Can you hear me?" I repeat.

Her eyes roll back in her head.

"Is . . . she . . . dead?" I cry, looking up at Mrs. Jane.

Smoke from the tailpipe bounces off the snowbank and snakes toward Pauline. I shift my body to shield her from the fumes.

Seconds later, Aunt Mable and Grammy reach us and throw blankets over Pauline.

"Open your eyes, Pollyanna. Open your eyes. Don't go to sleep. Stay awake, hun," Aunt Mable says, dropping to her knees beside me and repeating the same lines over and over.

"Go get your parents, dear. And tell 'em the ambulance is on the way," Grammy says.

I sprint down the snowy road and burst through the mustard-trimmed door.

"Pauline's been run over by a car." These words come out of my mouth and make me burst into tears all over again.

Mum throws on her red galoshes, and Dad, his boots. I turn and head back to Pauline, and they take off behind me down the slippery road. When they reach her, they collapse beside her.

"Don't go. Stay, Pauline," Mum pleads with a gut-wrenching sob. Her words send an icy shiver up my spine.

I look for proof my sister is alive. A puff of white breath, a finger twitch, another eye roll. But nothing.

"Why don'tcha go to The House and wait with Jerry and the kids," Grammy says. "You don't need to see this."

Snot mixes with tears and freezes to my upper lip. I shake my head hard and fast.

No! Please! I don't want to, I say with my head motion.

"Do it, damn-it!" Dad points with his bare finger toward the rooster weathervane, his nose and hands as red as poinsettias.

৩৩৩

Two hours later, the phone rings. I cross my fingers and hold my breath. The creaking of the rocking chair stops. Grammy sits up straight.

Aunt Mable crosses the brick linoleum to answer it. She stands at the tiki bar with her back to us and talks low and slow.

Please God! I mouth, eyeing Charlene from the oval poker table. She gnaws on her nails.

"Ayuh... ayuh... ayuh. I love you, too, Franny. I'll tell Ma and the twins," Aunt Mable says.

My heart pounds in my ears.

Don't let her be dead, God. I'll be wicked good. Pretty please with a cherry on top, I beg Him. All the while, pushing back the thought, *It's not like He's listened to this nine year old's prayers before.*

Aunt Mable places the receiver back on the hook and turns to face us.

"Franny said, 'Pollyanna isn't respondin'. She's broken all but two ribs, punctured a lung and has internal bleedin'. The doctor said that he 'wouldn't give a penny for her life'."

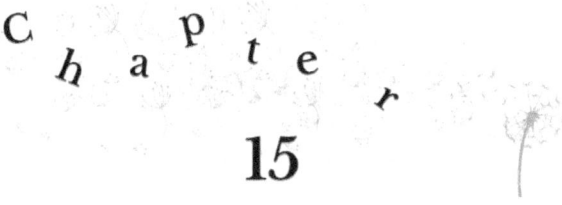

15

CAT AND MOUSE

Nine months after Pauline's near fatal accident I step out onto the rickety stoop with a five-gallon bucket in my hand. It's dusk and the purple glow of the bug light lures unsuspecting winged creatures to it, zapping those that fly too closely. I hang the five-gallon bucket on the water pump's lip and wrestle with the rusty brown handle. I jump up in the air, throwing all sixty-two pounds onto the handlebar. It doesn't budge, so I plant my feet on the ground, dig my toes into the long grass, reach back up, grab the bar, and pull it hard. My body lifts off the ground and back down, up-down-up-down-up-down, until the bucket has enough water to satisfy Dad. I then must carry it with the *heave, tug, rest, repeat method* across the grass and into the house.

The words "It's my lucky night" send an alarm up my spine and into my hairline. I stand stock-still with my ears perked. A deep cringe starts at my dingy heels and works its way up my dirt-streaked legs, through a belly full of cheesy shepherd's pie, forcing its way out my throat like a screech owl in the night.

He's behind me. Or is he in front of me? I can't tell.

I blink the darkness away, and there behind the driver's side tire of the Titanic, an inky image slowly emerges.

It crouches on all-fours, barely visible on a September evening when the long shadow of darkness arrives early and stays late. The image moves toward me slowly like a cat stalking a mouse.

As a ten-year-old, I am older, wiser, and wearier of the foot chases and games he likes to play. It seems these days I'm on the run more than the Duke boys from Cletus and Rosco. And as the episodes of *The Dukes of Hazard* goes, those who witness the frequent chases pay it very little mind. I eyeball the side of the rickety stoop and the warm yellow glow emanating from the gap under the door.

Should I run to the left or to the right?

Three feet from the stoop, he unfolds from his stalking position and stands up straight with his shoulders back, making himself big like a giant. The giant stands between me and the warm glow. The thought—*If I win, there'll be another chase tomorrow*—rears its ugly head. I shove it back down into the trunk of my mind and think about the light.

How do I get from here to there without getting caught?

I already know what happens when the cat gets the mouse, and I can't let that happen. Not tonight. Not if I can help it.

"I have a dollar bill for my little girl," his voice slices through the darkness.

Keep your damn money! I wish the bug light would zap you! I want to say, but all that comes out is "What are you doin' here?" I say these words softly and slowly as if in surrender.

When he's not expecting it, I let go of the rusty handle, shoving the half-full bucket of water to the ground, greasing the grass with it. As he lunges toward me, he slips in the grass, giving me a head start. I sprint to the far side of the 1978 Dodge Omni, broken-down in our side yard, where the weeds grow up around it.

We slow waltz around the Omni—he steps one direction, I step the other, blocking me here, and blocking me there, blocking me everywhere. My blood pressure climbs like rungs on a ladder, and instead of tunnel vision, I have tunnel hearing. Voices fade in and out, and my heart beats louder than quads on a drum line.

The porch light next door comes on, swallowing the lesser light, and the storm door opens. Voices flitter in the night air.

It's Aunt Mable and Grammy. A small smile lifts my face and my hopes.

A second wind rises like eagle's wings on the tops of their voices, and I sprint from the Omni to the Titanic.

In the porch light that splays across the yard, Grammy and Aunt Mable's silhouettes talk and walk across the deck, down the stairs, and over the blacktop toward the footpath.

Grammy wears her polyester slacks and white blouse with a white sweater over it. I make a mad dash past Grammy and Aunt Mable, now both on the footpath, and book it around the backside of the trailer, past Aunt Mable's prized snowball bush, and around to the front again.

"Give that girl a break, ayuh," Grammy says, interrupting Aunt Mable's spiel on how the pit we dump our pisspots in smells worse than the chicken-manure Old Man Peabody uses in the cornfields.

"Leave her be, Jerry!" Grammy says fitfully.

She sweeps her milky hair with gray badger streaks back, drawing attention to her long Gran Torino nose in the porch light.

"We're just playin', Ma," Uncle Jerry says, giving her a smile. But she doesn't see how his face changes into the scowl he gives me.

The foot chase continues. This time, I zip between Aunt Mable and Grammy, knocking loose Grammy's cat-eye shaped frames and spilling the bottle of Coca-Cola she holds in her hand.

"Wicked sorry, Grammy," I say, looking back without stopping.

"Why I oughtta'," Aunt Mable says with her fists up,

pumping the air. "Your ass is grass, and I'm the lawn mower. Why don'tcha put that in your pipe and smoke it."

"Now Mable," Grammy says in a calm steady voice, "Francine didn't mean anythin' by it."

The vision of Pauline's bloody rabbit fuels my running. Barefoot, I leap over the ditch by the mailbox with the red flag pointing up at the stars and high step it down Nelson Hill Road. All the time stumbling over potholes and stepping on sharp pebbles cemented into the compacted dirt. Here and there a rock, here and there a pothole, I wince and keep going. His boots pound the road behind me like a jackhammer on my heels.

Coming upon Grammy's crabapple tree by the road, I eye the ditch which separates me from it. When I go to jump, my legs fold like Mum's old wooden ironing board and I land in a pile of sticky wet leaves.

"Ouch!" I grab my thigh and blink back tears as a piercing somethin' or rather' stabs my leg and pains me.

My face puckers as if biting into the crisp stalk of a rhubarb plant. Blood mixes with the damp smelling leaves.

How bad is it?

I finger the wound.

Deep, I think. Will it need stitches like on my chin when I was three? I hate needles.

"Here. Take my hand." Uncle Jerry's arm unfolds toward me like the drop-down staircase.

He pokes his bottom lip out as if to make a pity face.

I want to believe him. I want to think he could be nice.

It's nectar. He's trying to lure me with his sweetness like the Venus flytrap.

"Go away. I'm not fallin' for it." I clench my fist and grit my teeth.

At the top of the hill by the garage, an image floats down the footpath and I realize it's Grammy in her white sweater. Her gait is slow. She stops at the corner of the garage and peers in as if wishing upon the solo star in the sky to hear Grampy's tinkering on a car one more time.

Uncle Jerry retreats along the shaggy hedge of roses, leaving me there. Moments later, the light flickers in the upstairs window. His image peers down through the glass darkly.

A small win.

The blood wets my sweatpants. I wait for the florescent light over the kitchen sink to turn on, then hobble up the grassy hill toward the empty garage. A torn piece of tar-paper flaps against the windowless wall like a pair of wet trousers on a clothesline in a windstorm.

I pass the rhubarb patch at the back of the garage, where the light on the pole doesn't stretch, and approach the hand pump where the empty bucket lays.

The closer I get to the rickety stoop, the louder the television and my family become. The dingy curtains open for me to see, and I spy on them from the top step, mentally preparing myself to Double-Dutch my way into the chaos within.

Through the smudge and bug guts on the window, I observe the book each one holds: Charlene with her Trixie Belden mystery book, Dad with his Louis L'Amour, Mum with her Harlequin romance, and Pauline with her Stephen King. I can't recall the last time I read a book for pleasure, if ever.

What's wrong with me? Why am I the odd ball?

"Category's Before and After, babe," Dad says loudly, his voice bursting through the barricade of a window, a wall, and a door.

He slouches on the divan with his white work shirt unbuttoned and his round belly hanging out. I watch through the window as he blows his nose and tosses the handkerchief on the coffee table where he props up his dry foot with the jagged yellow toenails.

My eyes shift to Mum, who shakes her index finger fitfully in her ear hole chasing an itch she can never seem to catch. Then she sprinkles salt with the waxy finger on a green apple.

"Is there a *p*?" Mum says.

I pan over to Pauline. She lowers the Steven King book and peers over her thick eyeglasses. Her cheeks pucker with the laugh she holds back as she listens to Mum and Dad quarrel over which vowel to buy next. Then she dog-ears her book the thickness of a brick and leans forward in the armchair to squeeze her way into their conversation.

Pauline tilts her head.

"There's a cake recipe I wanna try, Mum. It's a—" her voice rises and falls.

"Is there an *s*?" Mum says, interrupting Pauline's interruption. "Ayuh, I'm listenin', Pauline. Go on," Mum says, as she calls out the letter *n*.

"Like I was sayin'..." Pauline continues.

Their words twist together like a soft-serve cone. The art of talking over one another and hearing what each one says is a necessary skillset in my house. It's the only way to get a word in edgewise.

Headlights flicker down Nelson Hill Road. The cone shaped light splays through the corn, and before it reaches my celery green shirt and pink sweatpants, I open the door and Double-Dutch my way into the noise.

Dad's dry foot with the jagged yellow toenails slides off the coffee table and onto the mishmash of carpet samples. He belches, rubs his round belly, grabs his handkerchief, and stuffs it in his back pocket with most of it hanging out the way Grampy used to do with his grease towel. Dad scoots forward on the divan and rocks to stand up.

"What took you so damn long, girl?" he says. His tone hurling judgement.

"I—I—"

He steps toward me with an empty coffee cup, then stops in his tracks and peers down at me.

"Where the hell's the bucket?"

"Well, I—"

"Well, nothin'. Go and get it!" he demands as he pours himself a cup of old coffee.

When I turn around to go back outside, Mum straightens up in her chair and sets the apple and the saltshaker down.

"Come here. Lemme see what you've done," she says, her tone hurling more judgement.

Pauline thump-step-thumps past me, snarling her lip at the injury.

"Geesh, and I thought I was the pits," she says as she grabs the Band-Aids and iodine for Mum. "It's official," Pauline adds, "we're gonna haveta' wrap you in bubble wrap."

Her belly tumbles with laughter beneath her Rod Stewart T-shirt.

I narrow my eyes.

"It's not funny, fatso!" I ball my hands. My fingernails dig into my palms.

"It ain't?" she says with a wide gap-tooth grin.

"Helluva gash you've got there, birdbrain." Mum redirects the light from the fisherman with the yellow slicker lamp. She reaches up, plucks out the leaves and the dirt with her fingernails. "If you were doin' what you were supposed to be doin' this never would've happened, now would it have, ding-ding?" she says, pulling a dried shard of a leaf from the cut.

Which is it? Birdbrain or ding-ding? I ball my fist tighter in frustration. *You think you're so darn smart. You think you know everything. You don't know beans.*

"If you say so," I say, wishing to tell them the truth. That Uncle Jerry keeps chasing me. That he keeps hurting me. That the whole world feels like it is closing in on me like a Venus flytrap. But I can't say any of those things.

Mum makes her Dr. Mom face as she examines the gash on my thigh about the size of a quarter.

She swabs the blood away and applies iodine before

squeezing the flesh together and giving me three butterfly stitches with Band Aids. "This oughtta' do you. Now go get the water bucket and scrub-a-dub-dub 'em dishes before they grow legs and walk off."

"But Charlene said she'd wash the dishes tonight," I reply.

"Your hands ain't broke," Dad says from the kitchen as he dips his fingers into the rectangle pan and grabs a corner piece of chocolate cake, his hand doubles as the plate and the utensil.

"I never said they were."

"Somethin' fishy is goin' on here," Mum says with suspicion, changing from Dr. Mom to Sherlock Holmes the detective.

Mum pauses for a moment.

"Didn't Charlene have dishes last week? A matter of fact, you had rubbish duty, and Pauline had the slop buckets. Yeah, that's right," Mum says, agreeing with herself. "And if I remember correctly, you have 'em this week, Charlene has the slop buckets, and Pauline has rubbish duty."

Dad makes his way back across the mishmash of carpet samples with the slice of cake in one hand and a cup of coffee in the other. The springs on the divan creak as he settles in his spot.

"Somebody damn well better tell me what's goin' on," he says. He opens his mouth wide. Crumbs tumble over his bottom lip like trapeze artists and into his open shirt pocket.

Charlene's gaze flickers toward me and then away.

"It's her fault!" she stutters, her index finger pointing at me. "She said I haveta' do her dishes for a month, or she'll tell Aunt Mable what wicked awful thing I said 'bout her."

"This oughtta' be good," Pauline says with a grin, dog-earing her page and looking up, so not to miss a word.

Dad's eyes dart back and forth between Charlene and me. "Well, spit it out, damn-it. I ain't a mind reader."

"Aunt Mable's a w-w-itch, fell in a ditch, found a penny, and thought she was rich," Charlene says in her sing song voice.

The room is silent. All but the television.

Then Pauline throws her head back and lets out her annoying half-chuckle.

"Damn, daughter," Mum says, eyeballing me. "Don'tcha know blackmail's illegal? You can go to jail for it."

What do you mean jail? And what's blackmail?

I swallow hard, remembering the class trip to the jailhouse in Skowhegan, where the nice policeman locked our entire class in a cement cell.

Charlene's words "So, this is where our uncles spend the night when they're drunk," ring in my ears.

Dad presses the small of his back into the flowered divan.

"Looks like you've got dishes for a month. Go get the water bucket before I put somethin' on you Ajax won't take off."

A whole month?

"That's not fair!" I stomp my bare foot on the burgundy carpet square—one time, then two.

Mum grabs the saltshaker and her apple and continues where she left off. She chews and talks. Bits of apple flying.

"No one ever said life's fair, dingy."

I scowl down at Mum as she takes another bite.

"I hate it when you say that!"

"Watch your mouth," Dad says, "before you have dishes for two months."

"I can't see my mouth. My nose is in the way," I say under my breath.

Why did I say that? I always have to have the last word.

"That's two, Nimrod," Dad says. "Keep it up and I'll make it three."

"That's not fair," I say again. "I have eczema on my hands. The dish soap makes it worse. It will be Thanksgiving before—"

"You poor abused baby," Mum says with a mouthful of chewed fruit.

These words: YOU POOR ABUSED BABY make me cringe. I hate it when she says that more than anything else in the world.

If she knew it were true, would she still say it?

Smoke billows from Dad's nostrils.

"You ain't a damn door. Now move it!" His hand shoos me from in front of the television.

❦

THAT NIGHT, WHILE WASHING THE DISHES, I HATCH A PLAN TO get even with Charlene for tattling on me. As the family watches television and reads in the living room, I sneak the rubber Frankenstein mask off the top of the Frigidaire and tiptoe down the striped carpet into the bedroom to Charlene's bottom bunk. I place the mask on her pillow and stuff it with a shirt, then take an armful of clothes from the floor and form a body for Frankenstein. Afterward, I pull her covers up and tuck Frank in.

Standing back by the bookshelf in our bedroom, I cup my chin with my hand and eye the monster.

Something's missing. But what?

Then it hits me.

Feet. Frank needs feet.

I dash across the hall to my parents' room and return with a pair of Dad's old boots, propping them up at the foot of Charlene's mattress.

With the payback in motion, I pull the chain in the middle of the ceiling. All goes dark and I join my family in the living room to watch reruns of M*A*S*H.

When the sitcom ends, Mum and Dad lower their books in sync, a sure sign that it's bedtime.

"Good night Eeny, Meeny, Miny, and no Moe," Mum says.

I line up behind Pauline and Charlene for our nightly ritual. I watch as my sisters kiss them both on the forehead and say goodnight, then disappear into the back of the house, one by one.

A mischievous smirk curls up one corner of my mouth. Before I can get the first kiss out, a blood curdling scream rips through the house, sending Dad's western book and Mum's romance book flying. They spring up and rush to Charlene.

Oh, boy!

"Francine Marie Dodge!" Dad shouts with a voice like thunder. "Get your ass back here!"

I thread my way between Mum and Pauline in the hallway and peek my eyes around the doorframe into my bedroom where Dad and Charlene stand.

"Closer," Dad says, curling his index finger at me.

"What is it?" I take one small step, then another, and another, stopping short of his reach.

He snatches the mask from the pillow and holds it up. "What's this?"

"A head," I say.

"I know that smart ass. What's it doin' in your sister's bed?"

"I dunno'." I clasp my hands together. My big toe rubs a hole in the particle board floor.

"Geesh. You look like a little angel, but you've got two horns holdin' up your halo," Pauline says. Her Woody the Woodpecker laugh vibrates my ear holes.

"Closer," Dad says again, his finger doing the curling thing at me.

His tone is strangely alluring like the purple bug light, and I take a step closer. Then his hand reaches out, snatches my ear, and clamps down like a lobster.

"You're hurtin' me," I whine.

"It's meant to," he says.

My nose presses into his chest.

Dad breathes heavily and stares down at me. His coffee and cigarette breath spray me. In his shirt pocket a single cake crumb peers out.

"What the hell's wrong with you, huh, girl?" His index finger and thumb still pinching my earlobe.

I have a name, it's Francine, I want to say, but what comes out is, "I. Don't. Know."

Charlene wipes her eyes. A hiccupy cry catches in her throat.

"I'm sorry, geesh. It was a joke," I say, feeling bad.

Mum shakes her head.

"There's never a moments peace with you, Francine. Now get in bed."

❦

STARING UP AT THE CLEAR PLASTIC THAT COVERS THE HOLE IN my ceiling, I think about Mum's words, 'You can go to jail for that.' They make me think of Uncle Jerry's words while we were on the green school bus, 'If you tell, we'll both go to jail.' A tear sneaks down my cheek. 'Once a jailbird always a jailbird.' That's what Mum says.

Am I a no-good jailbird like my drunk tank uncles?

I squeeze both fists tighter than the bark on a tree.

The fall crickets chirp loudly outside my window, and the sound of them rubbing their legs together mix with Charlene's sniffles. Peeping through the hole in the plastic, light from the moon shines on Festus, our Saint Bernard in the backyard. The tops of the trees, white birch and pine, sway in the night breeze. The rickety old window is level with my mattress, and one small, rusty, bent over nail holds the window shut. I watch for uncertain shadows and movement in the woods, in the field, near my house, anything that might say, *He's back!* Fear fills me as I wait for Uncle Jerry's hands to reach through the window any minute now and yank me out.

Festus growls and lunges at the line of pines behind his doghouse. I press my nose against the pane and pray for a bear, a moose, or a Maine bobcat. I inhale, and when Festus retreats to his doghouse, I release the air and close my eyes. I take a shuttering breath as the werewolf in the mechanic suit, the six-legged octopus, and the giants that stalk the four corners of my mind, crawl, creep, and slink their way back into my dreams.

Chapter
16

SCARECROWS AND L-SHAPED TOES

A searing pain shoots through my foot and I tumble mid-cartwheel to the ground.

My small toe sticks straight out off the side of my foot and makes a visible L shape. Pushing myself up into a standing position, I limp across the yard and through the mustard-trimmed door. I hobble past Pauline who is pulling a skillet of burnt cornbread out of the oven, past Charlene who is reading a library book under the living room window, over to Mum doing a crossword puzzle in her sad old chair.

"What's another word for a dog chewin' a bone?" Mum asks.

"What do I look like?" Pauline says with a smirk. "A dictionary?"

They laugh.

"I've got one. What's another word for broken?" I say, drawing everyone's eyes down to the burgundy carpet square where I stand.

Their laughs turn to gasps.

"Damn, girl. Excuse my French," Pauline says. Her chin plunges like a submarine into a black hole of puzzlement. "If it wasn't for bad luck, you wouldn't have any at all."

"Shut up, fatso."

"I still vote we wrap you in bubble wrap," she says, slicing the burnt off the cornbread. Her tongue clicks against her cheek.

"And I vote, you never cook again. Whatcha' tryin' to do, send Smokey the Bear to our doorstep?" I snipe before turning back toward Mum, who sits Indian style in her worn turquoise housedress without underwear on, as usual.

Mum sets the crossword book on the end table with the fisherman in the yellow slicker lamp and places the pen in the "V" where the two pages meet. Then she looks at me cock-eyed.

"Give it," she says, wiggling her fingers at me, palm up. "Lemme see what you've done now," she says low and slow, blowing a plume of smoke over my head as I settle on the carpet square and rest my foot in her lap.

Mum starts by wiggling my big toe.

That one isn't hurt. My brow makes a question mark.

But Mum ignores my brow and continues to wiggle my big toe up and down.

No sooner than, *You're not as smart as you think* leaves my mind, the answer comes by way of a nursery rhyme.

"This little piggy went to market," Mum begins, squeezing my big toe and choking back laughter.

My eyes shift from the cloud of smoke above me to the tears squirting from Mum's eyes as she slides her fingers down to the next toe. She wiggles it and continues with the nursery rhyme.

Then she wiggles the next toe, and giggles even harder.

I roll my eyes as her fingers slide down, and she tugs on the next toe and then the next, as she rattles off which piggy went where.

"It's not funny!" I say, hissing in pain.

By now Pauline stands over me.

"It's not?" she says, tilting her head. Her belly and breasts tumble like in a dryer, her face red with laughter.

Mum, unable to contain herself, breaks into a full fledge belly laugh.

"How is this funny?" I ask.

I lean up on my elbows and see Mum's fingers doing the Yellow Pages walk toward the L shaped toe. Pauline eyes Mum with a devilish grin, egging her on.

"Don't you dare," I say.

"I can snap it back," Mum giggles. "Save us the gas."

"Jiminy Crickets! That has as much to do 'bout nothin'," I say, sliding my foot off her lap and out of her hands. "I'll be in the car."

۞

A FEW WEEKS AFTER THE CARTWHEEL, CHARLENE AND I PEER out the school bus window and point at the many festive decorations peppering the yards in Canaan—jack-o'-lanterns, black caldrons, spiderwebs, skeletons, life-sized witches, scarecrows, and a ghost made from bed sheets.

The decorations cause me to squirm in my seat and rub my hands together. I think about the finishing touches Mum is putting on my E.T. costume for tonight's annual haunted house. The thought of having the best costume in the school gives me the wiggles, and I let out a happy squeal.

The bus stops at the foot of our driveway. I hurry down the aisle, down the steps, and across the road. My feet move me past our mailbox with two sheaves of towering cornstalks tied to it, past the spree of Indian corn hanging from the purple bug light, and past the half-stuffed scarecrow leaning against the stoop, decorations that in my mind makes us look normal to those driving by. *Mallard duck decoys.*

I dump my Trapper Keeper and pencil bag on the table, quickly picking up the E.T. mask and alien hands Mum meticulously cut out of cardboard and painted. The elastic bands slide easily over my head and hands. I raise my alien index finger at Pauline.

"E.T. ph—one h—ome," I practice saying.

Mum smacks me upside the head and snatches the mask away.

"Stave it up why don'tcha? I've got costumes to finish and popcorn balls to bag."

"Ouch," I say, "I wasn't stavin' it up."

I grab Charlene's hand and head outside in the direction of the cornfield to gather more stalks. This time, to give our scarecrow arms.

The slumped-over half-stuffed scarecrow wears a pair of Dad's frayed dungarees and a red checkered smock.

As we hurry down the path and through the wooded area that separates The House from the cornfield, we see our sumac hideout and the kitchen table we made by rolling a large wooden spool down the path from the garage.

"Wanna play? I'll be the mum. You be the baby," I say.

Charlene lets go of my hand and peers up at me. "But what 'bout the school's haunted house?"

"That's not until seven o'clock," I remind her.

Inside the sumac hideout, I stand at the make-believe stove and mix sweet clovers with milk weed juice. I set the food on the wood spool in front of her.

"Eat it up yum," I say.

Charlene pretends to chew the food.

On the second bite, she whirls her head around, looks over her shoulder, and straight out the door.

"W-W-What was that?" she asks.

"What was what?" I say, scooping another invisible serving of food into her bowl.

"That—" she whispers.

I perk my ears and listen.

"It's probably Grammy's mutt. Go on now, eat up."

"What if it's not?" her voice quivers.

I step to the entrance of the sumac hideout and clap my hands together.

"Come, Missy. Come, girl. Here, Missy."

A stick snaps nearby. I pause.

"Little pig, little pig, let me come in," Uncle Jerry's scruffy voice says. His image emerges from the trees.

I spread my arms and legs out in the entrance like a star fish to keep him out.

"Not by the hair of my chinny, chin, chin," I say back. My stomach twists into a pretzel.

I make eye contact with him, begging with my eyes for him to hurt me and not Charlene.

Ignoring my silent plea, he pushes past me, picks Charlene up, and sits down on the stump with her on his lap.

"I'll be the daddy," he says. He bounces her on his knee.

My cheeks inflate with anger.

I need to save her!

I can only think of one thing that will make her run home where she will be safe. So I cross my arms, push my bottom lip out, and look her dead in the eyes.

"Go home, crybaby. I hate you!"

A quiver forms in the corner of her mouth, and she looks at me with a deep sadness.

"You heard me. Go home! We don't want you here! You're stupid and you stutter."

"B-B-But..."

"But nothin'," I say, blinking back tears.

Charlene doesn't budge.

I narrow my eyes and hold my fist up to her cheek.

"Go, or I'll knock your block off!"

After a long pause, she scurries away.

My knees knock together as Uncle Jerry stares down at me with eyes as dark as blackberries. He forces me onto a bed of dry leaves. They crunch and crackle beneath me. I lay still and wait for his body to close in around me like a coffin.

He kisses me with his three-day old whiskers, while I stare at the embroidered dragons on my purple China flats—shoes I got out of a bag of hand-me-downs which look like the shoes a

China doll wears. I think about princesses in faraway lands and the cornstalk arms I'll never make. The whole while, ignoring the tears that sluice down my cheeks.

When he's done, he jumps up.

"Count to fifty slowly and then you can leave," he tells me.

He reaches into his pocket for two dimes and a nickel and places them in my palm before jogging up the hill toward The House.

I lay there wanting to escape the nightmare but not knowing how.

Make him go away. Make this stop. Please.

But I feel even worse knowing that God doesn't hear me, except for the time He brought Pauline home from the hospital. I'm still thankful for that. On fifty, I stand up and wipe his kisses from my face.

As I pass the rhubarb patch, Dad steps out onto the stoop wearing a Robin Hood hat with a feather in it, along with a white dress shirt with a red paisley design on the shoulders and chest, and rhinestone buttons. A cigarette hangs from his mouth.

"Get your ass in the house and get dressed." His nostrils pulse. "Didn't you hear me callin' you?"

I wish I could tell you why I didn't answer you! I really do, but I can't. He'll kill me.

Charlene sits on the stoop. Her skin is blue and she wears the white Smurf hat Mum made out of felt. She frowns up at me and I frown down at her.

Don't you start with me too! I'm not in the mood. If you only knew what I went through for you. Maybe then you'd be more grateful!

Then, as if she heard my thoughts, she bites her blue lip and casts her eyes away.

Inside, the lazy-eyed Jolly Green Giant stands with a frayed green T-shirt on, green body paint, and a pair of cut-off white pants.

Mum wears a frilly dress and bonnet. "Little Bo Peep found her lost sheep," she says in her deep smoker's voice as she swaddles me in a flat brown bed sheet that she secures with safety pins.

I push back a tear.

Wrong again! I wasn't lost.

When the swaddling is done, she pulls the back of the sheet up over my head like a hood and then stuffs old sheets down the front to create the low-hanging belly. I go through the motions and smile, but my excitement from earlier fades with each thought of Uncle Jerry. A part of me wants to follow in Pauline's footsteps and run away, but I wouldn't know where to go or who would want me.

After Mum stuffs the low-hanging belly with sheets, she slides the hand-painted cardboard feet over my shoes and then slides the hand-painted alien hands over my hands. Lastly, she slides the mask over my face. The mask hides who I am. I don't have to force a smile and pretend I'm okay anymore. This thought gives me the permission to exhale the breath I feel like I've been holding since we moved back to Maine, nearly six years ago.

"You look g . . . g . . . g . . . I like your costume," Charlene says, smiling forgivingly, and my heart lurches at how much I love her.

For a moment, I am better knowing that at least I protected my sister, just like the time Pauline protected me. But how protected are any of us with a monster living next door?

"Hold still. Lemme take a picture," Mum says as she grabs the Polaroid camera from the boxy, blue oak television stand, where the Polaroid pictures of both Smurfette and the Jolly Green Giant lay developing.

"Say cheese," she says.

"Cheese," I say with a stiff, small smile.

HALLOWEEN 1984

Pauline as the Jolly
Green Giant

Me as E.T.

Charlene as a
smurf

Pauline, Charlene, me,
Charles Jr., 1984

Pauline, me, Charlene, 1981

Me, age 11

Me, age 10 ←

→ Me, age 9

Dad
1968

Dad & Mum
1984-ish

Mum
1969

Me &
Charlene,
1984

Me &
Charlene,
1973

Me, 1981

Chapter
17

CHEESE AND CRACKERS

The orange Jell-O jiggles on my tray as I make my way across the gymnasium to the lunch table where Charlene blows bubbles in her milk carton. The bubbles round the top and trickle over the sides.

"Cut it out, Nimrod! Fifth graders don't blow bubbles!"

"S-s-says who?"

I take the straw from her.

"Says me. Now quit it before you draw attention to us."

As I hold the straw, a leather arm reaches over my shoulder and snatches my unopened milk. I crane my neck to see the new girl, Sandy Shaw, holding my milk above her head.

"Give . . . it . . . back," I say, raking my fingers through the air as if to take it away.

"Make me," Sandy says.

I grit my teeth and stand.

"Give . . . it . . . back," I repeat.

The boys pound the tables in anticipation of a brawl as Sandy Shaw squares her shoulders.

"Let's take this outside, Dodge. Me and you on the blacktop!"

"I ain't afraid of you, Sandy!" I say as I swallow deeply and snatch my milk from her.

At recess, I hide on the blacktop behind the hop-scotchers, double-dutchers, and Chinese jump-ropers in hopes that Sandy would forget about the altercation in the lunchroom minutes earlier. But when she rounds the corner with her friends, she spots me and makes her way toward me.

I take small steps backward. Each step causes the knobs on my polyester draw-string-pants to knock together—reminding me of the metronome the music teacher uses on Tuesdays.

Sandy scowls.

"Know what I'm gonna do to you, Dodge?"

"No. What?" I step backward until the small of my back presses into the white wood siding.

"I'm gonna choke you with this—"

She holds up a nude knee-high nylon and winds it around her hands.

I glance down and see her foot missing a nylon.

She wraps the nylon around my neck and pulls. My eyes widen—skin pores and dust particles from the stocking suspend in the air.

I struggle to breathe and claw at her hands.

The laughter stops—the half-court basketball game stops—the jump ropers stop. Suddenly, all the attention is on me and the Knee-high Stocking Killer.

Sandy Shaw drops her hands and smacks me on the back.

"I like you, Dodge! You've got guts!" she says as she kicks off her shoe and slides her nylon back on.

❧

AS THE SUN SETS, I STEP ONTO THE RICKETY STOOP WITH MY cardboard 3D glasses on and a pan of dish water in my hand. I fling the soapy water in the grass near the stoop, so not to fill up the slop buckets. A chilly breeze blows my nightgown sideways and tangles my knees. The purple bug light sizzles, and a moth flails in the ultra-light like a fish out of water.

Uncle Jerry appears from around the corner. His pockets jingle and he high-five's the purple light, then trots up the rickety stairs. The tail on his mechanic shirt hangs out and he smells of sweat and motor oil.

"How's my little girl? Hope you got a pair for me," he says, roughing my hair with his sandpaper hand and knocking my 3D glasses off, before stepping over the threshold and onto the peeling linoleum.

What's he doing here?

I follow him inside with the empty dish pan.

"What's up, Dolly Parton?" Uncle Jerry announces, when he sees Pauline.

I wait for Pauline to respond with the usual, "Nothing but the sky here." But she doesn't.

Pauline growls at him, dog-ears the page in her book, and limps behind the hanging blanket to the back of the house. Mum appears from behind the same blanket wearing her pin-striped bowling shirt and cherry lipstick with blue eye shadow.

"What's he doin' here?" I demand to know, following him to where the free carpet samples and the linoleum meet. "I thought Aunt Nina was babysittin' us tonight?"

Unlike Mum's usual frizzy ponytail, her hair is sprawled across her shoulders like an ebony shawl. A cigarette teeters between her lips, and she fills her tall green travel thermos with coffee.

"Thanks for comin' on such short notice, Shithead. You're a wicked good Samaritan, you know it?"

The cigarette bobs from the corner of her mouth. Her lipstick stamps a red ring on the paper.

"That's what I've been told." He grins and pats himself on the shoulder, stirring a pot of something wicked inside me.

His eyes shift from me to Charlene and Tonya, who both sit on the divan in their pajamas, and both have on cardboard 3D glasses, the glasses Dad brought home from the flea market so we could watch *Jaws* in 3D on television tonight.

I place the empty metal basin in the sink and flop across the armchair in the living room, kicking the double-oven stove beside me with my heel.

I warn myself, *Don't let him see you afraid. Fear excites him.*

Mum twists the silver lid onto the thermos. The tip of her cigarette recedes from a glowing red tip into a flaky ash, and she taps it on the rim of the Maine-shaped ashtray, then puts it back in her mouth.

My stomach twist and turns like a murmuration of black birds.

"Not every bowlin' night I hope?"

Mum sweeps her hair back.

"It's two nights a week. Stop bellyachin', damn-it. It ain't gonna kill you!"

It ain't? If you only knew, you would never let him watch us again. Just out with it already, Francine.

But I don't. Shame and fear keep me silent.

Uncle Jerry reclines on the divan between Charlene and Tonya. Lady Bug, our three-legged cat, lays on the back of the divan, and Patches, our pregnant calico cat, curls up in his lap. She purrs like a V-8 engine.

"I brought a game. I know how much you pissants like games," he says, stroking Patches.

My thoughts turn into a wishing well: *Wishing an engine would fall on him. Wishing he would move away. Wishing he would choke on his own vomit. Wishing Mum and Dad would quit bowling. Wishing I had enough guts to tell on him. Wishing God would do something.*

"You girls like Go Fish, ayuh?"

He digs in his pants pocket and pulls out the jackknife used to kill Peter Rabbit, then digs some more and pulls out a deck of cards with a bunny on the box that matches the tattoo on his arm.

"Playboy," he says, flexing his tattoo.

Mum stuffs her burgundy cigarette pouch in her pocketbook, throws the beige strap over her shoulder, and grabs the green thermos.

"You girls behave and don't give Shithead any problems, ayuh? There's Jiffy Pop in the cabinet, and you can have a cup of hot chocolate before bed."

The smoldering cancer stick teeters between Mum's lipstick speckled teeth.

"Charlene, be sure to go whiz before bed, or you and Tonya might float away," Mum says with amusement.

Charlene scowls up at her from the divan.

"Don't give me that look," Mum says. "Not my fault you still wet the bed."

Mum takes three steps from the table to the hanging blanket and whips it aside.

"Get to gettin' it, babe. We're gonna be late," she yells into the back of the house.

The buckle on Dad's belt clanks as he comes down the hall.

"Charlie," Uncle Jerry says with a nod as Dad steps through the blanket, taking the one step down into the front of the house.

"Shithead," Dad returns the nod.

"Smells like somethin' crawled up in you and died," Mum says, still chuckling from her floating away comment. "Did you put the lid on the pisspot?"

Dad's hands grip his hips, and he slides one dusty boot forward.

"Whatcha' think?" he asks, half serious and half sarcastic.

Please, don't go, I want to say, but the words get stuck in my throat.

Mum and Dad make their way out the door with their bowling bags, coffee mugs, thermos, and cigarettes. I stand in the open doorway and watch until the taillights disappear beyond the cornfield to the left, and then I withdraw into the lion's den.

"Who wants Jiffy Pop?" Uncle Jerry says. He shakes the disposable popper like a tambourine in the hand of the tele-evangelist we watch on Sunday mornings.

"Me!" I wave my hand. Anything to delay the games.

Uncle Jerry lifts the hanging blanket and yells to Pauline.

"Hey, tub-a-lard, get out here and pop this."

A thump-step-thump echoes down the hall. She tosses the hanging blanket aside and steps down onto the linoleum. Her forehead wrinkles as she grabs the Jiffy Pop pan and glides the disposable popper in circles over the glowing red burner until the aluminum erupts. Popcorn shoots like fireworks through the air and replaces the unpleasant smell Dad left with a savory one.

Uncle Jerry shuffles the cards in a rainbow formation, licks his grimy thumb, and deals five cards to each of us.

"The loser will be my partner in the next game."

What kind of next game?

Collywobbles multiply in my stomach as he mouths the words, "Hide-and-seek."

Charlene's blonde bangs hang unevenly around her face. She sweeps them aside and looks at Pauline.

"D-d-do you have any queens?" she asks.

Pauline's head tilts toward her.

"Go fish," she says.

With gnawed-on fingernails, Charlene leans over the table and draws a card. She smiles with glee and throws it down on the table with a matching card.

Uncle Jerry straightens his back and presses the small of it into the wooden chair.

"Go again," he says, shedding a smile like a snake sheds its skin.

"D-d-do you have any eights?" Charlene asks Tonya.

As quickly as the game began, it ends, and I sheepishly watch as Uncle Jerry takes my hand, and without fight or fuss, leads me to the bottom bunkbed where self-hate, anger, and hope bleed out.

He counts loudly as Charlene, Pauline, and Tonya hide. My stomach churns.

I wish I were dead. I wish I could run away! I wish God would strike him with his most powerful lightning bolt.

"Stop cryin'. It ain't that bad!" He slides my nightgown up.

"Now kiss me," he says.

I squeeze my lips together.

His mechanic shirt is open, his belly hangs out, and he forces my chin up with his jagged fingernail.

"I love you, ayuh?"

My eyes catch the blanket over the doorway as it moves. Tonya peeks in at us.

"Kiss me!" he says as he raises my chin with his index finger, his breath smelling worse than a bouquet of stinking Benjamins.

"Sixty Mississippi—" he yells out as his lips connect with mine.

I squeeze my eyes shut so not to see Tonya's eyes and lean into his prickly beard. His pants are around his ankles as his hips lunge forward.

"That hurts," I yelp.

"Damn-it, if you ain't gonna play, I'll find someone who will." He pauses a beat, then calls out, "Seventy Mississippi."

I'll do whatever you want. Just leave them be!

"I'm sorry!" I say softly. Tears fill my eyes.

"Eighty Mississippi," he calls out.

The pitter-patter of feet shuffles up and down the hall in search of a hiding place. I calm myself, knowing everyone else is safe because he is with me.

"—Ninety Mississippi, ninety-one Mississippi, ninety-two Mississippi." The counting speeds up and when he stands to fix his pants, he says, "One-hundred Mississippi. Ready or not, here I come."

He traipses toward the hanging blanket. I cling to his shirttail and drag my heels through the pile of clothes on the bedroom floor to the striped carpet in the hallway, then to Pauline's doorway.

With one sweep of his arm, Pauline's hanging blanket rips from the nail and cascades onto the floor.

"Here, Pauline. Here, Charlene. Here, Tonya. Come out, come out, wherever you are." He clicks his tongue like a cowboy does to get his horse moving.

With a second sweep, he knocks me off. I tumble into the bookshelf and jar loose a collection of dust and cat hair. He flips over boxes and searches under beds, before spotting a shivering bundle of blankets in the corner.

He kicks the bundle with his boot and out pops a blonde head with a white eye patch. He extends his hand, she takes it, and then limps past me, clutching his hand all the way to the living room.

When Uncle Jerry is out of sight, Charlene pops out from behind a teetering stack of what-nots in the back of the hallway. Tonya pops out from behind the Red Ryder sled next to Charlene. Together, we tiptoe into the bedroom, through the sea of dirty clothes on the floor, past the bunk beds to the built-in toy box Dad made of particle board and two-by-fours. We lift the lid, then climb inside, burrowing beneath the stuffed animals and girly magazines Dad hides from Mum, where it is dark, and it is safe for now.

Pauline's words, "I hate you! I hope you die! I'll spit on your grave," float like a ghost through the house and into the toy box with us.

A tear trickles down my cheek.

What's it gonna take to be free of him?

❦

Two days later, Charlene and I play *War* on our stoop with the deck of cards Uncle Jerry left with the bunny on them.

Tonya wanders down the path to show us a new magic trick.

She pops a handful of blackberries in her mouth, chews a bit, then swallows. Afterward, she sticks out her tongue.

"Ahhhh. See, all gone. Now watch this."

She snakes her neck and opens her mouth again.

"Tah-dah—" she says. Her tongue holds a regurgitated pile of berries on it. Only the seeds are identifiable.

"Wicked cool!" I clap my hands. "Teach me the trick."

"Sure, but first we gotta pick some more berries," she says.

Tonya leads the way. Charlene and I skip behind her to the tangle of blackberries near the garage where a layer of neon green slime covers the frog pond like monster skin.

Surrounded by cattails and thistles, Tonya wipes the berry juice on her shirt. She stares down at her right palm in silence as if reading it.

"What's wrong?" I ask, breaking the silence.

"I can't tell you. He made me promise," Tonya says.

"We won't tell. We pinky swear. Right, Charlene?"

Tonya pauses. Her eyes dart around the yard, back and forth, up and down the path, up and down Charlene and me.

"I don't wanna spend the night at Grammy's anymore," she says as she reaches into her pocket and pulls out two dimes and a nickel.

You too? I knew it!

"That's it! I'm runnin' away. Who's with me?" I say.

Charlene chews on her thumbnail. "No w-w-way, Jose. You can't make me," she says.

My hands move to my hips, and I slide one China flat forward.

"Would you rather have Uncle Jerry babysit us next week on bowlin' night?"

"N-N-No," Charlene says.

"Alright then—we ain't got a choice!"

"But I don't wanna hurt Mum and Dad's feelins'," Charlene says.

"Have it your way," I say, as I spin around to Tonya. "You a chicken, too?"

My cousin's heart-shaped front teeth appear as her lips part, and a light in her eyes begins to twinkle.

I glance at my Smurf watch.

"Good deal. Tonya, meet me back here in five minutes with two big sticks."

She nods, then takes off into the woods beyond the neon green frog pond. I hurry inside to grab saltine crackers and cheese slices, then scurry down the hall to pillage a bag of hand-me-downs to find two shirts with long sleeves.

On time, Tonya meets me at the blackberry bushes with two large sticks. I spread the shirts on the ground and place the crackers and cheese in the center. Once they are situated the way I think will work, I tie the long sleeves around the sticks to make bindles like the hobos do. Then without a word, we hop on the brown bike with the yellow banana seat and hang the bindles over our shoulders.

"Last call," I say, offering Charlene a seat on the handlebars.

She shakes her head no, her eyes as big as fish bowls.

"Don't you dare tell." I narrow my eyes at Charlene, then place my right foot into the stirrup on the pedal with the broken reflector and push.

With Tonya on the back of the banana seat, I pedal up Nelson Hill Road, leaving Charlene standing at our mailbox with the milk can base. I pedal past the cornfield, beyond the bend in the road and the vacant red shingled house, and up the hill leading to the horse farm.

"Where will we sleep?" Tonya asks, as I climb the hill with the bike.

"I dunno'," I say.

"What 'bout the Camp Modin killer?" she says. "The one who buried the girl in the shallow grave at the lake."

"What 'bout him?"

"What if he catches us—"

"He won't."

"How do you know?"

"I just do."

"What will we eat when our supply runs out?" she asks.

I shrug and continue pedaling.

There's a small pause, where all I hear is the rattle of the broken reflector in the spokes.

"What 'bout Grammy Dodge?" Tonya says, when we reach the top of the hill.

"Look," I say, "if we go back, Uncle Jerry will keep doin' bad things to us. Is that whatcha' want?"

"But Grammy's feelings will be hurt," Tonya chokes out.

"Fine then." I coast to a stop. "You hungry?" I ask, forgoing our plan.

"Ayuh, wicked. All I ate was a piece of toast with mint jam on it," she says.

We jump off the banana seat and sit in the field with our bindles open, eating cheese and crackers. We might not have gotten far, but for a moment, I felt the hope of being free. In my little girl's mind, I wonder if any of us kids will ever be free from the monster next door.

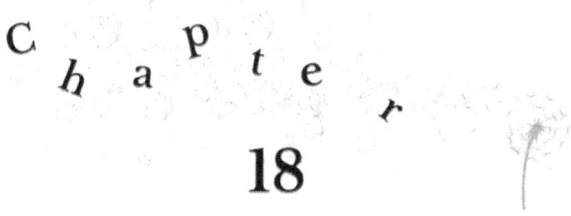

18

NEW BEGINNING

Mum opens the privacy blanket to my bedroom with a cigarette between her teeth and releases a plume of smoke. The smoke ascends into the hole above her head, where a bat flew down the other day, and Dad clapped his hands together and squished it between his palms.

"Rise and shine, sleepy head. Better put a boogie on it or your father's gonna leave you," Mum says.

I throw the covers back and sit up, yawn big, and prop up Buster, my stuffed dog, so he can look out the window while I'm gone.

Mum leans against the door jamb in her see-through nightgown. She holds a cup of coffee and a pack of cigarettes.

"It's your weekend to help your father with the flea market at Scarborough Downs. It's a hundred miles, so get to gettin' it." The blanket falls and Mum disappears down the hall.

I roll off the top bunk with only a T-shirt on and a pair of Pauline's hand-me-down underwear synched at the waist to fit. I grab my pants with the ketchup stain and hurry to the front of the house, where Dad sips his coffee and eyes Grampy's silver pocket watch in his hand.

"Get dressed, damn-it!" His eyes bulge and nostrils flare.

"But Mum said—"

"Did I stutter?"

"I thought you were gonna leave me," I spit out quickly, hopping on one foot, stuffing my left leg in the pant hole, then the right.

Dad sets his coffee down and reaches his hand into the large hole in the wall beside the kitchen cabinet, where the outside light switch is. He dodges the exposed wires and insulation to flick on the porch light.

"You gonna stand there like a statue or help?" he says, his voice rising with the sun.

He lifts a stack of red and black milk crates and totters down the rickety stairs with them to the back of the Titanic.

I follow behind him with a crate and set it in the driveway for him to pack, then scurry back inside for another, and another, back and forth, up and down the stairs.

In a careful manner, Dad loads the wagon with friendship bracelets, spoon rings, turquoise pendant necklaces, feather hair clips, hanging dice, glow sticks, sports cards, jumping beans, comic books, decorative pillows, and other what-nots, then slams the hatch, securing it with a bungee cord.

The Titanic idles loudly and jitterbugs as he presses the gas to keep it from stalling. The tail pipe blows grey soot, and the wire-rigged muffler rumbles like bowling pins for a strike. On the dinged-up bumper and back hatch is Mum and Dad's collection of bumper stickers, the newest being *The Maine State Bird* with a picture of a mosquito on it. It's placed beside the *Honk If You Love Jesus* and *Shit Happens* bumper stickers.

The plastic soles on Mum's slippers scuff across the peeling linoleum and stop in the doorway beside the large hole with insulation and wires springing from it. The glow of the porch light meets the sunrise and outlines her pear-shaped figure in the see-through gown.

"Better get a move on, babe, or you'll be late," Mum says loudly over the rumble of the muffler.

I grab the green thermos, the mug of coffee, the cash box, and the extra pack of cigarettes out of Mum's hands, race down the rickety steps, and climb into the ripped front seat with yellow foam springing from it.

The cloth ceiling sags over Dad's head. The console and carpets harbor years of grey ash and coffee stains, and the interior smells like a blend of stale cigarettes and the pine tree deodorizer dangling from the radio.

Dad sticks his arm out the window and waves goodbye. The station wagon bunny-hops down the driveway and onto Nelson Hill Road, over the potholes, through the canopy of trees, and toward the highway. The orange glow of his cigarette highlights his top lip, but that's not all that glows. I love going to the flea market when it's just me and him. Normally, Dad would speak in short sentences or bark commands, but not today, not when it's the two of us.

He flicks the smoldering filter out the window.

"You ready for some hard work?"

I rest my heel on the ripped blue seat and slide my grey Velcro sneaker on.

"Ayuh! A little hard work ain't never killed anyone," I say.

⚜

An hour and a half later, we arrive at Scarborough Downs and rent a booth in the middle of the gigantic glass building. I help Dad unload the crates and set up the table. Pillows go with pillows; feather earrings go with spoon rings and friendship bracelets; glow sticks go with the jumping beans, the Hulk dolls, and My Little Pony knock-offs; the hanging dice and the dream catchers go with the black hanging number eight balls.

After everything is set up and the cash box is stocked, I take out Dad's western book, top off his mug with coffee from the thermos, and set his cigarettes on the table before opening his metal folding chair.

Dad tosses me a ten-dollar bill to browse the other booths and get a snack from the concession stand. I return with Nerd rope candy, blueberry flavored bubble gum, and a roll of stickers.

By mid-afternoon, the foot traffic slows, and Dad's thermos is empty. I crawl under our booth and lay my head on the decorative eagle and Harley pillows we haven't sold.

When my cat nap is over, I crawl out from under the table, where Dad hands me a wad of ones.

"Get me a red snapper with ketchup," he says.

As I skip through the building past the other booths to get Dad a red skinned hot dog, I spot a unicorn with big sparkly wings and stop.

"Sell it to you," the man says. His offer is as alluring as the purple bug light.

I toss the wad of ones on the table.

"I have five bucks."

The man counters with six.

"Be right back!" I say.

I place the unicorn back on the table and race through the building to Dad in his folding chair with his book. His right leg crosses over his left leg. It bounces as he turns the page.

He looks up over the cowboy on the cover. "Hey, you! Where's my damn hot dog?"

"I need more dollars," I say.

⚜

AT FOUR O'CLOCK, WE LOAD THE CRATES INTO THE TITANIC, and begin the ride back. On the way home, Dad pulls the visor down to retrieve his sunglasses, and as he does, Grampy's obituary flutters through the air and lands on his dungaree leg.

He studies the picture of Grampy in the newspaper clipping that he's held onto for the past few years.

"Grammy's house is too big for her to take care of any longer," Dad says, popping the visor up and placing the obituary above it.

My lips curl down.

What do you mean any longer?

He chokes back emotion, and his Adam's apple bobs in his throat.

"Grammy's gettin' married and movin' to Clinton."

"Wait! What?"

"You heard me."

"Who's she gonna marry? I hope not Harold. He don't even like us kids. And where's Uncle Jerry gonna live?" I hold my breath and picture the wishing well.

"Shithead's movin' out, too. I dunno' where to yet."

"Your Aunt Fawn and Uncle Bo will be rentin' The House from Grammy."

"When?" I ask with a wide smile and big voice.

"Don't act so damn happy," Dad snaps. "Next month some time. They keep foster kids and need more space."

"When can I meet 'em?"

"Meet who?"

"The kids," I say. I wiggle in my seat and rub my hands together.

Could it be? Did God really answer my prayer?

"Hand me the lighter, will you?"

I pull the automatic torch from the console and press it to the end of his cigarette. The warm summer breeze pours in and makes me feel new like a pair of shoes.

The news makes me happier than the early sighting of a fiddlehead. I hug my unicorn and count the telephone poles whizzing by. I'm excited to play new games with my new friends and not play the same old hide-and-seek anymore. It'll be the first time I'm able to stand in the yard or sit or walk or do whatever I want without the fear of foot chases.

No more Goliath.

Dad inhales deeply and blows smoke my way. "Did you see what I bought you?"

"No."

"It's in the back."

"What is it?"

"An Atari," he says. "It comes with Pac-Man, Pitfall, Missile Command, and two joy sticks. We'll hook it up when we get home and see if it works."

"That's wicked cool," I say, sitting up on my knees and squeezing my unicorn with the sparkly wings.

A FEW WEEKS LATER, ON MOVE-IN DAY, CHARLENE CRAWLS OUT of bed with a yellow ring on her pajama's. The scent of urine fills my nostrils and makes my eyes water like an onion being sliced.

"I wish we were normal," I say, climbing down off the top bunk and blinking the burn away.

"W-W-We are," Charlene says, slipping out of her wet clothes and into some dry ones.

"No, dummy, hauling water and emptyin' pisspots ain't normal."

"I'm sure we're not the only ones?" she stutters.

I want to add that having an uncle chase you and play painful games with you isn't normal either. I don't think any of my friends at school have uncles like ours. But I don't say anything. I don't want to upset Charlene too much.

It's laundry day, so Charlene balls up the wet mound in her arms, and we head to the kitchen to help Mum roll the wringer washer across the linoleum, over the threshold, and down the rickety stoop to the driveway. It takes all three of us.

Charlene tucks the wet mound into one of the stacks of

clothes Mum has separated out on the floor. Then we grab the two buckets off the counter to help Mum fill the washer and the rinse tub.

I push and pull the handle, up and down, until the first bucket is full, and together Charlene and I lug it over to the wringer washer, where Mum helps us pour it in.

When we return to the pump, Charlene fills her bucket with water in the same up-and-down motion.

"Do you think they'll like us?" I ask, watching her straw-sized arms pulling and pushing the handle. Her hair is in a tangle of knots.

"Will w-w-who like us?"

"The foster kids, dummy. Aunt Fawn's movin' in today, or did you forget that already?" I stand like a lookout with my hand over my brow and peer down the footpath at Grammy's empty house, three telephone poles away, hoping to see a U-Haul and not a ghost. I see nothing.

"Why w-w-wouldn't they?"

The wind shifts and the scent of dried urine on her skin bristles my nose. My shoulders dip. I turn to observe the weeds licking the sills, the unfinished exterior, the recycled windows, the tarnished ice-chest, the mildewed mattress, the bee infested junk car, the empty rabbit cage, the mangled bicycle parts, the rotted lumber, the rusty brown hand pump, Snoopy the basset hound, Festus the Saint Bernard, Lassie the collie, Moose the Great Dane, and a football-sized bullfrog named Lumpy within view.

They'll see this and instantly hate us.

After filling the washer and rinse tub, I wrestle the antique push-reel-mower from the tangle of weeds beside the house, where the grass reaches my knees and Lumpy the bullfrog hides. The wart on my pinky finger is probably from holding Lumpy because, as Mum says, "a bullfrog's pee can cause warts." I push and pull the rusty mower through the tall grass in choppy, uneven patches.

An hour later, I head inside for a cup of strawberry Kool-Aid and sit on the top stoop to drink it. My eyes scan the grass. It looks like a tattered patch-work quilt of dandelions, tall grass, pig's weed, and sweet clovers.

I return the cup inside and grab the orange handled sewing scissors from the end table, where Mum's red pin cushion and jar of buttons sit. I need them to trim around the gray tree trunks in the front yard. Then I stack the warped two-by-fours strewn along the house into neat piles, wrestle the tarnished ice-chest out of sight, and finally drag the mildewed mattress around back.

More Mallard duck decoys.

When done, I flop down on the mildewed mattress I dragged over to the clothesline behind the house and prop myself up by an elbow. The dark windows of Grammy's house extract an eerie scene on the hill. The tire swing spins under the oak tree as though an invisible foot propels it, and the iron weathervane twists and creeks.

"Tell me again 'bout the ghosts that haunt The House. The pig eyes my aunts saw," I say with one dry gulp. Then two. I stare up at Mum as she hangs the laundry on the line above me.

Mum holds the cigarette to her lips and inhales deeply, then points down the path, as a stream of smoke funnels from her nostrils.

"If I've told you once, I've told you a thousand times," Mum begins. Her voice throaty and deep like Lumpy the bullfrog.

"In the 1700's, twin girls married twin boys," Mum says, quickly adding, "and lived across the road from each other."

Mum points next at the road across from Grammy's crab apple tree, where a cavernous hole remains, overgrown with decades of brush and briar—the foundation of a house.

"When one twin brother died, the other twin brother pulled his house up the hill using the horse and cart method and attached the two houses together. That's why Grammy's house is so big," Mum says. "Matter of fact, the side of The House facing us belonged to the widow woman. The upstairs window to the left was probably her bedroom because it's the largest."

The stream of smoke stops, and Mum's fingers disappear into the dangling bag of clothespins.

"How'd her husband die?" I ask, sitting up straight as if it were the first time hearing the answer that was about to come.

"Can't be sure," she says as she takes another puff of the stick hanging from her lips.

Just then, she crosses her legs where she stands and releases a gagging cough, hunching over. Her face turns red, and she struggles to catch her breath. She thumps her chest.

"Must be the pollen," she says after the cough eases.

But of course! It's never the cigarettes' fault.

Mum uncrosses her legs and resumes hanging the pair of worn-out underwear Charlene had her accident in earlier. Mum clears her throat and continues with the story.

"Back in 1968, The House shook like an earthquake. I was babysittin' for your Grammy when it happened. I got all the kids out of The House. It sounded like the wood planks on the exterior were being ripped off and thrown down to the ground. Then it stopped. As suddenly as that stopped, a hammerin' sound started, like The House was rebuildin' itself. That's when I heard the ghost say, 'Hang him!'"

I wring my hands and swallow hard.

"Hang who?"

Mum shrugs. "Later in years, The House served as a posting inn to trade out horses. That's why the large circular driveway. And over there," Mum points, fingering the direction of the frog pond and chicken coop, "was where the stable stood to keep the horses. A covered breezeway once connected the stable to The House. There's not even a trace of it now," Mum adds.

My brow raises.

"Back in that day, they had travelling judges that would hear cases." Mum's nicked hands shake out a wet T-shirt, and she reaches into the clothespin bag for two more wooden pins.

"After I heard the words, 'Hang him,'" Mum says, "that's when I heard another ghost say, 'I'm innocent I tell you'."

My eyes widen.

"Then what happened?"

"Whatcha' think, ding-ding? They hung him. Come to think of it, one of your uncles found the trial letters and a noose in the attic a couple of years back."

I sit up even straighter and stare up at her.

"What'd the letters say?"

The tip of the cigarette recedes into a gray ash, and smoke rises from the tip. Mum puckers her mouth and inhales, blowing smoke down at me on the mattress.

"The trial letters disappeared. The ghost must've taken 'em, like when the ghost in Florida took you girls' gold-plated silver dollars before we moved back to Maine. You remember that, don'tcha?"

⚜

LATER THE SAME EVENING, PAULINE, CHARLENE, AND I follow Mum to The House to say hi to Aunt Fawn and meet the foster kids. When we enter the chipped red door, we hear footsteps thunder down the stairwell and look up with big wide eyes at the two strangers. Not kids at all.

"Girls, meet Abby, she's thirteen, and Roger, he's sixteen. They're brother and sister," Aunt Fawn says.

"Hi!" we say, still in shock.

I bat my eye lashes at Roger and tuck a rogue curl behind my ear.

He's wicked cute!

Mum slides her cigarette pouch into the ripped pocket of her housedress and exhales a rosette of smoke.

"These are my twins, Francine and Charlene. They're ten. And this is Pauline, my oldest. She's thirteen. I wouldn't count on seein' much of this one right here. She hibernates like a bear most days," Mum says, eyeballing Pauline.

We look at Pauline, who cocks her head, tucks her chin into her chest, and peers up at us with her one good eye.

The sound of laughter echoes in the distance and reaches the chipped red door. The cousins who live nearby flock to meet the new kids. Laurel and Tamara, who live just up the road, and Lottie and Dottie, who live in the trailer right next door to us, gather in the kitchen where the giant oval table and rocking chair used to be.

"Guys, this is Abby and Roger," Pauline says. "Let's make 'em feel welcome by showin' 'em around the property. Ayuh?"

From the chipped red door, the seven of us Dodges lead them around the property, showing them the flowering apple trees, the junkyard, and the frog pond. Then we hang a left at the mailbox, walk down Nelson Hill Road a few yards to where the entrance to the cornfield is and stop.

From the entrance, Roger notices his bedroom window through the thicket of birch trees lining the road.

"Hey, that's my room," he points. "Wanna come see my posters?"

Abby turns on her heels toward Roger. "Your light's on. I cut it off."

My sisters, cousins, and I glance at the curtainless window and quickly turn away for fear that the headless doohickey or glowing pig's eyes will appear. Our eyes rotate from one Dodge girl to the next until they reach Roger and Abby.

Pauline cocks her head and looks up. "Didn't Aunt Fawn tell you The House is haunted?"

"I-I-I ain't goin' upstairs," Charlene says. She raises her fingernail to her mouth. Her cuticles are as raw as the tips of her big toes.

Roger's brow bends with disbelief.

"You're kiddin', right?"

He gives Abby a quick wink, turns around to face the

window, jumps up and down in the road, waves his arms wildly and shouts at the ghost in The House.

"Come and get me. I dare you!"

The light flickers, on then off, on then off again.

A prickle goes through my spine and up the back of my neck. Goosebumps stand on end, and my heart pounds like feet chasing dragon flies. I wait for a dark shadow to appear and drag Roger away.

Roger ceases jumping and turns to Abby.

"See! It's an old house with old wirin'. There's no such thing as ghosts. They're tryin' to scare you."

"A man was hung. My dad found the noose," Laurel says sternly.

"You're full of shit. Where's the noose now?" Roger asks.

"The ghost took it," I blurt out in her defense.

Roger straightens up and covers his mouth to hide his laugh.

"How do you know? Did the ghost tell you this?"

Pauline dabs her head, her lazy eye rattles back and forth.

"Mum wouldn't lie 'bout a thing like that! Go ask her for yourself if you don't believe us."

"Yeah, ask her," we seven Dodge girls say in sync.

"I'm a big boy. Big boys don't believe in ghosts."

Roger rolls up his plaid sleeve and makes a fist like to fight the ghost if it were to appear.

"I'm not scared. I'll go up there right now. Double-dog-dare me?" he says.

Pauline scrunches her nose at the circular marks on Roger's arm.

"What happened? You get the mumps or somethin'?"

"It's from cigarettes," he says.

Pauline's lazy eye shuffles back and forth. She peers up over her glasses. "Hell boy, you smoke?"

Roger rolls his sleeves down and fastens the button on the cuff. "No, but my Old Man does."

Pauline pauses and hangs her head.

I don't get it. Why's she so upset about him having the mumps?

"G-e-e-s-h, Roger, I'm sorry. I didn't know." Pauline's mouth frowns down and her voice crackles.

What don't I know?

"Don't worry 'bout it," Roger says as he takes Abby's hand and pulls her around front and toward the chipped red door. "Thanks for showin' us around. It's late and we've got some unpackin' to do."

The seven of us follow them inside to the kitchen, where Mum slides the wooden chair back from the small table.

"Perfect timin', birds. Your father will be home from his weekend of reserves at the Navy base shortly. Thanks for the coffee, Fawn. It was wicked good catchin' up. Come, girls," Mum says, motioning to the door.

When Mum and the three of us reach the backside of the garage, where the torn tar-paper hangs, she wrestles the cigarette pouch from the ripped pocket of her housedress and points at the roof of the garage.

"I ever tell you 'bout the UFO I saw land on the roof? It had itty-bitty tinfoil legs."

Mum holds the lighter up to her lips where the cigarette hangs and purses them. With three sharp strikes the cigarette glows and so does her nose.

"You girls be nice to 'em kids. Fawn told me Abby was raped by her father, and Roger was forced to watch."

A stream of smoke funnels from Mum's nostrils, and she slides the lighter into the pocket of her sad housedress.

I frown and look away from Mum. I didn't think other kids got hurt like us. It makes me sad.

"You should see where Roger's dad played chicken on his arm. What a douchebag," Pauline mutters angrily.

That's it. I decide Roger and Abby are going to be our friends. After I make that decision, I feel a little better.

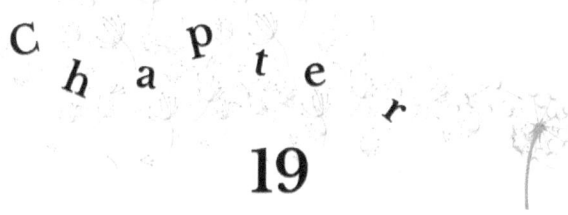

19

THE TROJAN HORSE

Much like the three reading groups and the three lunch groups, the bus also has three age groups—high school, middle school, and elementary school. In the afternoons, we all ride the bus home together.

When the dismissal bell rings, I make my way from my fifth-grade classroom to the line of elementary students boarding the bus, where the middle school and high schooler's noisily wait.

Charlene climbs the three steps and strolls down the aisle in front of me. A tangle of hair protrudes off the back of her neck like the tail-feathers on a peacock. I try not to focus on the unsightly tangles, unsure as to when she last brushed them.

When I don't hear singing coming from the back of the bus, I peek my eyes out from around the back of Charlene's head, hoping the Cooley sisters—Michelle and Angela—had caught another ride home. The younger, Angela, is in middle school and the older one, Michelle, is in high school. They like to serenade my sisters and me with the *Old McDonald Had a Farm* song on the way home each afternoon. They are never alone in their serenading. The Goode brothers always join in. My eyes bounce over the seats, each bounce collecting wisps of hope like Mum's button jar, until I spot the sisters in the back sitting by the Goode brothers.

My eyes quickly backtrack six seats from them to Pauline, where she sits alone, head down, pencil in hand, sketching like Picasso in her sketchbook. She's in the eighth grade and boards the bus before us with all the other middle school and high schoolers in Skowhegan, securing Charlene and me a seat for which I'm thankful. Otherwise, where would we sit? It's not like anyone wants a Dodge sitting with them.

I hold my Trapper Keeper in my left arm because my right arm is in a thick plaster cast held up by a blue sling with a long white strap around my shoulder. The plaster of the cast wraps around my fingers and thumb and stops at my elbow, an injury that happened shortly after Roger and Abby moved in. Uncle Chester gave us kids a ride on his new tractor in the front-loading bucket—and I, being the tomboy that I am, jumped off the tractor while in motion, hitting my wrist on the loading bucket. Fracturing my wrist ended all the fun.

When Charlene reaches Pauline's high-back seat, she stops in the aisle, while Pauline swings her legs out so we both can squeeze in with her.

Lottie and Dottie sit two seats up from us, while the Goode brothers, Lyle and Eddie, sit in the back with the Cooley sisters. The Goode brothers, along with the Cooley sisters, plug their noses with their thumbs and index fingers while making loud farm animal sounds.

"Oink. Oink. Oink. It's the three little pigs," the Goode's and the Cooley's announce, like four court jesters heralding our arrival.

"I wish they'd leave us the hell alone!" Pauline mutters under her breath. Her words spit ice.

"Why doesn't the bus driver make 'em stop?" I ask in a small voice, sinking down into my seat and opening my Trapper Keeper to look over my collection of puffy Care Bear stickers.

"Because . . . he's . . . old," Pauline responds as she pencils in the grey pupils of the fairy she draws. "He probably can't hear 'em. Lucky for us, he can see...at least, I think he can," she says with a small grin.

The singsong starts, and I wait for the bus in front of ours to leave, so we can leave, knowing salvation—our little brown house with the rusty brown handpump—is only ten-minutes away.

"Grrrr," Pauline mutters loudly as we wait, her irritation visibly builds with each "oink."

I elbow her to be quiet so not to draw more attention to us.

"Maybe they're oinkin' at somebody else," I say in her ear.

Pauline turns the growl on me.

There is the potent scent of urine on Charlene's skin, the odor from Pauline's overly active sweat glands, and the cigarette smoke on our clothes, in our hair, coating our skin.

It's definitely us!

The diesel engine rattles as our bus pulls out onto Main Street. We pass the purple cow statue, the thirty-five-foot rocket ship, the red tin man made from muffler parts, and the water wheel before turning right at the antique shop.

A series of "clicks" and "snaps" catch my ear. I glance over my shoulder at the Cooley's and the Goode's lowering the windows around them, before beginning a new round of *Old McDonald Had a Farm* with added emphasis on "everywhere an oink, oink—"

"Shut up before I rearrange your faces," Pauline yells, chugging those words down with a deep throated snarl.

This time her volume isn't quarantined to our seat. It penetrates the noises on the bus—the chit-chat, the laughter, and the singsong—bringing the triune of noises to a halt.

Pauline pushes her thick glasses up and continues sketching.

A beat of silence follows. Then two. And three.

I breathe a sigh of relief and lean my head back against the seat to rest my eyes.

No sooner than I close my eyes, the words, "Make me," break the silence.

The voice is hauntingly close.

I peer over my shoulder again. The collywobbles churning summersaults in my stomach as Michelle makes her way toward our seat, breaking rule number one to remain seated when the bus is in motion.

I gulp.

Michelle breezes past our seat. When she does, she slaps Pauline's sketchbook out of her lap, scattering the drawings all over the floor.

"Take a seat, Michelle," the driver says firmly.

Michelle steps on the sketches, grinding them into the floor with her Converse, before taking a seat further down the aisle toward the front.

My eyes water but not from the pungent smell of urine and sweat but from anger and hopelessness.

Why can't they leave us be? Just one time.

I melt into the green high-back seat like a crayon in the sun.

The bus buzzes past the vacant, red-shingled house on the left, past the private road Laurel and Tamara live on, past where the pavement on Nelson Hill Road stops and the dirt road begins, toward the bend where Mr. P's corn grows.

There it is—The giant antenna on our roof.

Never so glad to see my house than on the bus rides home in the afternoons, I close my Trapper Keeper and take a deep breath.

Michelle looks back at us and smiles.

I ignore it.

The bus stops at the foot of Aunt Mable's driveway. Lottie, Dottie, and Charlene scramble down the aisle and off the bus, while I stay behind to help Pauline collect her sketches.

We kneel in the aisle, reaching under the seats to find them all. And when we're done, I assist Pauline in getting her awkward, nearly two-hundred-pound body up from her knees to a standing position.

I then follow her slow, lop-sided gait down the aisle, toward the bifold door, closer to where Michelle now sits.

As Pauline approaches Michelle's seat, Michelle flashes a mischievous grin. Then, out of nowhere, Michelle slides her foot out into the aisle.

Before I can put two-and-two together, before I can make sense of what I see and warn Pauline, she trips over Michelle's black high-top sneaker with the star on the side and crashes to the floor like a box of rocks.

Pauline's glasses fly off. When she sits up, I notice the grate marks from the floor leave impressions on her face. She feels around blindly for her glasses, while choking back tears.

"Don't anyone move," Pauline commands. "I can't see a damn thing without my glasses."

I kneel beside her and grab her glasses from behind her in the aisle.

"Got 'em," I say in her ear. "Don't let 'em see you cry." I sweep a strand of her greasy hair out of the way with my plaster-cast-hand before sliding the thick Coke bottle glasses onto her face. They hang lopsided off her nose.

While still on our knees in the aisle, Michelle jumps up from her seat, stands over us, and looks down with her hands on her hips.

"Have a nice trip last fall?" she mocks.

Her words make my blood boil.

I slowly slide my casted arm out of the sling, make a tight fist around the plaster overlaying my palm. Drawing my arm back, I spring to my feet as hard and as fast as I can, landing a solid right hook with my plaster-casted-fist to Michelle's jaw.

Michelle's eyes close, her feet lift off the floor, and her body falls backward in what looks like slow motion, landing like a rag doll in the aisle.

The bus erupts with cheers and celebration.

Pauline, who is now the one standing, looks down at Michelle sprawled out on the floor.

"Have a nice trip last fall? Teach you to mess with a Dodge!" Pauline says.

"Is she dead?" I ask.

"Hell naw, she ain't dead. C'mon, before she wakes up."

She grabs my arm and spins me around. I follow Pauline's thump-step-thump the rest of the way down the aisle, down the steps, and across the road. When we reach Aunt Mable's driveway, my sister stops and gives me a cockeyed grin.

"Thanks! I owe you one."

I think of everything we've been through and shake my head. "You don't owe me a thing."

⚜

ON THE WEEKEND, PAULINE, CHARLENE, AND I DRAPE A queen-sized quilt over a low hanging branch in the front yard and secure the corners with four big rocks from Mum's flower bed. A breeze blows the grass sideways and redirects the fumes from the pit that we empty the pisspots in. The smell shifts from the backyard to the front.

In my left hand, I hold a mason jar with five scrappy lightning bugs, and in my casted right hand, a lid with holes poked in it. I screw the lid on and watch the lightning bugs sparkle against the darkness.

My dungaree covered hip leans against the Titanic, and I hold the jar up to watch the lightening bugs crawl up the glass and slide down, crawl back up, only to slide down again. Their butts' glow on and off, on, and off.

Roger and Abby show up with an armful of camping supplies. Julie, a friend from school, arrives with snacks and more camping supplies.

When Roger leaves for the evening, Abby, Julie, Charlene, Pauline, and I crawl into the flowery tent we made. We lay long ways like sardines with our heads sticking out and our faces pointed up at the stars. Taking turns, we point out the only constellations we know, the Little and Big Dipper.

Then Pauline rolls over, flicks on her flashlight, and grabs the collection of Garbage Pail Kids trading cards Abby brought with her.

Pauline tilts her head awkwardly and holds each card close to her face so she can see the picture and read the caption out loud.

"Ewww, Ray Decay," she grins, pushes out a dry laugh, and points at the Garbage Pail Kid with the rotten teeth, sitting among half-eaten sweets and empty soda pop cans.

She hands the card of Ray Decay to Julie. After Julie views it, she hands it to Charlene. After Charlene views it, she hands it to me. After I view it, I hand it to Abby. Abby hands it back to Pauline. She puts it back in the deck.

Pauline eyes each Garbage Pail Kid card closely, before passing it on.

"Ewww," Pauline says, stopping at Heavin' Steven, a picture of a Garbage Pail Kid spewing puke. Her belly bobs with amusement.

"Adam Bomb," she says next. "One of my favorites."

"Hey—" Julie interrupts, "let's tell ghost stories."

Suddenly, Pauline swats the air, then her arm, and then her neck.

"These damn mosquitos," she says, her tongue clicks. "What do I look like, dinner? I'm goin' inside. I'll see you fools in the mornin'."

She hands Abby back the stack of Garbage Pail Kids cards. Grabbing her pillow and blanket, she exits the tent.

Abby sits up and chugs a can of Moxie.

"Ghosts don't scare me." Her words follow Pauline over the gravel and up the stoop.

Pauline's signature thump-step-thump magnifies on the wood steps. The front door opens, the television blares, and the light from the living room funnels through the tent wall and dissolves.

I sit up along with Julie and Charlene and hold the flashlight to my chin. The light shines up my face as I tell the same story Mum told while hanging the laundry.

Charlene gnaws her fingernails. Julie holds her breath.

A whispery sounding "booooo" comes from outside the tent. It rises and falls.

My eyes bounce from Abby to Julie to Charlene to the tent door. I wonder if they heard it too or if I imagined it.

Their eyes tell me yes.

The "boo" sound comes again. Louder this time. I lean my ear against the wool wall—ear facing out.

Maybe Pauline didn't go inside and she's trying to scare us, I reason.

"Sh-h," I say with my finger to my lips.

"It's a ghost," Charlene says, her eyes wide with fear.

The "boo" gets louder. An outside force causes the tent walls to collapse in on us. We break free from the wool prison and run through the darkness screaming.

Roger chases us with his hands raised and spread like monster claws.

Next door, the porch light comes on. Aunt Mable storms across her small deck and down the steps to the tree where her barking dog is chained. She swats his snout with the rolled-up newspaper in her hand, then turns to face our house.

Her fists pump into the light illuminating the blackness.

"Your asses are grass, and I'm the lawnmower. You kids hear me? It's ten o'clock. Why don'tcha put that in your pipes and smoke it?"

Aunt Mable turns around and storms back inside. The porch light cuts off. When the darkness returns, I count the inky shapes of Charlene and Abby.

But where's Julie?

A muffled scream wafts through the air. I follow the sound to the ditch, where Roger is on all-fours. The leaves come up around him.

A hand pops up from the leaves and waves for help from beneath Roger.

"Get off her!" I say with a gasp.

Abby charges at Roger with a flurry of fists and knocks him sideways, freeing Julie from him.

Julie trembles and shakes.

"He held me down and put his hand up my shirt. Call my mum," she demands, "I wanna go home!"

Julie runs up the rickety stoop and into the house, while the three of us that remain stare at Roger in shock.

Without saying a word, he gets up and snakes his way through the darkness toward The House. The upstairs light in the window comes on and I'm hit with a strange sense of deja vu.

❦

THE NEXT WEEK, THE TITANIC PULLS INTO THE DRIVEWAY, and Dad steps out of the wagon wearing his chef jacket and black non-slip shoes.

The driver door slams.

"Francine!" Dad hollers from the driveway.

My heart pounds.

I didn't do it, I want to assure him, but instead I say, while hanging upside down from a tree branch, "Over here." Blood rushes to my head.

Dad hauls a five-gallon bucket with a lid from the back seat. It lands with a "thud" in the driveway.

"Go feed Festus."

I wrestle the bucket around to the back of the house to where Festus, our Saint Bernard, waits for his dinner—leftovers from the restaurant where Dad works.

As I dump the roast beef and gravy into his bowl, he thanks me by planting his paws on my chest and knocking me backward.

"You okay?" A voice comes seemingly out of nowhere.

From the corner of the garage, Roger sprints toward me and helps me to my feet.

"You ain't mad at me are you? I was just playin' with Julie. It ain't my fault she can't take a joke. Hey, you got your cast off?" he says as if to change the topic.

"No," I say because I don't know what else to say.

"C'mon, I wanna show you somethin'."

He takes my arm with skin like crepe paper and leads me past the garage to Grammy's chicken coop, where I had found the puffball when my cousin Richard and I played cops and robbers. *I was six.*

"Close your eyes and step inside."

I feel the splintery door jamb with my fingers and step up into the old chicken coop.

"Open your eyes. This is our new hangout for me, you, Abby, Charlene, Pauline, Lottie, Dottie, Laurel, and Tamara," he quickly lists. "Pretty cool, ayuh?"

My eyes scan the space. I remember Grammy's white geese, Lulu and Larry, and the harem of chickens with the one rooster, Rex, leading them around.

To the right, the back seat of a car leans against the wall and two bucket seats take up space under the chicken-wire window. Against the beam, a broom handle leans with a pile of straw and feathers around it.

Roger lets out a strangled laugh then stoops down and scoops up a handful of straw and tosses it in my hair.

The straw tickles my throat and sticks to my curls.

"Whatcha' do that for? I just washed it." I flip my hair over and shake my head, activating a snow globe of dandruff. *It's not easy washing my hair*, I want to say, but I don't. He doesn't know what it's like to not have running water.

"Here, I'll get the straw out." He falls backward onto the bucket seat and points at the dry planks on the floor. "Get on your knees."

"Okay," I say. Something doesn't feel right, but I do it anyhow.

He picks a piece of straw out of my hair and runs his fingers through it.

"Your hair smells wicked good, like strawberries," he says, taking a whiff.

"Thanks." *I think.*

He pushes my head down and continues to push until my nose touches the zipper on his pants.

I place my good hand on the floor and I push up.

Roger yanks my hair and jerks my head back down. He rubs my face against the metal teeth of his zipper and closes his thighs around my head. His hips rotate in big wide circles.

I'm woozy, lightheaded, and angry at myself for letting this happen.

"You're my girlfriend, ain'tcha?"

Right. Wrong. I don't know? My thoughts are garbled with fear and confusion. I remain stock-still.

What did Uncle Jerry do? Leave a guidebook on how-to's and who-to's for Roger to find?

His thighs squeeze my head like a pimple.

"Well, ain'tcha?" His voice is angry.

"Ain't I what?" I say into his zipper.

"My girlfriend," he says. "You like me. You think I'm cute."

This is all my fault! If I never would have told him he was cute when he first moved in, he never would have started calling me his 'little girlfriend.'

Pauline doesn't approve of him hanging out with me alone and she doesn't like that he calls me his "little girlfriend." Her words: "Sixteen-year-old boys don't hang out with ten-year-old girls" ring in my ears.

Roger lets go of my hair and opens his legs.

I sit up on my knees and see the cigarette burns on his arms, where his father played chicken. My bottom lip quivers. All I want to do is make like a magician and disappear.

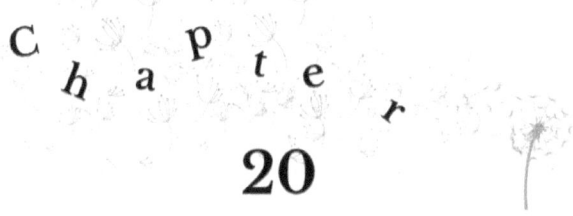

20

FIRE IN THE HOLE

While waiting on the toaster, I mix cinnamon with sugar and fill the glass shaker on the table with the yummy concoction.

Mum enters the kitchen with a beamy wide smile and clutches a Baby Book of Names.

"Your father and I are expectin'!"

Expecting what?

Mum points to her belly. Her smile widens. She flips open to where her thumb holds the page and points to a name.

I'm too shocked to smile, but Pauline giggles warmly and gives Mum a gappy-toothed grin.

"Congratulations!" Pauline says with a mouthful of cinnamon toast.

A cigarette bobs between Mum's teeth, and she turns to me and waits for my response. I bite down on my lip and eye the name her finger points to in the book, *Charles*.

You can't afford us! I want to scream.

"Don't look so damn cheerful." A cloud of smoke dances from her lips. "If you've got a problem with it, why don'tcha say so?"

"You can't take care of us," I say, pushing back tears.

"Who made you God?" Pauline asks. Bits of toast churn with her tongue.

She leans on the table and pours herself a cup of milk made from the powdered milk in the government food box.

"Well, I'm happy for you Mum," Pauline adds, still smiling.

My eyes narrow.

"Shut up, fatso. No one was talkin' to you! I'm... happy... for... you," I say, mocking her.

I ball my fist up and hurl the butter knife across the room. It lands between the large wooden spoon and fork hanging on the wall by the dingy deer tapestry and topples to the floor with a clatter.

"Next time it'll be you!" I grit my teeth and eyeball her as she chews.

Mum blows a plume of smoke and hangs her head with a sigh. "It's a boy! Thought you'd be happy, that's all."

"I'm h-h-happy for you," Charlene pipes up from the armchair with muted orange flowers.

How can you two be so stupid? Mum and Dad don't even know what's going on in our lives. The last thing they need is another kid.

Mum lifts her head and the corner of her mouth curls up.

"Your Father always wanted a boy. We're gonna name him Charles, after your father and your grandfather and your grandfather's cat. Do you wanna know what the name means?" Mum points to the page in the book.

I let out a series of sharp sighs. My arms wave wildly with annoyance.

"Dad never wanted us girls. I get it," I say.

"That's not what I said, ding-ding."

"No. It's whatcha' meant to say." I correct her.

"That's not fair. You're puttin' words in my mouth."

Life never is, I want to tell her, but instead ask, "Am I?"

I stomp my foot three times on the peeling linoleum, then continue. "Dad hardly ever speaks to us girls unless he's givin' us orders."

Smoke streams from Mum's nostrils. Her lips quiver. "That's not fair." Her eyes swell with tears.

"It's not? You're the one who said Charlene and I weren't supposed to be born. That we're here because the doctor screwed up!"

"He did screw up, but that doesn't mean I don't want you."

Mum's recent words to Charlene come back to mind: "I wish you were never born."

I stomp my foot again and rub my knuckles white. My windpipe shrinks to the size of a thin coffee stirrer.

"We go to the bathroom on buckets and draw water from a hand pump. Is that your *idear* of fair?"

The skin between Mum's eyebrows scrunches, and she stares at me with pain in her eyes.

"Watch your mouth, damn-it." Her voice shakes.

I ball my fists.

"You can't afford us three! How can you afford a baby?"

"What gives you the right to judge me? Why can't you be happy like your sisters?" More grey smoke funnels from her nostrils. "You haveta' wreck everythin', Francine!"

As a family mantra, the words "You wreck everything" is frequently used in conjunction with my name. The more I consider the baby announcement, the more my muscles tense. I squeeze my eyes shut, clench my fists tighter, lift my shoulders.

My body shakes from my toes to my eyeballs.

You couldn't even protect me, I yell the words in my head. *Or Pauline and Charlene. Aren't parents supposed to keep us safe?*

"She's fixin' to blow," Pauline warns as she hobbles behind the plaid blanket with her cinnamon toast and glass of powdered milk.

My head tips back. I cover my ears with my hands and scream at the top of my lungs. I feel the capillaries burst under my eyes as I push out the roar until my breath is gone.

My arms flail and I knock over the kitchen chair. It lands with a thud.

"I'll kill the baby!" I shout. A blood curdling scream follows. Mum's face is red with frustration. She lets out a tearful sob.

"What am I gonna do with you, huh, girl?"

Francine. My name is Francine. Not girl.

"I don't care whatcha' do with me." I snatch the baby book of names from her hand and storm outside to the playhouse that Dad built for Charlene and me out of two-by-fours and particle board.

The playhouse is attached to our house. I sit on a stump inside it, cupping my face with my hands. My elbows rest on the small table that Dad built.

Tears pour down my face. I am so upset that I can barely think straight. Guilt sets in.

Mum was happy. Why did I have to ruin it?

As my emotions calm down, I stare at the book that I had grabbed from Mum. I thumb through the pages of names and stop at the name "Charles." It means *man*. I flip through the pages in search of my name and prickle at the meaning of Francine. *Free one.*

Is this a joke? I'm anything but free.

I grab Mum's two-sided make-up mirror that we keep in the playhouse and hold it in my hands. Staring at my reflection, I can't help but study the things I hate most about myself like my tiny ears, wide nostrils, wrinkly forehead, thin lips, and red-hot temper.

The skin under my eyes is puffy and peppered with red dots from where the capillaries burst when I screamed with all my might, something that happens frequently.

No longer wanting to look at myself, I shove the negative thoughts back down, and toss the mirror on the ground. It lands with the magnifying side up. I decide to head inside to watch my favorite afternoon show, *The Bloodhound Gang,* and then hook up the Atari to play Pac-Man. I want to see if I can beat my high score of 300,000.

At five o'clock, the Titanic rumbles into the driveway.

Dad's home! I hope Mum doesn't tell him about my tantrum. But I know she will. She always does.

"Fire!" Dad bellows at the top of his lungs, his voice like rolling thunder.

I spring forward on the divan and look out the window. Dad's chef bag tumbles through the air, and his recipes, arranged by colored tabs, fall like jacks in the grass.

Mum springs from her sad old chair and grabs the two five-gallon buckets on the counter and sprints outside to the hand pump. We three girls follow.

The flames rise from the roof of the playhouse, and I clasp my hands together.

God, please don't let our house burn down. It's all we got! I won't complain any more...I promise!

Charlene, Pauline, and I stand frozen in the grass.

Dad and Mum fill buckets and throw the water on the flames until the fire dies down and the playhouse collapses into a pile of rubble.

"You okay, babe?" Dad asks Mum.

"Ayuh," Mum says as she makes her way to the smoldering remains.

Pauline, Charlene, and I creep closer to look at the make-up mirror which Mum points at.

"I know exactly how it started," Mum says as she looks at Dad.

You do? She really does know everything. How?

"The sun reflected through a cork-sized hole in the roof of the playhouse and reflected off the magnifying side of the mirror to start a fire," Mum continues.

Is that even possible?

Dad's nostrils flare, the muscles in his neck flex, and he glares at Pauline, Charlene, and me.

"Which one of you three dumbasses left the make-up mirror magnifyin' side up?" Dad demands to know. He stomps his black chef shoe in the grass. A florescent green grasshopper leaps and lands on his pant leg.

"Well, don't speak all at once." He stomps his foot again.

Charlene and Pauline look at each other, then at me, and back to each other.

"It wasn't me," Pauline says.

"It w-w-wasn't me," Charlene says.

Their balled-up fist with thumbs sticking out point my way.

"Why's it always gotta be me?" I cross my arms over my chest and push my bottom lip out.

Dad leans down with his long nose touching mine. He smells of coffee, cigarettes, and roast beef from the restaurant. His eyes staring me clean through.

"Who else would it be, Nimrod?"

"I dunno'," I say.

Mum eyes bounce between the smoking ruble and the patch of grass where I stand, back and forth.

"If it wasn't for bad luck, dingy, you wouldn't have any at all," she mutters, cradling her small round belly and my baby brother growing inside her.

Dad lets out a wince and grabs his back.

"Fill the water buckets and bring 'em inside. And when you're done with that, pick up my damn recipes." His leg buckles from the pinched nerve in his back.

As my family walks away, the meaning from the baby book flashes in my thoughts—*Free one*.

Yeah, right.

I shake my head and retrieve the buckets.

Chapter 21

EAT THE RUBBISH

A few months later, after Charles Jr. is born, Dad lifts his head from the divan and scowls up at me with a tiny white sock in his hand.

"You ain't a damn window," he says. "Move it so your mother can see the television."

"She ain't even watchin' it," I sputter.

"So—"

"So, I'm not in the way."

"You're this close," Dad says, holding up his index finger and thumb with a small space of air between them.

I step back three carpet squares to the right to the armchair, where Charlene reads a book.

"I was gonna ask if you wanted to play Pac-Man, that's all. It's been a while," I huff.

"Later," Dad says. "Can't you see I'm playin' with your brother?"

"What's new? You're always playin' with him."

Charles Jr. coos from the cushion on the divan where he lays. Dad hovers over him, pulling his sock off and putting it back on.

Charles Jr. coos again, and his tiny coos turn into a string of giggles.

Pauline slides the shepherd's pie into the oven and peers up at me over her thick round frames.

"Can someone take the rubbish out for me? I'm cookin' supper."

I pretend not to hear her and look down at Mum's mail order plants, pluck a dry leaf, then two.

"Make yourself useful and take the rubbish out," Mum says, looking up at me from her sad old chair. She shakes a baby bottle full of formula.

"Why can't Charlene do it? She never does anythin' but read dumb books."

"Hark, big mouth, and do it," Mum says, testing the temperature of the formula by squeezing a drop on her wrist.

I roll my eyes almost to the back of my head.

"Why don'tcha eat the rubbish," I say boldly.

The springs on the divan creak, and Dad's bare right foot with yellow toenails hits the carpet, then the left. I take off running down the hall as the chain affixed to his wallet clanks after me.

He catches me at the back of the house and locks his hands around my head, lifting me off the floor until I'm eye-to-eye with him.

"What the hell did you just say to your mother?" His nostrils pulse like a current moving through them.

"I-I-I—"

"You're grounded!"

"But—"

"But nothin'. Did I stutter?"

His grip tightens around my head. I squirm to get free. My legs dangle in the air like two Pixie Sticks.

"You're squishin' my head. Put me down. You're hurtin' me!" I demand.

"Keep it up, wiseass, and I'll give you somethin' to gripe

'bout." This Dad says as he lowers me back onto the striped carpet. "Now shut your damn mouth and empty the rubbish like your mother told you. If I hear you speak to your mother like that again, I'll whoop your ass so good, you won't be able to sit for a month."

After supper, I soak the shepherd's pie pan in the sink to loosen the burnt-on cheese before breaking out the scouring pad. A knock at the door causes my heart to skip and the hairs on my arms to raise.

Go away! I scream in my head. Knowing the tempo of Roger's knock—two quick wraps and one delayed.

"Ayuh, it's open," Dad announces from the divan. His voice carries over the television.

The doorknob spins and my belly becomes nauseous.

"Hi, Mr. Dodge, can Francine come out?" Roger asks.

"You ain't a damn mouse, boy. Speak up," Dad says loudly.

Roger clears his throat and repeats his question.

Dad waves his hand in a shooing motion at me.

"You pain in the ass—go on! Get, before I change my mind!"

My shoulders slump.

"But I haven't finished the dishes, and I thought we were gonna play Pac-Man."

Dad tosses the TV Guide on the coffee table. With his nostrils already in a flare, he rocks to stand up.

"Let 'em soak. You got peanut butter in your ears, girl? Go on, get!"

"You grounded me remember?" I say. *I don't want to go! Pretty please with a cherry on top, let me be grounded!*

My eyes dart around the room.

"I want to do the dishes...I want to clean the kitchen. I was mean to Mum. I deserve to be punished."

"Go before I plant my foot up your ass so far it comes out your mouth." Dad's tone rises like the smoke from his cigarette.

He slams his empty coffee mug down and glares at Charlene reading her book in the armchair beside the stove.

"Damn it all! Fill this, will you?" he says to her.

My eleven year old brain tries to think of an excuse. Why is it I can smart-mouth my parents, but when it comes to telling them the truth about monsters, I get tongue-tied? As the months have passed, the swooning crush I first had over Roger has morphed into fear and a bitter hatred.

Dad's sandpaper heels scuff across the mishmash of carpet to the peeling linoleum. His thin lips make a straight line. He glares at me with his blood shot eyes, his bare belly hanging over his dungaree belt loops.

"No . . . I . . . uh . . .!" My tongue's in a bigger tangle than Charlene's hair. With a heavy sigh, I fling the dish gloves off.

Dad opens the front door and shoves me outside with Roger, slamming the door behind us.

Roger grabs my fingers and twists.

"What were you tryin' to pull in there, huh?"

"Nothin'. Honest."

His words, "Never make me mad," weave through my thoughts.

I twist and turn, standing on my tippy toes to keep my fingers from snapping off.

Roger pulls me by the hand down the footpath to a rusty old car near the garage.

The metal door creaks open. He holds his hand out, signaling for me to get in. The faded sign above the garage door reads *Dodge's Auto Salvage*. I slide across the ripped front seat, wondering who will salvage me? There's a colorful bedsheet on the floor. He tugs on it—red, blue, green, and yellow. I wait for him to say, *ta-dah*.

Worry forms pockets in my mind as he hangs the corner of the sheet out the window for privacy and rolls the window up.

"Quick. Take your pants off."

My eyes water. I shake my head feverishly.

He makes a fist and holds it up.

Just give him what he wants. I hate the thought.

It's the thought I had every time Uncle Jerry cornered me. I stare at the shattered windshield and do what Roger says, hating myself and hating him.

He unzips his zipper. His pants and underwear come down. Then mine come down. My legs tremble as he pushes my thighs apart and he pumps his naked hips between my open legs.

I wince and ball my fist tightly at my side, wishing for the courage to deck him in the jaw like I did Michelle Cooley.

My knuckles turn white. I stare at the cracked glass as though it's my own reflection and think about Mum's stories of miniature UFO's, ghosts, Big Foots, and rainbows with pots of gold at the end.

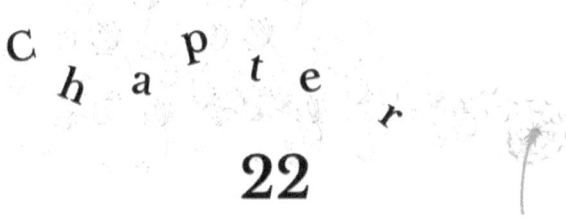

22

FIGURE EIGHTS

Dad grabs the empty water bucket off the counter.

"Make yourself useful, girl." He shoves it at me.

"Why me?" I ask, taking my eyes off the television.

"Their hands ain't broke." I look around the living room at the others: Charlene who bounces Charles Jr. on her knee, Mum who works on a crossword puzzle, and Pauline who writes a short story that begins, 'The boy stepped off the bus.'

"Because I said so," Dad says sharply.

I snatch the handle away, slide my snow boots and coat on, and step out onto the icy stoop. I tuck my chin in to my chest and walk down the deep, white-walled pathway of shoveled snow to the pump. Icicles hang from the mouth of the pump like monster fangs. I smash them loose with the bucket and hang the handle of the bucket on the iron lip of the pump.

The handlebar is cold to the touch. An arctic wind whips my hair around. I sweep it out of my eyes and tuck my chin back down to my chest. My hands wrap around the handle, and I squeeze. The wind beats against my coat and whips snow in sideways spirals. My eyes water from the cold temperature. I pump the handle harder and faster, but nothing comes out.

"What are we? Little House on the Prairie or somethin'?" I growl up at the northern lights swimming overhead in a sea of stars and throw my hands up in frustration before traipsing back inside with the empty bucket.

At least Little House on the Prairie had a handpump that was indoors, I mutter in my head.

"Pumps froze," I quickly say, returning the bucket to the counter.

Dad eyeballs me from his spot on the divan where no one dares to sit when he is home, not even Lady Bug or Patches, the cats.

"Well, boil some water idget, and then go prime it."

"There ain't any to boil," I remind him. My tone seething with sarcasm.

"Looks like your shit outta' luck, girl," Mum says with a glint of amusement in her voice. Her crossword puzzle book open, pen in hand, long johns on.

"Go next door and borrow some," Dad barks.

"What? No! Aunt Mable's gonna kill me. You know how she gets. Last time she went on a tirade 'bout how she feels bad for us girls, and how you should've taken her up on the offer to put plumbin' and a septic system in."

Which reminds me, why didn't you? I want to ask, but instead say, "It's wicked embarrassin'! If Aunt Mable goes into that same spiel again, I'll just die," I add in dramatic fashion.

Dad rubs his mustache with his index finger, his thin top lip barely moving.

"Just do it, damn-it!" he sputters. "That's what you get for lettin' the water run out."

"How's it my fault?"

"Fran...cine," Dad sighs. "You're this close." He holds up the same two fingers he always holds up to demonstrate.

I step out onto the icy stoop with the northern lights—red, green, and purple rolling and dancing overhead—and slam the door behind me, dragging the empty five-gallon bucket at my side over the thick snow. I trek the one telephone pole length, placing my small black boot into the big wide footprints Uncle Chester left earlier. The birch trees outline the night sky like a city scape—some trees taller and wider than others. In some places, I sink to my thighs and crawl out, sink again a few steps later and crawl back out.

By the time I reach Aunt Mable's storm door, I've got my fingers crossed and I'm praying Uncle Chester will be the one that answers, because he's nice. But before I'm able to knock, Heidi, the hot-dog dog, sounds the alarm and the porch light cuts on. In one of the three diamond windows of the trailer door Mable's beady eyes appear.

I hold the bucket up to a diamond and point at the white plastic container.

Aunt Mable hisses and tosses her head to the side, showing her annoyance before unlocking the door.

I step inside with my eyes downcast at the snow caked on my boots.

"Can I borrow some water?"

"Borrow?" she says with her hand on her hip.

"Have, I mean."

"Make it quick," Aunt Mable huffs out. "And tell your father that this is the last time. It's damn near nine o'clock. I've already mopped, and the girls are in bed. It's a bit late, don'tcha think?"

"She ain't hurtin' anythin'," Uncle Chester says, coming down the hall.

I bang my boots off and walk the bucket down the carpeted hallway past Lottie and Dottie's room, where whispers spill out.

When I reach the bathroom, I turn the spigot on and set the bucket in the tub.

The red heat of humiliation creeps up my neck and into my face.

I only need a tea kettle's worth, I encourage myself, turning the spigot full blast.

Seconds later, I cut it off and hustle back down the hallway, past the whispers still spilling into the hallway, past Aunt Mable washing a small saucer under the light over the kitchen sink.

"Thank you," I say softly to Uncle Chester, catching his eye and drinking in his pity, the way Mum did in the car when he picked us up from the Greyhound station.

Aunt Mable calls my name. I turn around and prepare for the worst.

"I'm not mad at you, hun. I'm fed up with your parents, that's all. I feel so bad for you girls, like the other month when Charlene spent the whole day over here cryin' because your mother told her that she wishes she was never born."

I can't lie. Mum did say it. So, I hang my head and focus on the hole in my boot with the wool lining springing from it like the filling in a French cream horn.

If Mum wishes Charlene were never born, then what does she wish upon me? I'm the one who never gives her a moments peace. I'm the one with the smart mouth and the hot temper. I'm the one, as Mum puts it, that 'trouble follows me wherever I go.' Charlene's nothing more than a harmless bookworm with a stutter.

"You twins can spend the night tomorrow with Lottie and Dottie and take a bath, that is, if you want. I bought the girls some new Mr. Bubble's Bubble Bath to put in the water."

My eyes ascend, and my lips curl up.

"That would be wicked nice," I say, tripping over my own boots to get home and tell Charlene.

There're two kinds of kids that hang out next door with Aunt Mable: the full-time-favorites and the not-so-favorites. The full-time-favorites spend the night and go on trips to Disney World, Unity Raceway, and Blezdoe's swimming hole. While the not-so-favorites observe the favorites as they spend the night and go on trips. But every now and again, even the not-so-favorites get lucky. Charlene and I fall in the not-so-favorites category. But I would take a night over at Aunt Mable's with the heat, the toilets, and the running water any day.

I do a jig up the rickety steps and over the threshold. With the door wide open, I make the announcement that Charlene and I have been invited to spend the night at Aunt Mable's tomorrow.

"Close the door, whooze-it, we didn't raise you in a barn," Mum says.

Could have fooled me I want to say, but instead, bite my tongue, and say, "Sorry."

All eyes shift to me, not because the door is open but because I used the word 'Sorry.' It's a word not often spoken in our house, along with a host of other words like 'please' and 'thank you.'

"Who are you and what'd you do with my sister?" Pauline says with sarcasm, closing her book with her thumb in the page to look at me.

I scoop the tea kettle worth of water out of the bucket to boil on the stove. When the whistle sounds, I carry the tea kettle and the bucket out to the pump to perform a delicate balancing act of slowly pouring hot water with my left hand into the neck of the pump and pushing and pulling the handle with my right hand, until water comes out. But I don't even mind the cold handlebar and red palms, because I'm already fantasizing about a warm bath in a big bathtub.

❦

AFTER THE NEXT ALBERTA CLIPPER, I SHIMMY INTO MY HIGH-water ski pants and toss my ice skates over my shoulder and head out the door.

The moon glistens on the crust-covered-snow as, alone, I follow the glow to the ice rink behind Aunt Mable's trailer. I lean against the embankment—the one Uncle Chester made, when he plowed the ice off with his tractor yesterday—where I swap my boots out for the skates to practice making figure eights.

I pretend I'm an Olympic skater and with each figure eight, my speed increases.

As I skate, Festus lets out a deep growl. I slow down and perk my ears toward the trees. A snowball pelts me in the shoulder, and I skate toward the direction from which it came.

"Charlene," I say, "I thought you weren't comin' out."

With no response, I skate around and practice more figure eights.

A second snowball plummets onto the ice in front of me.

I crouch down, scoop up a handful of snow, and form a snowball with my mittened hands to throw at her.

Festus's growl softens, and I skate watchfully around and wait for Charlene to pop up from behind the bank to lambaste her with the snowball. The blades slice the ice and sound like an apple being peeled.

When she doesn't pop up, I skate to the embankment and peer over it.

"Come out, come out, wherever you are." And when she doesn't, I add with a nervous twill, "It ain't funny anymore."

A whiff of mint and Irish Springs wafts through the air and paralyzes me. From behind the snowbank, an inky image pounces. Roger's hand, with fingerless gloves, covers my mouth and smothers my scream.

A nervous tick starts in my right index finger and thumb. Shock and fear pumps through my veins and a crippling pain stabs me in my rib cage. I clasp my chest and hold my breath as the rogue air bubble travels upward—'a clinical heart murmur,' Mum always says.

"Do what I tell you," he says.

My eyes blinking back icy tears.

"Take off your coat."

"No. Why? It's wicked cold out."

"Do it!" His voice is low and garbled.

He grabs the back of my head and pushes my face into the snowbank and holds it there. One beat. Two beats. Three beats.

Then, he pulls my head back up. I feel the sting of the abrasions the crusty snow leaves on my cheeks.

Roger grabs me by my coat and spins me around, then glides me forward on my skates, unzips the coat, and yanks it off. My mittens come off with it.

His lips press against mine and I taste mint and fold like the leaves on Mum's coy tickle-me-plant. My coat makes a small thud as it lands on the ice.

It's no use. He owns me.

"Take your ski pants off," he instructs next.

I hesitate.

The words "Never make me mad" and "When I say jump, you say how high?" replay in my head and I swallow deeply.

My ski pants fall to my ankles and I stand cross-legged on the ice.

"Take those off, too," he orders.

My skates?

I bend down and untie the strings with my numb and frozen fingers, while trying to maintain my balance. The skates glide forward and backward in small bursts.

Roger spreads my coat on the ice and with his hands on my shoulders, pushes me down until I'm sitting on the coat. Then he yanks the skates from my feet and slides my ski pants off. His fingers fidget with the button on my corduroys.

"It's wicked c-c-cold—" I whine.

"Never. Make. Me. Mad," he says, grabbing my face and squeezing my cheeks.

My body trembles, and I stare at the sheep-cropped snowbank. My stocking feet burn from the cold seeping through them, and I pull them up onto the coat with me and hug my knees.

He pushes me over until the small of my back lands on the coat. My stocking cap head rests on the bare ice.

His pants slide down and his warm body lays on top of mine. His hips move up and down, driving my tailbone into the ice.

A beam of light stretches sideways across the rink and into the trees. Roger doesn't stop.

"Hey, Nimrod," Dad bellows from the front stoop.

"Hey, what?" I shout back loud enough for Dad to hear me.

"Get your ass inside. It's bedtime."

"Comin'," I say, trying not to sound too happy so that I don't anger Roger.

When the light from the door fades, Roger lets out a series of breathy moans and falls off me like a salted leech.

He immediately jumps up.

"You better not tell anyone, not even Abby, or else."

"I promise," I whisper.

I know I can't even tell Pauline, because this is my fault. Plus, I don't want to see the judgement in her eyes when she says, "See I told you so."

He fixes his pants. Without so much as a backward glance, his footsteps crush the crust-covered snow and he disappears into the darkness.

I grab my underwear on the ice and use them to wipe between my legs. Then slide my pants on and will my frozen fingers to pull the tiny tab to zip them up. I put my boots on, stuff my underwear in my pocket, and abandon the blades on the ice.

Inside, I plop down Indian style in front of the kerosene heater and hog the warmth by holding my coat out like a pair of wings.

"Where'd you get 'em scratches?" Mum asks, swabbing my cheek with her fingers.

"I fell makin' figure eights," I lie.

"Hey, you, numbskull," Dad calls from the divan.

"Hey, what?" I say without turning around.

I wish they'd leave me alone for a minute. I still shiver, and the pain of what just happened stings in my mind. My thoughts waffle from Uncle Jerry to Roger. *How ironic that my name means free one.* I sigh with despair.

I'll never be free.

"Whatcha' think? Bedtime. Now get," Dad says.

Pauline and Charlene skirt past me, stepping through the hanging blanket and into the icy back of the house.

"Just another minute," I say. "I'm still thawin' out."

Dad's command to go to bed hangs in the air as I ignore him and continue warming myself in front of the heater.

The divan creaks.

"You're cruisin' for a bruisin', girl," Dad says as a warning.

I still don't budge.

The divan creaks again and I turn to see Dad swinging his arm like he's harvesting air, the Louis Lamour book is his sickle.

"But—"

"But nothin'. Did I stutter?" Dad says, springing from the divan.

"Geesh," I say, jumping up. "You don't haveta' get so snippy."

At the table, Mum pours hot water into the yellow basin and places a clean washcloth and a green bar of soap beside it.

"Sounds like someone's up shit creek without a paddle. Now skedaddle—it's your father's night to bathe, and I'm gonna watch."

I prickle my nose.

Gross!

Knowing I lost this battle of the wills, I resign myself to being cold. I pause and kiss them both on the forehead.

The nightly routine of kissing my parents goodnight wipes my conscience clear until the next morning, when the little white lies, the name-calling, and the outbursts will start to accrue all over again.

I whip the blanket aside and step into the freezing hallway where warmth from the kerosene heater never ventures.

"Hey, nit wit," Dad calls. "Get back here."

I pop my head back through the blanket and look at him.

"I didn't do it," I quickly confess, remembering the extra piece of cake I snuck after supper. Another lie.

"Turn the electric blanket on for your mother."

A deep sigh escapes me.

"Why can't we have an electric blanket like you and Mum?"

Dad lowers his chin and peers over his readers.

"Because you can't. Now go before I put somethin' on you Ajax won't take off."

"Not fair," I say, stomping down the striped carpet in the hall, past the small room with the crib in it, to Mum and Dad's bedroom to flick the switch on.

"Life never is," Mum says from the kitchen. Her words race like a bobsled down the icy hallway, my ears being the finish line.

I hate it when she says that!

After flicking the electric blanket on and seeing the red light, I peek into the small room with the crib. Charles Jr.'s Glow Worm lights the ceiling. He lays on his tummy under layers of blankets. I tiptoe closer and touch his icy nose and tiny frigid fingers. When he stirs, I withdraw my hand and scurry out of his room to my ice-box bed. The fitted sheet feels like a sheet of ice. I arch my back and peddle my legs aggressively beneath the purple sleeping bag to generate heat.

My breath is visible like fog. Tiny droplets of water float through the air. I slash through it with my hand and rub the condensation between my fingers.

"You asleep?" I whisper down to Charlene.

Her teeth clatter.

"Zip it b-b-before Dad comes in and whips us both."

"But Charles Jr. is cold," I say. "What if he freezes to death?"

"He won't. Mum and Dad know what they're doin'."

They do?

"Now pretend like its summer and go to sleep," she stutters.

The eleven o'clock news ends, the television cuts off, and the kerosene heater knocks as the flame dies. Then two sets of slippers scuff down the hall to the only room with a door and a warm bed.

The house is eerily silent, except for my weary legs which bicycle in slow lopsided circles. I dread the giants, the six-legged octopus, and the werewolf that visit the little girl in my dreams.

A girl with chestnut curls and bright blue eyes huddles on a bed with black smoke and flames surrounding her.

I roll over to face the recycled window which is held shut by a bent over nail. The icy draft fills the plastic, and I poke at it, drawing a line with my fingernail down the center of the plastic.

Festus barks, and I stick my eyeball over the hole in the plastic to peek outside. I fear that Roger is back, or worse, that Uncle Jerry is with him. I study the shifting shadows, the movement the trees make, and the direction in which Festus faces.

What if they've teamed up and have come to steal me away and kill me in the woods, where no one will find me until the snow melts and the fiddleheads sprout?

I gulp.

Stop being ridiculous! I'm not! I argue with myself.

More thoughts of worry run through my head like the fact that we never lock our house at night. I hate the silence. It makes the noise in my head louder.

To settle my thoughts, I climb down from my bunk, sneak through the house in the dark to the living room, lock the front door, then sneak to the back exit and lock that too.

Back in bed, I squeeze my eyes shut, pedal my legs some more, and pray.

Dear God, please keep the six-legged octopus, the werewolf, and the giants away. A big order, even for You, I know, but please. Amen.

The snow crunches outside my window. My eyes snap open. I quickly grab my purple sleeping bag and Buster, my stuffed dog the elf gave me when I was five, and climb down into Charlene's bunk, where I sleep until a warm gush of fluid awakens me.

"Charlene Ann Dodge!" I shout, springing straight up and whacking my head on the underside of the top bunk.

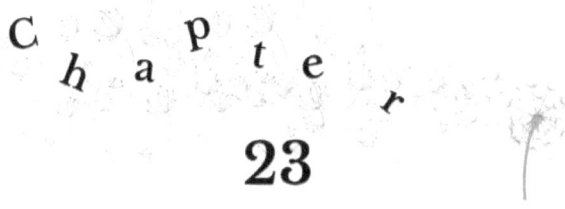

C h a p t e r

23

CONFESSIONALS

In May of 1985, daffodils and tiger lilies paint the woods around the school yellow and orange. After recess, I exit the main building to meet the Title I teacher in the trailer behind the school, where she helps me with my reading. When our time is up, she walks me back to class to listen to the Sex Education teacher who travels from school to school talking to all the sixth-grade classes in Somerset County.

"Boys have penises and girls have vaginas," the sex education teacher begins.

I shrink in my chair. My cheeks feel hot with embarrassment. *I know this already!*

The sex education teacher scans the room. Her eyes lock onto mine, and she holds my worried gaze. I fidget with my sleeve, then her eyes move across the room, and she holds up a plastic pair of breasts.

"These are for breast feeding," she says, holding the plastic breasts up.

The class giggles, and I stare at the clock.

Twenty more minutes until school ends. Thank heavens!

She rolls down the shades and turns off the lights.

"I have one last thing to share with you," she says as she turns the projector on.

My head rests in the crook of my elbow on the desk, and I watch quietly as a man gives candy to a small girl. He picks her up and bounces her on his knee. And then, when no one is looking, he slips his hand up her skirt.

I close my eyes and hear the little girl cry for help, then open my eyes and see her running away from him—she's screaming.

The words *The End* flicker on the roll down screen, and I sneak to wipe my eyes.

"It's never okay for someone to touch you and make you feel uncomfortable," the sex education teacher says.

It's not? Why hasn't anyone ever told me that?

The room is quiet. My heart pounds.

Can anyone else hear my heart beating besides me?

I wipe my nose on my sleeve. Glancing around the room, I look at Julie, my friend from our sleepover, and Charlene.

Don't her words bother anyone else but me?

When school lets out, I duck into the bathroom and crumble like shale rock behind the stall door. I wipe my tears.

Think on happy thoughts, I remind myself. But I can't.

The visiting teacher's words play over and over in my head. It's as if the visiting teacher opened Pandora's Box to my most horrid memories, and I don't know how to shove them back where they belong.

Charlene sticks her head into the bathroom and calls my name. I emerge from the stall and slowly make my way down the hall to the bus.

She sits in the same high-back seat as me and chews her fingernails.

"Are you al...al..., what's wrong?" she says, finding an easier question to ask.

"I'm fine. Leave me be," I say.

I gaze out the window feeling the rumble of the bus under my feet as the brakes release and the driver pulls onto Main Street. We pass Tom's Convenience Store, the purple cow statue, the thirty-five-foot rocket ship, the tin man made from muffler parts, and the water wheel.

The words, "It's never okay" churn in my head.

The bus veers right at the antique shop. It barrels past the horse farm, the red shingled house, the cornfield, and halts in front of Aunt Mable's driveway.

As I make my way off the bus and to the front door of my house, I'm greeted by the smell of the pisspots mingled with Mum's cigarette smoke and homemade cookies. I lean against the table and observe Mum as she slides each cookie off the baking sheet and onto the cooling rack.

I pick at the grey duct tape which runs in a straight line down the center of the kitchen table. It's there to keep the flour from falling into the crevasse where the extra leaf goes to extend the table. This way, Mum doesn't have to scrape flour out of the crack with a butter knife every time she bakes.

She swats my hand with the rubber spatula.

"If I've told you once, I've told you a thousand times. Stop pickin' at that tape."

My mouth quivers.

"That didn't hurt. I barely touched you," Mum says.

Her brow scrunches up.

"Did Mable say somethin' to you again? Last week she blamed you for trompin' on her tulips, and yesterday she blamed you for breakin' Lottie and Dottie's horse figurine. Let me guess, you looked at her wrong?"

"It's not her," I say low and slow.

"What then?"

I shake my head and take a deep breath as the words, *It's never okay for anyone to touch you and make you feel uncomfortable* continue to play in my head.

Mum stands with one moccasin forward and taps her right hip with the spatula.

"I ain't got all day."

My head drops and I cup my face.

"It's never okay for someone to touch me and make me uncomfortable, the sex education teacher said today."

Mum stops to study me, but I don't wait for a response. The words spill out of my mouth. I couldn't stop them.

"I was raped or molested. I dunno' which."

The blood drains from her face and she drops the spatula. It bounces off the linoleum and onto the carpet.

"What's-at?" she chokes out.

My eyes focus on her housedress and the loose threads springing from the purple armpit. I crumble to the floor with my forehead resting on the grimy linoleum. Once the tears come, there's no stopping them. Every painful memory releases itself and travels out through my tears. I can barely breathe—I'm sobbing so hard. But I can't anymore. I can't hold the secrets in. So, I release them, right there, onto the linoleum in front of Mum, Charles Jr., Charlene, and Pauline.

"Who hurt you?" Mum asks.

I cry with such pain that no words come out.

"Francine, tell me who did it."

"I can't. They'll kill me." I wipe my eyes.

"Whatcha' mean, they? There's more than one?"

Mum kneels on the linoleum beside me. "Look at me, String-bean," she says, directing my chin upward with her finger. "I won't let 'em hurt you again. Just tell me who."

"Uncle Jerry and Roger," I say. My voice is hoarse.

I take a shaky breath.

"Uncle Jerry said he'd kill me like he did Peter Rabbit if I ever told."

"I knew it!" Mum says in her Sherlock Holmes kind of way. "So Pauline didn't leave the cage unlocked."

Her voice and hands tremble as she opens her burgundy cigarette pouch, slides out a cigarette, and puts it to her lips.

"Please, don't be mad at me, Mum. Uncle Jerry said that if he gets in trouble, I'll get in trouble too, because we both wanted it. I don't wanna go to jail."

Mum's arms draw me in and she hugs me, which surprises me, and makes me uncomfortable in a good way.

"I'm not mad at you."

Her hug is warm and necessary. For the first time in a long time, I don't feel empty.

"I never wanted what happened to me to happen to you girls," she cries.

The scent of coffee and cigarettes clings to her breath. Her tears wet the side of my face.

"I knew somethin' was wrong. I should've listened to my gut."

"It's not your fault, Mum," I say through a landslide of tears, wiping my nose with my hands, rubbing snot up through my hair.

She exhales a plume of smoke.

"I never wanted any of you to go through what I went through at the hands of my own father and grandfather. How did I miss the handwriting on the wall?"

"Don't cry, Mum! It's not your fault!"

"It is my fault. I didn't protect you. Just like nobody protected me."

She takes a drag off her cigarette. Her floury thumbs wipe the tears running down my cheeks.

The sound of gravel crunching beneath tires causes me to spring forward like a punch to the gut.

Dad's home! What will he say?

My eyes fill with worry.

"Don't tell Dad, please!" I tell Mum, pushing myself up from the floor and sprinting down the hallway to my bed, ducking under the covers.

The front door opens and from my bedroom I hear "ka-plunk." It's the sound Dad's chef bag makes when it hits the floor.

"Who died?" Dad asks.

"No one yet," Mum says.

"What'd Francine do this time?"

Dad's heavy footsteps move across the living room, and the springs on the divan creak.

"She didn't do anythin'," Mum adds. I sense the hesitation in her voice.

"Then what?" he says.

I hold my breath as the words "Francine's been raped," leave Mum's mouth.

"What'd you just say?" Dad says.

"Jerry and Roger," Mum continues.

"I'll kill 'em!" His voice explodes.

"Settle down, babe, before you make her more upset than she already is."

"Where is she?"

"She's in her room."

The chain attached to his wallet clanks down the hall. The clanking stops at my bed, and he peels the covers back.

Dad's elbow is perched on the bed frame. Mum stands behind him in her sad old housedress with a long sad face and a cigarette between her lips.

"Are you mad at me, Dad?" my voice trembles.

"Not at you, hun."

That's a nice name for a change. Hun. I like it.

When Dad's eyes can no longer hold the tears, they splash down his cheeks. He whips his handkerchief out, honks his nose loudly, and crams it back in his pocket.

Boys don't cry! That's the rules.

My lips turn down. I've never seen him do this before, except for the time his eyes welled up in the car when he saw Grampy's obituary. But this, this is different. These tears drip from his nose and his chin and cause his voice to tremble. I want to scream *stop* and take his pain away. I want to take back my confession and tell him it's okay. But everything in me tells me it's my fault that he cries.

"Don't worry, hun," Dad says, "I'll take care of Jerry and Roger."

His arm falls from my bed to his side. He storms past Mum perched in the doorway and down the striped carpet in the hall.

"Babe, killin' 'em ain't gonna help," Mum says loudly, chasing after him.

"Wanna' bet?" he snaps.

The front door slams.

The Titanic's engine revs. The tires squeal off down the road.

"Come back!" Mum hollers from the stoop.

A list of 'what-if's' tumble through my mind. *What if Dad gets a hold of Uncle Jerry? What if Roger and Uncle Jerry kill me? What if they kill Dad? What if Dad goes to jail?*

While Dad heads to Grammy's house in Clinton, where she lives with her new husband, to hunt down Uncle Jerry, Mum calls Social Services. She reports Roger and what he did to me.

"I want him removed from The House tonight." She hangs up the phone and walks back down the hall toward me.

"He will never come near you again," Mum says. "At best, he'll be put in a juvenile delinquent center until he turns eighteen. If we're lucky, they'll hold him until he's twenty-one."

❧

NINE O'CLOCK THAT EVENING, I LAY IN BED AND STARE UP AT the plastic over my ceiling and listen for Grammy Dodge and Uncle Jerry to arrive at our house for the meeting that Dad called with them.

My heart thumps heavily in my chest. I thought about packing up and hiding in the woods. Uncle Jerry wouldn't be able to find me there.

Or would he?

He's like a god—all-knowing and everywhere present, even in my thoughts.

Three loud knocks followed by Dad's command to "come in" causes more fear to pump through my veins.

It's too late to run now.

I hop down out of bed and tiptoe to where Charlene and Pauline crouch in the hallway behind a stack of teetering whatnots from where we can spy on the adults sitting around the kitchen table. The hanging blanket is tacked open to allow the spring breeze to circulate through the house, giving us a clear view of the kitchen.

A lump appears in my throat, and I swallow hard as Grammy Dodge and Uncle Jerry take a seat at the table. It's a strange sight to see Grammy Dodge in our house. I've never seen her step foot in our doorway before. She goes next door to Aunt Mable's to visit all the time but never here, not once.

Pauline's tongue clicks and she tilts her head to the left to look at me.

"You scared?" Her lazy eye jitterbugs in its socket.

I shift my focus away from the eye.

"Big time," I say, lacing my fingers together, trying not to cry again. My bladder feels like it's attached to my eyeballs.

Pauline angles her head the other way, drawing my attention back to the dancing eye.

"What if he doesn't confess?"

Her words hang in the air.

"I dunno'," I say. "I hadn't thought of that." I chew on the tips of my hair. "You can back me up. You know the truth."

She narrows her brow and peers up at me over her glasses.

"Leave me outta' this. This is more than I can handle." Her eyes water.

"Sh-h," Charlene stutters. "We're supposed to be in b-bed."

The whistling of the tea kettle draws my attention back to the kitchen. I rest my head against the paneled wall and continue watching the adults through the space between the hanging blanket and the door frame.

Mum steeps a tea bag at the stove.

"One lump or two, Ma?" Mum asks.

"Two," Grammy responds. The silver chain around her neck rattles, and she slides her glasses up. "What's this all 'bout, Charlie? Why did you have us come all the way from Clinton at this hour?"

Mum drops two sugar cubes in the hot tea and carries it across the peeling linoleum with an open can of Carnation milk.

"Mable tells me you squealed the tires today, Charlie. What's got you all fired up?" Grammy asks.

Dad doesn't respond. He sits with his leg crossed and rubs his mustache. Charlene, Pauline, and I watch with faces full of angst.

The spoon clanks as Grammy stirs a drizzle of milk into her tea.

She sets the spoon down and turns to Uncle Jerry. "Do you even know why you're here?"

Uncle Jerry's shoulders dip. With a nervous half chuckle, he drapes his arm over the back of the chair and drums the wood with his grease-stained fingers.

A cigarette bobs from Mum's lips as she exhales a rosette of smoke. The smoke from Mum's, Dad's, and Grammy's cigarettes dance and twirl together over the table like the northern lights, only without the pretty colors.

"You're not pregnant again, are you Franny?" Grammy asks.

"No, Ma," Mum says with a sigh.

Grammy rolls the teacup between her hands and holds Dad's gaze.

"For Pete's sake Charlie, tell us why we're here."

Dad uncrosses his leg and leans forward with his elbows on the table.

"Jerry, had I found you earlier, I would've rung your neck."

Grammy spits her tea out with a gasp.

"Don't speak to your brother like that." Her mouth hangs open.

"I have good reason to, Ma," Dad says, adding, "Francine told us you sexually abused her."

"She's lyin'," Grammy spouts.

I prickle at her words and hold my breath.

"Ah nope, Ma," Dad rebuts, "Francine's eleven years old. She wouldn't lie 'bout somethin' like that."

Grammy sets her tea down and slides her chair back. "That's one helluva accusation, Charlie. C'mon Jerry, let's go home."

Dad's nostrils pulse. He slams his palms down on the table and stands.

"Go ahead, Ma, ask him yourself, why don'tcha?"

"I don't need to," Grammy says.

"Ayuh, Ma, you do. Ask Jerry, damn-it."

Grammy's eyes bounce from Dad to Jerry.

"For Christ's sake, Jerry, tell Charlie it ain't true."

I cross my fingers and hope for the truth.

Just then, Uncle Jerry cups his face with his grimy hands and his chest caves. His eyes hide beneath the brim of his ball cap as he sobs.

"I'm sorry, Charlie. I'm wicked sorry."

The corners of Grammy's mouth turn down.

"How the hell could you, Jerry?"

"I dunno', Ma. I'm sorry!"

Dad crosses his arms over his chest and glares at Uncle Jerry.

"You're my damn brother," he says. "I trusted you."

Dad's half-smoked cigarette rests in the ashtray shaped like Maine, sending smoke streaming up to the ceiling. Mum unclips her burgundy pouch. Her hands shake, she slides out another cigarette, and strikes the lighter with her thumb.

A ring of grey smoke pours from her nostrils and rises like a hot air balloon.

"We're callin' the police in the mornin'. Thought you oughtta' know," Mum says with a fierceness to her voice.

Grammy gasps.

"No, Franny, you can't! He'll go to jail."

"Good, Ma. I hope they put him under the jail. Now if you don't mind, I think it's time you both left," Mum announces with a twinkle of satisfaction in her voice.

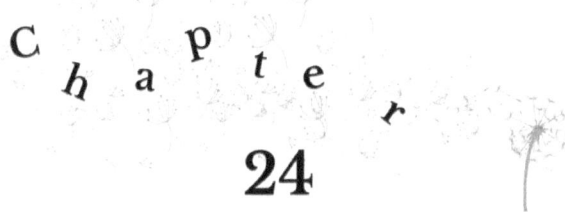

24

THE SIXTY-TWO FOOT GIANT

The next day, following my confession, the principal of the school interrupts my sixth-grade class. After an exchange of words between the teacher and the principal, the principal turns and makes eye contact with me.

My stomach lurches. The thought rattles around in my head that *I'm in trouble.* He makes a beeline up the aisle toward me. His corduroy pants rub together as he walks, and the noise stops when he reaches my desk.

I shrink in my seat and twirl my hair around my finger nervously.

"Get your stuff, Miss Dodge," he says whispering in my ear in slow level tones, a hand on my shoulder. "You won't be coming back today."

"I didn't do it," I say with a nervous laugh, doing my best to keep the rip tide of emotions at bay. I close my Trapper Keeper and slide out of my chair.

Charlene sits in the desk beside me. The color drains from her face. I cast my eyes on the ground and stare at the scuff marks on the principal's brown shoes as I follow him out of the classroom and down the hall to the main office, where two policemen wait, one bald and the other one pudgy.

"Miss Dodge," the bald officer says, "we're here to take you home."

"Home? Why? School doesn't let out for—"

"To file a report based on the phone call we received this mornin'."

I recall Mum's words last night before Grammy and Uncle Jerry left and cringe.

"Why you?" I ask, wringing my hands. "Why can't my mum come get me?"

"Your father's at work and your mum didn't have a way to get you, so we offered to pick you up on our way to your house," the pudgy policeman says.

The two policemen walk me outside to the patrol car with the words *Skowhegan Police Department* painted in bold black letters down the side.

I slide to the middle of the back seat. A cage separates me from them like an animal at the zoo.

The second and third grade classes and teachers pin their noses against the wall of towering windows, ogling me. I cross my arms and poke out my bottom lip.

Take a picture. It will last longer!

The policemen take a left onto Main Street. We pass Tom's Convenience Store, the purple cow statue, the thirty-five-foot rocket ship, the tin man made from muffler parts, and the water wheel on the right. At the antique shop, we take a right and stay to the left, passing the red shingled house near the bend in the road and the cornfield.

"That's my house," I say, pointing to the little brown house with the giant antenna and lightening rod on the roof.

The car slows to a stop and then turns up my driveway. Mum sits on the rickety stoop with her Maine shaped ashtray beside her and Charles Jr. on her lap. She wears her turquoise housedress and wool-lined moccasins.

My stomach drops at the sight of Grammy's car parked next-door in Mable's driveway.

Aunt Mable knows! Who else has Grammy told?

Realization creeps up my spine and I swallow hard. The thought of the entire family knowing what Uncle Jerry did to me makes me sick.

The bald policeman opens the back driver's side door, and as he does, Aunt Mable flies out of the trailer and plants both feet like an oak on the front deck. Grammy too. They glare at me across the yard and talk loudly.

I slide out of the back seat, stepping over the hole I dug to play marbles in. Suddenly, I wish I had dug the hole deeper, all the way to China, so I could disappear.

"There's that lyin' tramp now. You little slut," Aunt Mable shouts, descending the steps and streaming across the pavement, down the path toward me.

I'm an idiot! Uncle Jerry said this would happen. I should've kept my mouth shut! Maybe I can lie? I reason. *Tell the policemen I made it up.*

But I didn't lie, I tell myself as Aunt Mable draws closer.

"You got what you asked for," Mable says, bold and loud. "Not just Jerry, but from Roger, too. Lightnin' don't strike twice in the same place."

How do they know about Roger? Aunt Fawn couldn't have. She wouldn't.

Fear climbs my spine like a ladder and fills my eyes like two small ponds.

By now Mum's on her feet with Charles Jr. on her hip.

"She's a child, Mable. You got a problem with her—you take it up with me. Now leave."

"She teased my brother. She sat on his lap." Aunt Mable looks down her nose at me with a piercing stare. "Did you tell the police that?"

"I didn't ask for it," I say softly, fighting back tears.

I cover my face with my hands then dart over the gravel past the two policemen with puzzled brows. Once up the rickety steps, I dash inside the house and flop into the armchair with muted orange flowers.

"Go home, Mable," Mum demands as she ushers the policemen inside.

"Never mind her. That's Francine's aunt," Mum tells the policemen. "She's a loose cannon. I'm Mrs. Dodge by the way." Mum extends her hand and shakes theirs before showing them to the divan propped up by two-by-fours.

"Coffee, water, or Kool-Aid?" Mum asks, placing Charles Jr. on the gold carpet square between her feet and sinking down into her sad old chair.

"No thank you, ma'am," they say at the same time.

Their eyes zip around the space like hummingbirds pollinating the room, pinging off the peeling wallpaper, particle board ceiling, and curling linoleum.

The tips of my ears feel hot. I try not to crumble under the weight of Mable's words bobbing in my head like apples.

"When will this day be over?" I mutter.

Something tells me it won't ever fully be over. *Not really*. Mable won't let it. Tomorrow will be a run-on of today. And the next day will be a run-on of tomorrow and after that, more of the same. Mable will rub my nose in it—*it* being her dislike for me. She will achieve this through name calling and public humiliation, the way she does everybody on her blacklist.

The policemen write in their notepads.

What are they writing? Could it be the buckets on the counter? The double-oven stove in the living room? The wringer washer beside the Frigidaire? The particle board ceiling and one-by-four trim? The tittering stacks of what-nots? The pungent smell of pisspots?

"Let's begin," the bald one says. His voice deeper than the Grand Canyon. "We're gonna ask you some questions, so answer the best you can."

I nod.

"Who . . . touched . . . you?" the bald one asks.

"Uncle Jerry and Roger," I say, staring off to the side, still

feeling the burn of Aunt Mable's words—'LYING TRAMP.'
'LITTLE SLUT.'

"Can you tell me their last names?"

"Jerry Dodge and Roger Rhodes," Mum inserts with a
deadpan tone.

"Over or under your clothes?" the pudgy one asks.

"Oh . . . ah . . ."

I press my lips together, wishing the floor would open up and
swallow me like Korah in the Bible. Mum and the policemen
wait for me to answer, so I take a deep breath.

"Under," I push out.

"Were their clothes on or off?"

I clear my throat and fiddle with my thumbs.

"Oh . . . ah . . . off," I say, squirming in my seat.

"You're doin' great," the bald one says. "Now can you tell me
where?"

My brow turns down.

"Where what?"

"Where they touched you," the pudgy one clarifies.

Where didn't they? I want to say.

Images flood my mind. My tongue feels heavy and dry. I don't
want to talk about this anymore, but they're waiting. My hand
lowers and I point down between my legs.

"Here," I say. The saliva in the corners of my mouth thickens.

"You haveta' say the body part, the actual word," the bald one
says.

I wipe my sweaty palms on my knees. My heart pounds in my
ears.

"My p-privates."

"And by privates...you mean?"

My eyes stick to the wall above their heads like two thumb
tacks.

"Vagina," I say quickly.

My bottom lip trembles. I hold my hand to my mouth to try
and stop it.

"Can you tell me if they penetrated your vagina?" the pudgy one asks.

No, I can't! I don't want to! But they're waiting. Mum's waiting. Everyone's waiting.

So, I tell them. The heat from my ears moves into my cheeks. The balls of my feet bounce on the mishmash of carpets, and the room shrinks in size. There's so much pressure on my chest.

I can't breathe!

"I don't wanna do this anymore. I never should've told."

Pushing back tears, I throw my hands in the air and spring from the chair. Once outside on the stoop, the door slams behind me.

"Come back!" Mum shouts.

"It's okay, ma'am," one of them says. "Give her a minute."

Standing on the stoop, I release loud, gut-wrenching sobs. They rattle my insides and force me to my knees.

Suddenly, I hear Aunt Mable's laugh. It carries on the wind one telephone pole's distance.

"There's the little bitch now." These words waft across the yard on the wind with the laugh, interrupting my sobs. I sit up straight and wipe my eyes.

I lean forward on the stoop and peer around the corner of my house. Aunt Mable barrels toward me. Grammy's gait is slower but consistent as she joins Mable on the firing line. Mable's arms spin like helicopter blades.

As I wipe my eyes, I smear snot up through my hairline.

Mable stops in front of me. She sticks her index finger between my eyes and wags it.

"You're a liar!" she says through clenched teeth. Her eyes bulge out of their sockets.

"I'm not. I promise."

Her words cut deep.

"I'm tellin' the truth," I cry with breathy pauses.

Tears stream down my cheeks. Each time I wipe them away, they return.

I turn toward Grammy who stares down at the fringes on her loafers.

"Tell Aunt Mable I didn't ask for it," I beg as tears weigh my lashes down.

Grammy says nothing. She doesn't even look up at me, leaving me sitting there with no helpful explanation.

The front door opens. Mum lets out a gasp.

"What the hell do you want now?"

"She's a liar, a floozy-Suzy. The whole family knows it!" says Aunt Mable with steeliness in her voice.

Aunt Mable's wagging index finger shifts from my face to Mum's.

"You're meaner than a pole cat," Mum says, swatting her finger away.

Aunt Mable shakes fitfully from her fiery red hair to her rainbow flip flops.

The pain of Mable's words, "THE WHOLE FAMILY KNOWS IT," forces the wind from my lungs. I know deep down inside she has already threaded the family with her lies about me. A tsunami of tears hit and I cup my face with my hands.

The policemen instruct Aunt Mable and Grammy to return to the trailer. They bring Mum and me back inside and suggest we finish the report at the police station, in Skowhegan, when Dad gets off work.

❧

WITH MY FACE EDGED IN STREAKS FROM THE TEARATHON I'VE been on since my confession last night, I climb into the front seat of the Titanic. The yellow foam padding sticks out of the torn vinyl seat. I wait for Mum to grab her pocketbook.

Drumming my fingernails on my knee, I stare out the passenger window at Aunt Mable's trailer door and pray she doesn't come barreling across the yard at me with fists flying for a third time in four hours.

Hurry up, Mum! I silently plead.

Collywobbles flutter in my stomach, and my hands shake like two leaves blowing in the wind.

Aunt Mable's never called me the B-word before, only dirty ragamuffin and a pissant.

In this moment, I don't know who I hate more, Uncle Jerry or Aunt Mable.

Mum opens the driver's side door with the strap of her pocketbook draped over her shoulder and three throw pillows in her arms—two pillows to sit on and one to put behind her back so she can reach the pedals.

When she's done arranging the pillows, and before she puts the car in drive, she lights herself a cigarette, adjusts the volume on the radio, and rolls the window down.

Hurry up! I scream in my head, my eyes still glued to Mable's trailer.

The Titanic bunny hops down the driveway and onto Nelson Hill Road, where the wire-rigged muffler rumbles loudly. Mum's open window allows the wind to whip through my curls.

Twenty minutes later, as we round the rotary in Skowhegan, I gaze up at the sixty-two-foot Indian statue carved from a single pine tree and painted with an array of vibrant colors.

"You like it?" Mum asks.

"Ayuh. It's majestic!"

"The Indian's name is Skowhegan. It means, *Watching Place*," Mum explains as she pulls into the police station parking lot and parks.

A woman in a black skirt and white blouse greets us.

Is she a police officer? Her hair is in a bun, but she's not wearing a uniform.

"I'm Mrs. Kline," she says with a smile. "I've been expecting you."

Mum runs her hand over her sad old housedress, smoothing out what she could, and extends her hand.

"I'm Mrs. Dodge. This is my daughter, Francine. She was raped and we're here to complete the report."

"Mum!" I gasp, then picture the marble-sized hole I dug and me climbing into it.

Mums' frizzy hair springs from the rubber band.

The woman smiles. "Nice to meet you ladies. How are you holding up?"

"Could be better. Could be worse," Mum responds.

"I heard about the conflict today with the family member," the woman says with concern. "Sometimes family members blame the victim to protect the family name."

"Tell me 'bout it. Her Aunt Mable can be colder than a clam digger's hands in the middle of the winter."

The woman gives us a kind smile. "Please follow me, ladies."

The woman's heels click-clack up the steps and down the hallway to a private room. Mum's wool-lined moccasins scuff down the beige tile.

Inside the room, I sink into the leather seat beside Mum and pick at the cat hair on my shirt.

Mrs. Kline opens a camel-colored briefcase. She pulls out two dolls.

"I'm going to ask you a series of questions like the police did earlier. Are you okay with that?"

Do I have a choice?

"These dolls can help you tell me what happened. Would you like to hold one?"

I shake my head no.

"It's okay. You don't have to," she says, setting them down in front of me. "Can you tell me about your uncle?"

I wring my hands.

"Whatcha' wanna know?" I ask, trying to be brave.

"Well, to start, can you tell me what his favorite game is?"

"Hide-and-seek," I say. "I hate it when he chooses me to be his partner."

"How many times in the past has he chosen you?"

"A wicked lot."

"Can you give me a number?"

"Fifty or so."

"Does your uncle make you anxious?"

A beat of silence follows. Two. Three. Then four.

"Ayuh," I force out.

Another beat of silence follows, until Mrs. Kline breaks it.

"When do you get anxious?" Her long red fingernails wrap around the pen as she writes.

"Whenever he's around me."

"Very good," she says, "and has he ever taken his pants off in front of you?"

"Ayuh. Except once, when he didn't get a chance to."

"Oh," she says with a brief pause, "can you tell me about that?"

I push back a tear and stare at my hands in my lap.

"They put Charlene and me in Grampy Dodge's beat up car. The blue and cream mafia-styled one by the apple orchard—"

"Tell me, who is Charlene?" she asks. Her tone rising like a flag on a pole.

"Her twin sister," Mum says. "She's older by five minutes."

"I see. You said, 'They, *they* put you in the car. Who are they?"

"My uncle and his friend, Jud. They picked us up off the ground where we were sitting and carried us to the car."

"What did they do to you in the car?"

"They untied the straps on our shirts and unbuttoned their pants."

Mum's leg bounces nervously, and she fiddles with the burgundy pouch in her hand. The silver clasp opens and she slides a cigarette out. Then she glides it back in and pulls it out again before sliding it back in.

"And then what did they do?" Mrs. Kline asks as she uncrosses her ankles and slides back in the chair, putting distance between me and her.

"Played Mr. Tickle with us," I say. "I don't like Mr. Tickle. It makes me wicked uneasy."

"Yes. I'm sure. And what did they do after Mr. Tickle?"

"Two of my aunts knocked on the passenger window and dragged Charlene and me outta' the car and into the puckerbrush."

Mum looks up at me, her eyes watering.

"Nobody told me 'bout that! Had I of known, I would've stopped it," Mum says in a wounded tone.

"Yes, I'm sure, Mrs. Dodge," Mrs. Kline says as she returns her attention to me.

"Tell me, what did your aunts say to you and Charlene?"

"They said we were hankerin' for some trouble and that we knew better than to be hangin' out with older boys."

"I see. Tell me, Francine, do you think you're bad?"

"Ayuh. I know it."

"Why are you bad?"

"Because Uncle Jerry said that we both wanted it and that if he goes to jail, I'll go to jail with him, and because I took his money and bought zebra cakes at Tom's Convenience Store."

"Zebra cakes?" Mrs. Kline's honey colored brow forms a stiff peak.

"Sometimes I sneak across the street from the playground after school, before the bus leaves."

"Why does he give you money?"

The heat of the shame rises up from my toes.

"Let me rephrase that. When does he give you money?"

"After..." I whisper. My voice thick with pain.

"After what?" She picks up the dolls and hands them to me. "Maybe now you would feel more comfortable showing me?"

I close my eyes and count to *ten Mississippi*. After which, I take the boy doll and lay it on top of the girl doll.

"I love you. You know that right? This is our little secret," the boy doll says to the girl doll.

"Ouch! Stop! That hurts," the girl doll tells the boy doll.

Mrs. Kline holds up her palm to stop me.

"Thank you! That's sufficient. And tell me, Francine, does the boy doll have pants on?" Mrs. Kline asks.

"Ah nope. Well, ayuh. Kinda," I say, tugging on the shorts of the doll. "They were around his ankles like this."

"Good. Now does the boy doll have underwear on?"

"Ayuh. Kinda. They were also around his ankles."

I start to tug on the underwear the boy doll wears.

"No need," she says, stopping me. "Tell me, does the girl doll have pants on?

"No."

"Does the girl doll have underwear on?"

"No."

"The girl doll mentioned something hurt. Can you ask the girl doll to tell me what hurt? Does the boy doll do something to the girl doll?"

I nod hard and fast.

"Can you tell me what you told the officers earlier?"

"His thing...he put his thing in me," I tug on the doll's underwear and point to his male part.

"I see. Do you know what his thing is called?"

Shame reddens my face like a bucket of paint.

"Penis," I whisper.

"You're doing good. Now can you tell me the big person word for where he puts his penis?"

My brow scrunches up and I point between the doll's legs.

"Vagina," I say, closing my eyes so not to see Mum's face which puckers with sadness.

"Okay, thank you! You're doing great. Just a few more minutes. Now we need to talk about Roger. Can you pretend that the boy doll is Roger?"

"Ayuh, I suppose."

"Good. Now show me how Roger the boy doll plays with the girl doll?"

I lay the boy doll on the girl doll and move it up and down, the same way I did when it was Uncle Jerry.

"Do the dolls have clothes on?"

"No."

"Does the boy doll put anything inside the girl doll?"

"Ayuh. His penis," I choke out.

"Okay, that's enough. Thank you, Francine. You're very brave. You wait here with your mum, and I'll be back shortly."

Mrs. Kline puts the dolls back in the briefcase. Her heels click-clack out of the room and down the hall apiece.

Mum slides the unlit cigarette into the pouch and rest her shaky hand on my knee.

"I didn't know. I would've stopped 'em," Mum says.

I stare at her hand, unsure if it trembles because she needs a nicotine fix or because she's upset with me for not telling her about the mafia-styled car. So, I focus my attention on the tapestry of wild horses hanging on the wall above the desk and imagine riding one far away from here.

Several minutes later, the click-clack of the heels makes their way toward the room where we wait.

"Sorry to keep you," Mrs. Kline says, drawing me out of my fantasy of riding a horse. Her red fingernails caress a stack of carbon papers.

Mum pulls a pen out of her pocketbook.

"Sign by the "X' please, Mrs. Dodge. You are going to be required to attend family counseling. I'll get with Mr. Dave and schedule it for you. It looks like he's booked this week and next, so it will be a few days, maybe even a week, before we can get you in."

Mrs. Kline turns the page and points to another 'X'.

"Make sure the whole family attends. It will be once a week until Mr. Dave releases you. If you need to reschedule, please call him in advance."

Mum puts the burgundy cigarette pouch in her pocketbook and throws the strap over her shoulder.

"Let's go, birdbrain, I've got supper to cook." Mum pauses, then adds, "I'm makin' your favorite."

I smile up at her, hoping her next words will be—fried beef heart.

"Fried beef heart," Mum says, smiling back.

I walk with her out of the room, casting one more glance at the tapestry of wild horses.

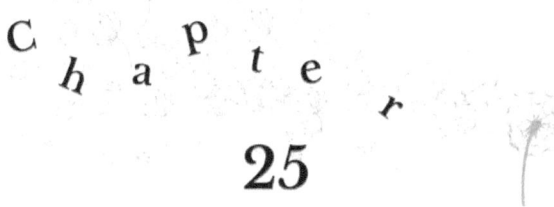

25

STICKS AND STONES

One week later, the afternoon school bus stops at the foot of Aunt Mable's driveway—Charlene, Pauline, and my cousins, Lottie and Dottie, and I make our way down the aisle and across the road.

My sisters and I ignore Lyle and Eddie chanting *Shack! Shack! Shack!* out the small rectangle window as we scurry up the paved driveway and across Mable's manicured grass to our overgrown grass.

As I approach the swing set, I leap over Aunt Mable's flower bed of pink, yellow, and red tulips. My landing falls short, and my heel comes down in her mulch bed. Aunt Mable flies out of the trailer, eyes ablaze, face as red as the tulip I almost stepped on.

"Why you little shit. I'm gonna knock your block off if you tromp my flowers again." She beats the air with her fists.

I gulp hard at the cyclone of fury spinning toward me.

"I didn't tromp on 'em, I promise."

"Lottie and Dottie aren't allowed to play with you anymore," she shouts as she gets closer. Her words spew hate.

The shock makes the corner of my mouth quiver.

"You see that property line?" she points to the pine tree with the chain wrapped around it and her dog, a collie, attached to the other end.

I eye the forked trunk.

"Ayuh," I say, low and slow.

"Don't...cross...it," she says, clenching her teeth.

The skin between my eyes wrinkles.

"I don't understand. Is this because I jumped over your flower bed?" I ask, pointing and showing her the heel mark where I landed in the mulch. A small miss.

"You're a troublemaker with a capital 'T'. A bad influence."

Lottie and Dottie watch from the deck.

How am I a bad influence?

My eyes plead with my cousins to tell their mother that I'm not bad. But a voice deep down inside me agrees with her.

"You seduced Jerry. Now he's locked up," Aunt Mable says with a haunting laugh, stepping around to the front of me and blocking my attempt to continue the last fifteen steps to my house.

Only then do I realize that it's not about the tulips.

Mable holds her breath. Her face changes from red to blue to purple.

Is she gonna pass out before she remembers to breathe?

I take a large step backward to stop her index finger from jabbing me in the chest.

She closes the gap. Her finger makes contact with my chest.

"Ouch! That hurts," I whisper. She continues jabbing me.

"You're a floozy-Suzy," she yells while bent over me. The veins in her neck stick out like strings on a weaver's beam.

"Sticks and stones will break my bones, but words will never hurt me," I say with a tremble in my voice, not sure what else to say.

My palms sweat and my heart beats loud in my ears.

Her beady eyes march back and forth across my face with a look of murder.

"You seduced Jerry. Why don'tcha admit it?" The cords in her neck twitch.

"What does seduce mean?"

"Don't play dumb with me, little girl." Her cheeks shake.

More tears fill my eyes and empty down my cheeks.

"You're a liar!" she insists. The tip of her nose presses against mine.

"Nah uh—"

"Uh huh—"

My voice cracks.

"You don't know beans," I cry out.

Aunt Mable bumps me with her big belly and pushes me backward two whole steps. My green plastic snake from the Shrine Circus falls out of my hand into the grass. Its red tongue sticks out.

Mable leans in, her lunch breath in my face. White spit foam collects in the corners of her mouth. She raises her hand and draws it back preparing to slap me. I squeeze my eyes shut and cover my head with my hands to shield myself.

Suddenly, I hear our front door open. Looking up, I see Mum scuttle the fifteen steps to where I stand. Her ponytail is flat against her skull and the creases from the lace on her pillowcase are embedded in her cheek.

"Pick on someone your own size, why don'tcha," Mum shouts, sweeping me behind her and shielding me with her body.

Mable clutches her fists. Her jowls shake.

"Tell your damn daughter to stay outta' my yard and away from my girls. She's a whore. A slut. A floozy-Suzy. The whole family knows it. Even her grandmother says so."

Grammy Dodge thinks I'm a slut? My eyes squirt tears.

"You're a bully," Mum tells Mable, grabbing my wrist and marching me the fifteen feet to the rickety stoop and over the threshold, past Charlene and Pauline who are staring in terror out the large, recycled picture window in the living room. Mum continues pulling me down the hallway to where Dad quietly works on his stamp collection at the folding table in his bedroom.

"Babe, you need to do somethin'. Your sister called Francine a slut again," Mum announces.

I wait for Dad to slide his chair back, to get up, to gallop down the hallway like a knight in shining dungarees. Instead, he squeezes a pair of tweezers that hold a gold plaited stamp. A magnifying glass hovers over the stamp and with a steady hand he places it on the empty space in the velvet covered collector's album.

Mum's hands rest in the pockets of her sad old house dress. Her foot taps the striped carpet.

"You're gonna do somethin', right, babe?"

He says nothing.

"Your sister's a damn bully and enjoys terrorizin' your daughter!" Mum's voice is hoarse.

Mum removes her hands from her droopy pockets, sighs loudly, and zips like a field mouse back down the striped carpet, past Charlene and Pauline still staring out the picture window at Aunt Mable screaming at the top of her lungs like a mad woman in the yard for me to come out and face her.

"FRAN—CINE!" Aunt Mable roars.

I hear my name being summoned as I step down into the front of the house. Mable's voice drowns out the television and Charles Jr. squalling on the carpet at Pauline's feet.

"Stay inside," Mum tells me as she makes the lonely trek back outside. I lean against the picture window with the coax cable leading up to the antenna on the roof and observe the quarrel. Standing sandwiched between Pauline, whose face is red with tears, and Charlene, whose frozen stiff with second-hand fright, I think about the Army of Israel.

Wonder if this is how they felt when Goliath taunted them?

Were they this scared?

Aunt Mable pokes Mum in the chest with her index finger

and pushes her backward in the long grass. One step. Two steps. Three steps.

"Don't blame me, Franny, because your daughter seduced my brother."

Mum wobbles, catches her balance, and squares her shoulders before looking up at Mable.

"If you have a problem with Francine, you take it up with me. Not her. She's a child, Mable."

Mable, who is a whole head taller than Mum and a hundred pounds heavier, flicks her brick-colored hair and cackles loudly. Her finger is planted almost like a permanent fixture in Mum's chest.

"The apple doesn't fall far from the tree, now does it Franny?"

"She's eleven years old, Mable," Mum reminds her.

"That has as much to do 'bout nothin'," Aunt Mable huffs, adding, "oh, thought you might wanna know, Franny, Jerry pled *not* guilty at his arraignment this mornin'. How do you like 'em apples?" A smirk of satisfaction paints her face.

Mum's jaw drops.

What's an arraignment? And why did he plead not guilty? These questions scratch at my skull.

"What's wrong, Franny. Cat got your tongue?"

Mable lifts her flip-flop. My plastic snake comes up for air. Its red tongue flickers before her flip-flop pushes its head back down.

Mable sees me in the picture window and takes three long strides toward me.

"You little bitch." The rat-a-tat-tat of her fingernail against the window, her cold beady eyes, and the heat of humiliation in my face all make me want to curl up in a ball and die.

"Leave her be!" Mum cries hoarsely.

Pauline looks at me. Her lazy eye wobbles in its socket.

"What if *he* wins?" she asks before returning her attention out the window.

I swallow hard through the lump strangling my throat. Fear pumps through my veins. My mouth is dry.

"Why I oughtta'—" Mable taps the pane harder and faster like a woodpecker drilling for insects.

Pauline, Charlene, and I stare out the window at Mable. Only a thin glass with smudges and bug guts separates us. Our faces pucker with tears.

"You're a whore," Mable shouts. "A slut." Her beady eyes bore holes in me like lasers.

Hearing those words makes me shrink back in shame.

I wish I were never born! I scream in my head. *Whoever said, 'Sticks and stones will break my bones, but words will never hurt me' is a big, fat liar!*

"I'm sorry I'm not strong like you," Pauline cries. Her voice trembles like a thousand waters. "I'm sorry you haveta' face this alone. I'm sorry I can't come forward." She tucks her chin in her neck, angles her head up, and pins me to the window with her good eye. "This would be the straw that broke the camel's back for me, if you know what I mean."

No, I don't! And what does a camel and a straw have to do with any of this? I want to ask her, but the look on her fourteen year old face tells me I don't want to know.

Despite my sisters on both sides of me, Charles Jr. twisting and squawking on the floor, and the clowder of cats on the divan, I feel alone.

My knees buckle and I collapse in anguish onto the carpet below the windowsill. I press the palms of my hands against my ears, close my eyes tight, and let out a blood curdling scream. I push out the sound until there is no breath left. When I am done, Dad's footsteps pound down the hall, out the front door, and onto the stoop.

"Enough, Mable!" he bellows.

His voice fills the air, and the three of us girls burst into tears as though it was the first time.

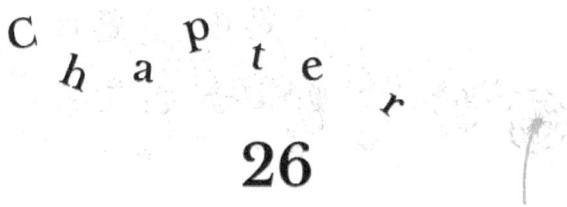

26

DAPPER DAVE

T hrough the bus's windshield, I see a U-Haul parked three telephone poles away at The House. Aunt Mable and Uncle Chester and some others march like worker ants up the small incline to the chipped red door carrying large pieces of furniture like breadcrumbs back to the nest.

Under the blue spruce tree, near the foot of our driveway, Mum weeds her oval shaped flower garden on her hands and knees. Beside her, Charles Jr. lays on a blanket surrounded by baby rattles. The blonde sprig of hair on top of his head folds into a perfect Boston curl.

"You didn't tell me Grammy was movin' back!" I hiss.

"Whatcha' think, ding-ding? The House can't stay vacant forever."

"Does this mean Uncle Jerry's movin' back, too?"

Mum roots around in the soil between the blue flags and the irises, pulling clumps of dandelions and purple pig weeds.

"Don't worry. Jerry ain't movin' back. He's movin' to Hartland with Valerie, his girlfriend, when he gets out."

Mum shakes her head.

"I pity Val's daughters," she says. "They can't be more than eight years old."

Mum plucks another handful of weeds and then sits up straight to stretch her back, twisting side to side. With the crook of her elbow she wipes the sweat from her forehead.

"I warned Val 'bout him," Mum adds.

Another clump of weeds flies by and lands in the heap at my feet.

"What'd she say?"

"That you're a liar and that Jerry wouldn't hurt a fly."

"He killed Peter Rabbit. Uncle Jerry's a monster! Tell me, how can Grammy let Uncle Jerry plead not guilty? She knows the truth."

"Doesn't matter," Mum mutters.

"But he lied. Can't he get in trouble for it?"

"Shithead's gotten away with murder for as long as I can remember," Mum says. "That's what happens when you're the baby of fourteen kids," she adds, whacking at a mosquito and smearing soil across her forehead.

Another clump of weeds flies by me. A light dusting of black soil covers the toes of my gray sneakers with Velcro-straps.

"Val told me to mind my own business, so that's what I'm gonna do. But don't say I didn't warn her."

Mum reaches into the sagging pocket of her housedress and slides a cigarette out of her burgundy pouch.

"If Val knows what's good for her, she'd take 'em girls and run." Mum flicks the lighter with her blackened thumb. The end of the cigarette dangles from her lips.

Even though I don't want anything to happen to Val's two girls, the relief that Jerry won't be living next-door to me makes me smile on the inside.

AFTER SUPPER, THE FAMILY LOADS INTO THE TITANIC FOR another session at the Family Counseling Center in Skowhegan.

Twenty minutes later, Dad parks in front of the sixty-two-foot Indian statue across from the town rotary. The Titanic rattles and bunny hops until coming to a stop.

Mum wears rouge on her lips and swallows her last bit of coffee.

I press the small of my back against the seat and cross my arms.

"I'm not goin'," I say.

The last two sessions brought out a lot of yelling and hurt feelings. I'm the problem in the family, and these sessions make me realize how much of a pain in the neck I am to everyone.

Mum dabs her cigarette in the pull-out ashtray and peers over her shoulder at me.

"You poor abused baby," she says. "You think any of us wanna go?"

I cringe.

POOR ABUSED BABY—I hate it when she says that!

I follow Pauline's thump-step-thump through the parking lot and across the street to the large rotary in the center of town lined with buildings. Mr. Dave greets us in his usual fancy bow tie and boat shoes.

Mum gives Dad a sneaky sideways smirk.

"Dapper Dave would be a fittin' name for him, don'tcha' think, babe?" she whispers loudly.

"Mmmph," Dad responds.

Mr. Dave escorts all of us into the room with chairs spread in a half-moon circle, where we met the prior two times, and opens his notebook.

"Last week, we left off with, with—" He pauses as he flips through his notes. "We left off with you, Charlene. Can you describe Francine with one word?"

Charlene gnaws on her already bleeding fingernails. Tufts of hair stand wildly like the snakes on Medusa's head. She catches my eye narrowing *don't-even-think-about-it* glare and glances the other way.

Mr. Dave slides one khaki covered leg with a boat shoe forward and scoots to the edge of his chair.

"You can't think of one word?" he says, prodding her.

The silence stretches, and Charlene pushes up her big red eyeglasses, the ones she got last week at the eye doctor that look like Sally Jesse magnifiers.

"Is Francine nice?" he asks her.

"S-s-scary," Charlene replies.

"I see. How is she scary?"

"She's got a wicked temper. It's more than a tantrum. Her eyes change and she goes into terrifying fits. It's like she turns into Mr. Hyde. She hits me, kicks me, throws stuff at me. One time it was the telephone in the back and another time it was a sneaker to my temple. I already know she's gonna kill me for talkin' to you."

Mum crosses her leg over her knee and bounces Charles Jr. up and down. As she does, her turquoise housedress rides up her thigh.

"Francine's the dominant twin," Mum informs him. "She's a tickin' time bomb."

"I see, thank you, Mrs. Dodge," he says, pausing to write something down.

They're right. My fits go from a low simmer to a teakettle blowing its whistle faster than Mum can light a cigarette. All I know is that I feel better afterward. Lighter. Cleaner. Though I don't think my family would say the same.

Returning his attention to Charlene, he asks, "Do you like Francine?"

"N-n-no . . . well sometimes, when she's nice."

"I see. So, she's not always scary?"

Charlene shakes her head. Her shake is a bit rusty.

Next, Mr. Dave turns in his chair and faces Pauline.

"What about you? What's one word you would use to describe Francine?"

Pauline growls, tilts her head down, and tucks her chin into her neck. Greasy strands of hair hang over her eyes.

"Dunno', don't care," she mutters.

"I got a word—" Mum interrupts. "More like two—Tasmanian Devil."

The family chuckles. Everyone except me and Charles Jr., who is asleep on Mum's lap.

Mr. Dave keeps his focus on Pauline who slouches in her chair and peers up over her thick frames. Her wobbly eye lands between two occupied chairs.

"She's a bitch. Pardon my French."

Mr. Dave tugs at his bow tie and clears his throat.

"Well, you asked, didn'tcha?" Pauline says.

"That's true, I did ask. Can you tell me if she's ever hurt you?"

"Duh, whatcha' think? Francine hits me, kicks me, and calls me names like Dolly Parton, fatso, tub-of-lard, Porky the Pig, Pollywog. Need I say more?"

"How does that make you feel?"

"You haveta' ask? Like I wanna kill her. That's how."

Tears run down Pauline's acne speckled cheeks and drip from the hair growing on her chin, pooling between her breasts in a patch of flaming red acne.

I hold up my right hand and point to my fingers.

"Pauline broke these three fingers for no apparent reason."

"You got what you deserved," Mum replies.

"Why does everybody always say that?" I fire back.

"You know what I mean," Mum answers.

Mr. Dave looks at me.

"Do you always get what you deserve?" he asks.

I stare at the wall with the poster of the happy family on it and blink away the scent of urine coming from Charlene's direction.

"What is this, Francine therapy or somethin'? Why do I haveta' go to counselin' and Roger and Uncle Jerry don't? I didn't do anythin' wrong, but I'm the one who's bein punished for it."

"Is that what you think? That you're being punished?"

My neck snaps back.

"Well, ain't I?"

"Sexual abuse can have long-lasting effects on the survivors and their families. Unfortunately, this kind of abuse is becoming more and more common amongst girls your age."

"Like hell," Dad spurts, rubbing his mustache like a cricket rubbing its hind legs together.

A beat of silence follows.

Dad uncrosses one dungaree covered leg and then crosses the other.

"What?" Dad says, eyeballing Mr. Dave and interrupting the silence. "Don't look so damn shocked. It can happen to boys, too. I should know."

Mum leans forward like she's the therapist now.

"Go on, babe. Tell Mr. Dave your big secret."

My brow raises.

What secret? How big is it?

"I'll talk when I'm damn good and ready," Dad says, honking his nose loudly into his handkerchief.

"I think now might be a good time, babe," Mum pushes. "What those men did to you way back when was despicable."

What'd they do? Something in me tells me, *I don't want to know.*

"What happened way back when doesn't matter now," Dad says sharply.

"Yes, it does," Mum responds. "You were an adolescent."

Dad reaches into his front pants pocket and pulls out Grampy Dodge's silver pocket watch and flips open the cover to expose the face.

"It's eight o'clock. You girls have school in the mornin'," Dad says.

The silver lid snaps shut, along with Mr. Dave's notebook.

"Same time next week," Mr. Dave says. "We'll pick up with you, Mr. Dodge, right where we left off."

"Like hell you will," Dad answers, half-way to the exit, his words trailing behind him.

As I exit the building and cross the street, the sixty-two-foot Indian statue named *Watching Place* stares out over the rotary, and I wonder what he would think of me if he could.

The trek through the parking lot feels like forever, and the flick of Mum's lighter is the only sound that registers. Charlene, Pauline, and I scoot into the back seat with Charles Jr. I gaze out the dingy passenger window with the Marvin the Martian sticker in the corner.

The silence is terrifying.

Does everyone hate me?

I taste the salt of my tears at the back of my throat, and without making a peep, I tuck my head in my elbow and let the tears flow.

The next day, Mum comes up behind me at the kitchen sink. She rests her hand on my shoulder. Her touch makes me flinch.

"I love you! I know I don't tell you like I should," Mum says.

My back is to her. I consider the warmth of her touch and how I long to say it back, but I jerk my shoulder away for fear of looking weak.

"Sure, you do," I respond with a sharp whisper.

Mum's hand slips from my shoulder. Her moccasin feet scuttle away, down the hall to her bedroom, where her sobs penetrate the thin paneled walls.

Why did I say that? Look who's the monster now.

⊗⊗⊗

SINCE MY CONFESSION FIVE WEEKS AGO, THERE'S BEEN countless confrontations full of sharp, painful words and name calling coming from the trailer next door. The deck is where Mable sits and waits for me to come home—whether from school or counseling or the flea market. From her perch on the deck, she shouts reminders at me—reminders that 'I asked for it,' that I'm a 'slut,' a 'floozy-Suzy,' a 'tramp,' a 'no good liar,' or a 'troublemaker with a capital 'T'.

If Mable's not shouting reminders from the deck, then she's bent over me, screaming them in my face, nose to nose, jabbing me with her index finger in my boney shoulder. And if she's not doing that, then she's calling my house and shouting reminders through the phone to whoever answers. If she's not doing any of those three things, she's mimicking a threat. This she does by making a beeline toward me, her eyes wildly ablaze, while I stand frozen with fright, waiting, wondering, worrying what she will do when she reaches me. At the last second, she breezes past me as if I'm a garden gnome and she doesn't see me. The beeline she makes is to our shared mailbox that sits in the milk can surrounded by tiger lilies at the foot of my driveway. It's her version of cat and mouse.

Since the start of the confrontations, I've spent more time inside my house driving the family crazy and playing Pac-Man on the Atari. One Saturday afternoon, to get me out of the house, Mum takes us girls on a surprise visit to our cousin's house, in Clinton, thirty minutes away.

Richard, my favorite cousin who gave me the Playdough Farm set when I broke my leg, shuffles the Uno cards at the dining room table under the chandelier for himself, Charlene, Pauline, and his two little sisters to play a game, while I play Chinese Checkers with Aunt Jenny at the two-seater table by the window.

Sunlight beams through the window and warms my back. Brimming with a smile, I jump my red marble seven spaces to Aunt Jenny's side of the board.

She then hops her yellow marble five spaces back and sets it down in front of my red marble, blocking my next move.

"Your go," she says with a grin.

As I strategize my next move, the phone rings and Aunt

Jenny answers it. There's an uncomfortable silence, and I notice how she twists the cream-colored phone cord around her hand and up her arm.

"Oh, hi Mable," Aunt Jenny says, swallowing hard.

All sound in the room is suddenly reduced to the noise a feather makes when hitting the floor.

"Francine there?" The voice trumpets through the phone.

My eyes widen with worry.

Aunt Mable's question wraps around me like a boa constrictor, and the whole room narrows to the size of a postage stamp.

A tumble of shame makes my slightly sunburned shoulders slump, and I pick at the large freckle on my arm. My stomach twists in knots.

I release a shuttering breath.

How does she know I'm here? Did she ask Dad where Mum was off to with us girls? Did he tell her? Then I remember I told my cousins next door where we were headed when they asked.

The heat of humiliation starts at my toes and works its way up to the top of my head. Her words bury me alive. My throat shrinks and I grab at it with my hands.

I can't breathe!

Pauline lets out a low sounding growl.

"That woman's brutal. She's got a nose like a blood hound." Her tongue clicks against the inside of her cheek. She tilts her head up. Her lips sink into a long frown.

"Jenny," the voice snakes through the phone, "I'm gonna give you the same warnin' I gave the rest of the family. Keep Francine away from your husband. She's liable to seduce him and then get him in trouble for it. I won't let my Chester anywhere near her."

Feeling the weight of seven sets of eyes looking at me with mouths wide open and ears bent toward the phone, I wring my hands and squeeze the color out of them.

Please God! Make it stop!

Mum reaches around Charles Jr. and snatches the phone away from Aunt Jenny.

"Leave . . . Francine . . . be!" Mum shouts into the receiver. "What if it were your daughter? It would be a horse of another color, now, wouldn't it Mable? Why don'tcha put that in your pipe and smoke it?"

When Mum is done, she slams the receiver down and disconnects the call.

After a beat of silence, whispers fill the room that has now shrunk to the size of a pinhead. My blood pressure rises, until the only sound I hear is my own heart beating. With eyes cast down, I dash to the bathroom and lock the door.

I inhale deeply, choking back sobs.

Whoever said, *Truth hurts*, didn't exaggerate. My truth about Uncle Jerry—hurts. My truth about Roger—hurts. My truth about Aunt Mable and Grammy—hurts. But my telling the truth —hurts the most.

"I hate you, Francine! You should've kept your mouth shut. This is all your fault," I mouth in the mirror.

My eyes sunken and swollen from weeks of crying, I clutch a fist full of hair and pull. When that doesn't ease the pain inside, I punch my legs until exhaustion takes over. Then I crumble to the floor in a fetal position, hugging my knees and crying tears enough to fill the claw-foot bathtub beside me.

On the way home, episodes of Mable's taunts fill my head like an overflowing trash can. I sink down into the back seat of the Titanic and try to make sense of everything.

Where it went wrong. What I did wrong. That I am something wrong.

My head rests against the window with the Marvin the Martian sticker on it. I close my eyes and listen to the hum of the tires on the pavement.

"It's like Aunt Mable's playin' Russian Roulette with Francine or somethin'," Pauline says loudly to Mum, over the rumble of the muffler. The Titanic takes a left onto Nelson Hill Road. "We never know which time it'll be when we come home that Aunt Mable will blow up on her. You see how livid she gets. Hell, that woman even scares me." Pauline pauses, then continues, "Aunt Mable's liable to snap one time and kill her. If looks could kill, Francine would've already been dead."

A shiver pulses through my body as we pass the cornfield coming up the hill and then The House. The loud muffler announcing our return. With our shared mailbox in sight, I twist a chestnut curl around my finger and choke back tears. A thousand questions nickeling at the back of my eleven year old mind.

Will Mable be waiting on the deck for me? What will her anger level be? Will she shout at me across the yard, catch me by the scruff of my neck, or pretend I'm a gnome on her perfectly timed trip to the mailbox? Will she kill me?

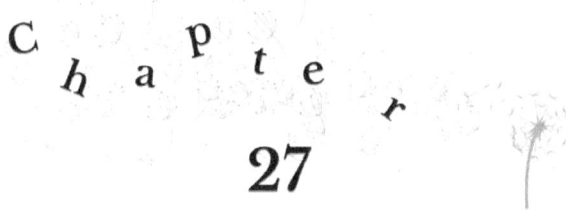

Chapter 27

GHOST IN A MAUVE DRESS

From the rickety stoop, tears sneak down my cheeks. I sit with my chin in my hands and stare down the footpath three telephone poles to The House, jealous that my cousins get to visit Grammy but I don't.

Thoughts that *Grammy doesn't love me, and I don't belong* play in my head.

Mum drops a basket of laundry on the ground in front of me and lights a cigarette. The wringer washer wobbles in the gravel behind her, spinning loudly.

"Why so glum, ding-ding?" she asks, blowing smoke my way.

I exhale a long breath.

"Why can't I go to Grammy's and play?"

"Because you can't," Mum says matter-of-factly.

"That's not fair. I didn't do anythin' wrong."

"Life never is," Mum says with a deep sigh as she slides her burgundy pouch into the sagging pocket of her housedress.

I sigh back.

Then Mum crosses her legs and bounces on the balls of her moccasin feet.

I roll my eyes up.

"What? You ain't ever seen someone haveta' go whiz before? My bladder's so full my teeth are floatin'. If I don't hurry up and go, it'll be my eyeballs," she snickers.

Charlene cuts off the television and heads down the path toward the voices calling out "gotcha'" and "tag, you're it." When she reaches the back corner of the garage, where our property line ends and Grammy's begins, she sits crisscross-applesauce in the grass and watches them play. I follow behind her to the property line and sit down beside her.

"It's all my fault. I never should have told," I say, staring into the distance at the cousins playing tag.

"It's not your fault—"

Charlene cranes her neck my way.

"Hey," she says, "remember when Dad t-t-took us to Santa's Village?"

"Ayuh."

"—an-an' we fed the reindeers?"

"Ayuh."

"An' an' we had our pictures taken on Santa's lap?"

"Ayuh," I say for a third time.

"That was fun. You were nice to me that day," she says with a small smile.

As we observe the cousins playing in the field, the chipped red door opens, and Aunt Mable and Grammy step out with towels and a box of popsicles in their hands.

"Who wants to go swimmin'?" Aunt Mable calls.

"Me! Me! Me!" The cousins yip.

Charlene jumps up and waves her arms. "Me!" she yips, too.

While knowing that drawing Aunt Mable's attention to myself could lead to more shame and blame, I leap up, wave my arms in big rainbow swooshes and call out "Me!" at the top of my lungs, in hopes to appeal to Grammy's softer side, if there still is one. The risk is worth it. I don't want to be the black sheep anymore.

Aunt Mable stops at the truck and looks long and hard down the path.

I know she sees us.

Seconds later, Aunt Mable climbs into the driver's seat, while Grammy in her polyester pants and sleeveless silk blouse gets in the passenger side.

The cousins pile into the back of the truck as Charlene and I continue jumping up and down on the property line, waving our arms in the air and yelling, "Me!"

The truck pulls away, and the cousins wave, suck on popsicles, and shout goodbye to us.

When we can no longer see the red taillights, we melt to our knees near the rhubarb plants and bawl a river, rolling in the purple pig's weed and crushing them.

"Should've known better than to hope," Charlene says with a wail so painful it starts in her toes and works its way up and out her throat with a long moan.

"You girl's hurt?" Mum calls from under the clothesline.

She rushes across the yard as fast as her short legs will carry her. When she reaches us, we sit up in the pig's weed with grass-stained knees.

"We didn't get invited—" I sputter between sobs. Tears shoot from my eyes like a sprinkler watering the weeds around my knees.

"Get invited where?" Mum asks. Her voice swells with anger.

"To the swimmin' hole," Charlene cries. "Aunt Mable t-t-took —" was all she could get out before bursting into tears again.

A cigarette bobs between Mum's teeth, and an unhappy tuck paints the corners of her mouth.

"And you're surprised why?" Mum asks with her hands on her hips. "That woman would cut her nose off to spite her face. Last week she took all the kids to the racetrack, this week to the swimmin' hole. What's it gonna be next week? Disney World. Oh, that's right," Mum pauses, then adds with a sarcastic huff, "almost forgot. Every year she takes her favorites to Orlando for two weeks with Lottie and Dottie over Christmas break."

"Why don't we ever get invited? It's like we're invisible or somethin'," Charlene says with a hiccupy cry.

"That's because we are," I say.

❦

LATER THAT DAY, WHEN IT'S DARK, CHARLENE AND I RETURN to the corner of the garage and spread a blanket on the ground. We sit Indian style on the blanket in the grass and face The House while enjoying the blueberry muffins Mum made.

I take a bite and watch Grammy in her doorway wave goodbye to the last cousin leaving for the evening.

Butter runs down my arm and I lick the salty goodness. The headlights flicker in the trees and vanish down the road.

Grammy closes the door. The porch light cuts off. The House is dark except for the small fluorescent light above the sink. I pop the last bit of muffin in my mouth, lay backward on the blanket, and gaze up at the canopy of stars.

"Why does Grammy love the others more than she loves us? What's wrong with us?" I ask.

Charlene is quiet and lays back on the blanket beside me. I peer over at her to see one tear in the moonlight sneak down her cheek and into her ear hole.

In the distance, Snoopy makes the whippoorwill sound he makes when tracking a racoon or a rabbit. It overrides the chorus of pond frogs croaking in the cattails and crickets rubbing their hind legs together. Yesterday, Snoopy dug up a rotten chicken foot from the cornfield, and the week before that, he brought home a mangled chicken beak with the eyeball still attached.

"Been lookin' for you—" a voice calls out from behind.

Charlene and I roll onto our sides to see Laurel pushing her red scooter down the footpath in the moonlight and carrying a mini cassette player.

"Whatcha' doin' here?" I ask with a voice full of delight. "I ain't seen you in a month of Sundays. Thought you were avoidin' me like everybody else in the family."

"Ah nope, been wicked busy that's all," Laurel chuckles. "Came to borrow some sugar from your mum. My mum sent me." She holds the clear plastic bag of sugar up and shakes it. "Thought you'd like to hear my new cassette tape before I head home."

Laurel squeezes in between us on the blanket and pushes play on the cassette player. With our hands behind our heads, we stare up at the inky tree line and listen to *The Gambler* play.

"Do you think the craters in the moon look more like a man or a sideways rabbit?" I ask.

"A man," they say with confidence.

"Ah nope. Look, it's a rabbit!" I insist. "See the ears?" I trace the sideways silhouette with my finger.

"See that cluster of stars?" Laurel points. "That's Orion."

"Like the cookies?" I ask.

"No, silly," she snickers. "Not Oreos. Orion."

The cassette tape ends, and Laurel props herself up on one elbow to flip it over and play the other side. As she is about to lay back, she lets out a terrifying shriek. It sends a chill through my spine, up the back of my neck, and into my hair.

"What's-at?" she chokes. Her mouth is as wide open as a garage door.

Charlene and I hesitantly follow Laurel's finger to the upstairs window of The House, where a woman wearing a long mauve dress gazes down at us. Her eyes glow like flames of fire and the moonlight shimmers off her mauve dress, illuminating her boney figure.

"G-g-ghost!" Charlene says with a high-pitched squeal.

Laurel scuttles backward over the blanket doing the crab walk.

"Where do you think you're goin'? We haveta' save Grammy," I say.

"No way, Jose," Laurel responds, shaking her head hard and fast before scuttling further away in the direction of the hand pump.

"We need to save Grammy," I repeat.

"You're not allowed at The House," Charlene reminds me, adding, "what if Aunt Mable gets wind of it?"

"She won't," I insist.

"How can you be so sure? What if Grammy tells Aunt Mable on you?"

"C'mon," I say with frustration.

"Ah nope! You can't make me." Charlene crosses her arms hard over her chest.

"Scaredy cat," I spout, springing to my feet and taking one giant step over the property line toward The House to rescue Grammy, even though she is a traitor, like the Benedict Arnold I learned about in class, because she knows the truth.

"You're not the boss of me," Charlene stutters, looking around for Laurel, who is nowhere in sight.

"Would you rather Grammy get killed?"

Charlene nods her head, yes.

"Don't be such a baby—" I say. "We can't leave Grammy to fend for herself. What's she gonna do—swat at the ghost with her flyswatter?"

"Maybe it's Grammy's sewing mannequin and someone put it there as a p-p-prank," Charlene suggests, taking a giant step backward as if not believing the story coming out of her mouth.

I throw my hand on my hip.

"You mean the headless doohickey? I'm pretty sure *that* woman has a head," I say, pointing at the window.

Frightened but not wanting to appear like a scaredy cat myself, I yank Charlene by the hand over the circular driveway and up the hill to the door with the chipped red paint.

"Please, please, please let me go," she pleads, trying to free her hand.

I squeeze her gnawed-on fingertips tighter and drag her over the threshold into the kitchen. The House smells like liver and onions with a dash of Avon. We stand with our bare feet, ten toes down on the yellow brick linoleum.

The door slams shut, startling Grammy in her rocking chair. Her flyswatter flips through the air.

"Jesus, Mary, and Joseph!" she yelps. "You twins tryin' to give me a heart attack?"

"G-g-ghost," Charlene says, pointing up at the ceiling where we stand.

"Anyone else here?" I demand to know.

"Nope, dear, why?" Grammy asks, leaning forward to retrieve her flyswatter.

"There's a ghost in the upstairs window with glowin' yellow eyes—" I say, pointing up.

Grammy chuckles.

"You're not the first ones to tell me that and you probably won't be the last."

Charlene and I exchange silent glances between us.

The many stories about glowing pig's eyes staring into the windows at my aunts and uncles when they were kids, along with the story of the recent séance held at the oval table when a candlestick floated across the kitchen accompanied by the sound of invisible bootsteps, quickly heap up in my mind like a towering stack of what-nots.

"And you're positive no one else is here?" I ask with a tremble in my voice.

"Go on, dears. Go see for yourselves," Grammy says.

I put my shoulder into Charlene's back and push her across the linoleum to the dark stairwell behind the tiki bar.

"You first," I tell Charlene.

"W-w-why me?"

"Because I said so—"

She digs her heels in and refuses to budge.

"Fine, I'll go by myself."

I push past her up the dark stairwell. My bold march tapers into tiptoeing. By the time I reach the top landing, I inch along the creaky floorboards to the room where the ghost was. Feeling for the chain attached to the naked bulb, I get more scared because I can't find it. The only light upstairs comes from the moon shining through the curtainless window.

The headless doohickey stands in the corner far away from the window draped in cobwebs. An icy gush of air sweeps through the room. The hairs on my neck raise. The floorboards groan and creek in front of the window where the woman stood minutes earlier. At break-neck speed, I retreat down the stairwell to the rocking chair.

A peel of laughter fills the kitchen. Grammy rocks back and forth in her chair, tapping the flyswatter on her knee.

"You twins better get goin' before Mable catches you here."

She presses her hands into the wooden arms of her chair and pushes off. On her feet, she takes three steps to the large oval table, places the fly swatter near the butter dish, and then takes five more steps to the counter. She reaches for the switch to turn off the small florescent light over the sink.

"Goodnight, dears," Grammy says.

"Goodnight," I say, elbowing Charlene to say it back.

Charlene doesn't respond and stares past the wood stove into the darkness with her mouth wide open. She raises her arm slowly and points straight ahead into the living room.

Something tells me not to look, but I crane my neck that way anyhow and follow the direction of her gnawed-on fingertip. In the corner of the living room stands the woman in the mauve dress with glowing yellow eyes.

"Ghost!" I scream, yanking Charlene by the hand and running out the chipped red door and down the footpath to where Laurel waits on the rickety stoop.

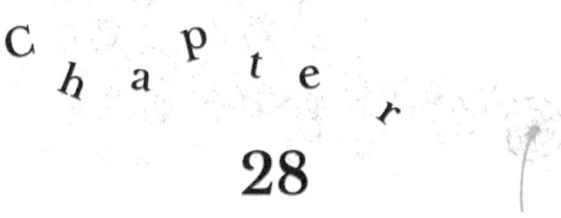

28

BLACK AND BLUE & GRAMMY, TOO

Ignoring the 'No Trespassing' sign, I climb over the rickety fence and enter the back way into the neighboring field to hunt for four-leaf clovers.

The sun beats down on my shoulders making them burn. I lay on my belly in the long grass and rake my fingers through a thick patch of clovers, counting the individual jade hearts. Each trio of leaves is topped off with a pink and white pom-pom which shoots from the center of its paper-thin stem. Sweat beads on my neck.

Your grandmother thinks you're a slut knocks at my little girl's mind, and a trail of tears trickle down my cheeks to water the clover.

For thirty minutes I scour the patch, spreading the miniature shoots apart, one by one, in hopes of not overlooking a four-leaf gem.

Finally!

I smile and pluck the clover from its stem and make a wish— the same wish I make when breaking the wish bone, blowing out the birthday candles, and rubbing Pauline's lucky rabbit's foot —*to be free.*

Armed with my special clover, I decide I will press my luck and sneak down to The House to visit Grammy.

I miss her, I sigh deeply. *I miss the tobacco and Avon scent of her skin. I miss dipping my fingers into the bowl of cucumbers and vinegar on the oval table. I miss shooing bottle flies from the butter dish.*

Does she ever think about me except with dislike?

Grammy didn't tell on me the other week, or at least, I didn't get in trouble for it, when I crossed the property line to rescue her from the ghost. Maybe she won't tell on me this time either. Besides, if Aunt Mable isn't there everything will be fine. I'm sure Grammy will be happy to see me. How could she not? She knows the truth.

The hands on my blue Smurf watch tell me it's three o'clock.

Aunt Mable has ceramic class at three. A smile stretches upward from my soul and makes the announcement on my face.

Now's a wicked good time.

I brush the grass from my knees and climb the rickety fence by the *No Trespassing* sign and walk twenty yards to the edge of the field where the junkyard begins, rehearsing what I should say when I get to the chipped red door.

Hi Grammy, how would you like to pick dandelion greens? I can get the trowel and bucket for you.

Or this. *Hi Grammy, how would you like to make homemade honey? I know your recipe: 50 pink clovers. 100 white clovers. 25 pink roses. Sugar. Water. A pinch of alum.*

Or better yet. *Hi Grammy, would you like me to steep you a hot cup of Red Rose tea, just the way you like it?*

Or maybe this. *Hi Grammy, I'm not mad at you even though you didn't stick up for me. I thought you should know.*

Or this, simple and to the point. *Hi Grammy, I'm glad the ghost didn't murder you.*

As I wind through the vast lonely junkyard, I pass row after row of rusty, crumpled up vehicles, piles of mangled bumpers, cracked windshields, rusty radiators, flat tires, and mis-matched hub caps. When I reach the mafia-styled car by the apple trees, I take a hundred more steps to the end of the junkyard road where the circular driveway starts. I look to the right at the garage, to the left at The House, and then down at the lucky clover peering up at me in my hand, before hanging a left and taking the thirty steps up the small hill to the chipped red door.

I breathe deep and push the door open. "Hi Grammy," I say.

My smile melts when I see Aunt Mable looking at me from the sink.

She's everywhere, I gasp. *Like purple pig's weed.*

"I didn't know you were gonna be here," I say. My throat dry.

Blotches appear on Aunt Mable's freckled neck and work their way to her face.

"Why wouldn't I be? It's my mum's house ain't it?"

Run! Don't stay. Come back when she's gone, I scream in my head.

Grammy and Aunt Mable whisper back and forth loudly. Against my better judgment, I tiptoe to the rocking chair and focus on the fly zipping from the honeycomb of beef tripe on the table, to the bowl of sliced cucumbers in vinegar, and to the pound of melting butter next to them.

When the whispering stops, Aunt Mable rolls her head around on her neck and glares at me in the rocking chair.

"Why don'tcha' ask your grandmother if she wants you here?" the voice from the rotating neck says.

A twill of nervousness fills my throat. I know Aunt Mable doesn't want me around, but it never dawned on me that Grammy might not want me around either, since she knows the truth and all. My eyes water and I stare up at the ceiling speckled with dried-on fly blood-and-guts.

"Well, go on, ask her." Aunt Mable's flip-flop taps the yellow brick linoleum.

I swallow hard, but the lump stays lodged in my throat.

"Is it all right Grammy?" I force out.

Grammy holds the fly swatter in her hand. Her eyes dart around the kitchen as if chasing a bottle fly and she says nothing.

The awkward silence stretches on. One beat. Two beats.

Three. Then four. Five beats. Six. With each passing beat my heart sinks lower in my chest.

"For a few minutes, dear." She glances away when she says it.

The delay tells me what I already knew—*she doesn't love me* and *I'm not welcome here.* In response to it, I fly out of the rocking chair, take five quick steps toward Grammy, and haul back and kick her with my shoe in the shin bone.

Traitor! I scream in my head.

Grammy yelps and grabs her leg.

Oh, no! What did I do?

My eyes widen, and I drop my lucky clover on the yellow brick linoleum.

Aunt Mable lunges at me and we volley around the oval table.

"Your ass is grass and I'm the lawnmower," she says as she cuts to the left.

I take the first opportunity to bolt out the door and down the footpath past the garage.

Before I can reach the hand pump, Mum and Dad fly out of the house and barge toward me.

"Turn your ass around," Dad barks. He points his finger in the direction of the lawnmower waiting for me at The House.

I stand stock still.

"Move it or lose it, girl," Dad bellows.

A second wave of regret hits me.

It's not going to be Mable that kills me. It's going to be Dad!

My knees jitter. Collywobbles do acrobats in my stomach as I turn slowly around and follow Mum and Dad in the direction from which I fled.

With my eyes glued to my shoes, I enter through the chipped red door and make my way back to the rocking chair.

"Look what Francine did," Grammy hisses in pain as she rolls her polyester pant leg up.

Against her pale skin, purple spider veins shoot like Silly String from the welt on her shin.

Mum's brow makes a question mark.

"Whatcha' mean, what she did?" she asks as she takes a seat beside Dad at the table.

Aunt Mable hands Grammy a frozen bag of peas to hold on the welt.

"Your daughter kicked me," Grammy says, still searing in pain.

"By accident, I'm sure, Ma." Mum blows a plume of smoke across the table.

Dad takes his handkerchief out of his back pocket and lays it over his worn dungaree knee.

"Well, girl, whatcha' gotta say for yourself?"

"I dunno'."

"That's not good enough," Dad responds. His voice rises along with the smoke that streams from his nostrils. He stares hard at me. His thin lips press together as he strokes his mustache.

Mable marches across the kitchen to where I rock in the chair. Her index finger wags in my face, and the nail clips my nose. I flinch and reel back. She clips my nose again, and I draw my head back further.

Her angry red face bobs up and down in front of me like a balloon on a string.

"You think you're so damn smart. I've got news for you, you're not! Put that in your pipe and smoke it, why don'tcha!"

Grammy places the frozen bag of peas on the table and rolls her polyester pant leg down.

"All I know is that Jerry doesn't deserve to be locked up," Grammy says, pushing her cat-eyed frames up with a finger.

Mum's forehead wrinkles and she burst into tears.

"Yes. He. Does. Ma! How can you say that? Look at what he did to her. The doctor doesn't know if she can ever have kids because of that monster."

Aunt Mable spins around to face Mum.

"Monster? Everyone knows your daughter's a liar, Franny. If you ask me...she got what she deserved!"

"Poppycock! How did Francine deserve that?"

"Don't play dumb with me, Franny. You know damn good and well that lightnin' doesn't strike twice in the same place— Jerry and Roger, duh." Her mouth hangs open for an extended amount of time, allowing for the full effect of the *duh* to sink in.

Mum stamps her cigarette out and lights two more cigarettes, one for her and one for Dad.

"Nobody asked for your two cents, Mable," Mum says.

Aunt Mable's chest puffs out.

"Truth hurts, huh, Franny?"

Grammy reaches for the swatter and whacks at a fly. The chain attached to her glasses rattle.

"Charlie," Grammy says, "I don't want any more trouble. All I'm sayin' is Francine's makin' more outta' this than need be."

Aunt Mable throws her head back and lets out a cocky half chuckle.

"Francine's attention starved, Franny, not abused. There's a difference."

Mum's eyes well again.

"Say somethin', babe." She looks at Dad, who rubs his mustache and gives her a blank stare.

Tears drip down Mum's cheeks, and her voice is hoarse.

"If you ain't gonna protect your daughter, then I'm gonna pack the kids up and leave for good. I'm not gonna tolerate this anymore."

"You'd be doin' us all a favor then," Aunt Mable says with laughter.

"You're crazier than Gideon's geese!" Mum shouts.

Mum's hands tremble as she jams the burgundy cigarette pouch into the pocket of her sad old housedress, the tear on the pocket stretching toward the floor from the force. She takes the cigarette between her fingers and dabs it in the ashtray angrily, sliding the ashtray back hard and fast until it clatters against the butter dish.

"If you ask me, Shithead deserves more than jail time," Mum says.

Aunt Mable sheds a grin like a snake.

"Go ahead, Ma, tell 'em why they're really here."

Grammy taps the flyswatter on her leg and stares down at the fringes on her loafers.

"Francine isn't welcome here anymore," Grammy says low and slow.

There's a pause.

"Whatcha' mean? Francine ain't been up here but one time in two months, and that was today," Dad says.

"Twice," Mable remarks.

Dad whirls his head around like an owl and looks at me. His nostrils pulse.

"There was a ghost," I try to explain.

Mum shoots Dad a sharp look, her eyebrows dip in the center.

"C'mon Francine, we're leavin'," Mum says, standing to her feet.

I slide like a Slinky out of the rocking chair and onto the linoleum for fear of never seeing Dad again, and I reel in pain. The flood gates burst and tears, so many tears, follow.

Aunt Mable cackles at the sight of me floundering on the floor.

"What'd I tell you, Ma? The apple doesn't fall far from the tree. Put that in your pipe and smoke it, Franny."

Dad slams his fist down on the table. The butter dish jumps and the vinegar sloshes over the cucumbers in the bowl.

The thud startles me, and I sit up on my knees on the linoleum. I stare at my lucky clover five feet away being trampled over on the floor and recall the wish I made when I found it. A sigh follows.

I'll never be free.

Dad grabs his handkerchief, scoots his chair backward, and stands.

A small amount of relief sets in when I realize Dad is coming with us, and Mum isn't going to pack us kids into the car so that we will never see him again.

"Shut your damn mouth, Mable! I've heard 'bout enough from you," Dad barks, "and leave Francine the hell alone!"

Dad stuffs his handkerchief in his back pocket and spins on his heels my way. "C'mon, girl, let's go home."

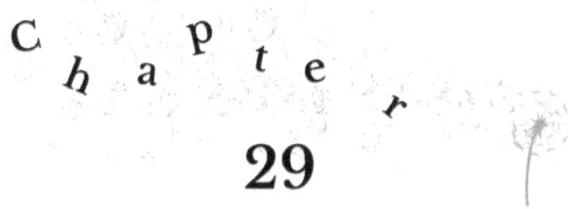

Chapter 29

THE CHAMPION

On a rainy Wednesday evening, Mum pulls out three ninety-nine cent plastic ponchos from her cream pocketbook.

"Eeny, Meeny, Miny, and no Moe," Mum says, chuckling at her own joke as she hands Charlene, Pauline, and me each one.

I open the package, shake out the creases, and slide it over my head before dashing out to the Titanic, slamming the cobalt-blue door behind me and locking it.

Although it's raining 'cats and dogs' as Mum likes to say, I wouldn't put it past Aunt Mable to barrel toward me in a pair of galoshes with her own disposable poncho on, so I watchfully look out the passenger window, prepared to jump over the seat and into the very back of the station wagon at the first sign of her.

How many more weeks of Mr. Dave is there? What more is there to discuss? Although, we never did make it back to Dad's secret Mum so desperately wanted him to tell.

The worn windshield wipers screech against the glass as we travel Route 2 all the way to Skowhegan.

Mum sings baritone with a cigarette bobbing between her

teeth and her left hand in its usual travel position—up high and between Dad's legs. Dad encourages her with a side-smirk that cradles his own cigarette. Pauline and Charlene cover their mouths to keep their giggles in, while our brother and I cover our ears to keep the noise out.

My head leans against the window. The rain pelts the roof, and I contemplate the upcoming trial. My lawyer called Mum while I was at school today and told her that she wants to prep me on the stand Saturday morning, when court isn't in session. She told Mum that she will be asking me uncomfortable questions like Mrs. Kline and Mr. Dave. I ball my fists and clench my teeth. The salt of my tears collects at the back of my throat. I think about facing Uncle Jerry in the courtroom and seeing Aunt Mable and Grammy there to support him.

Liar, liar, pants on fire, hanging on a telephone wire! I want to tell them all.

Collywobbles wreak havoc in my stomach. The closer we get to Skowhegan, the more the collywobbles churn. When the sixty-two-foot Indian statue is within sight, Mum stamps out her cigarette in the car's ash tray.

The windshield wipers thrust back and forth. The door cradles my chin. I sweep a tear aside.

Dad parks at the base of the statue. I gaze up, way up, at the hands of the *giant* holding the fishing spear and a fishing trap. I feel small, real small, like a grasshopper. My eyes continue to ascend, and when they reach the feathery headdress, Dad's command to 'move it or lose it' snaps me back to reality, the reality that nothing will ever change.

Dad reels around to the back seat. His hand slices through the air between my head and Charlene's, barely missing her mare's nest of tangles.

"Want a swift kick in the ass?" he asks.

"Can't say that I do," I respond.

"Well, then move it!"

At Dad's urging, I pull the silver handle on the cobalt blue door and step out. My shoe lands in a puddle. Water splashes up my leg, and I yank the plastic hood with both hands, holding it closed, tucking my chin in tight to my chest. Mum carries her umbrella with one hand, and my brother on the opposite hip.

Last week, Mr. Dave assigned our family homework. The assignment was to speak civilly to one another, no sarcasm, no name-calling, and no talking over the top of each other.

Who knew communicating could be so hard? Learning to ride a bike was way easier.

"Good evening," Mr. Dave says.

"Not good. Just evenin'," Pauline mutters.

The chairs are already set in the half-moon circle in the middle of the room, the same poster of a happy family hangs on the wall, and the sand in the hourglass drips like the rain from my poncho.

I sink into the hard chair. The small of my back presses into the cold metal, and I clear my throat.

Mr. Dave smiles wide like the Kool-Aid man on the television commercials.

Pauline leans toward me in her chair. "I'd like to wipe that smile off his face," she mumbles.

I roll my eyes in agreement.

No one can be that happy.

Raindrops snake down my poncho and puddle at my feet.

"How's everyone doing?" Mr. Dave asks.

"G-g-good," Charlene says with her thumbnail in her mouth as she chews bits of cuticles.

"It is?" Mum questions as she peers up at Mr. Dave with a mischievous look, the one she gives just before she says something corny or inappropriate. Or both. Mum seems to enjoy the attention she receives from oversharing.

"The damn ceilin' is leakin' like a sieve. We've got every pot and pan in the kitchen on the floor catchin' the rain. Might need a canoe and some paddles by the time we get home. Other than that, I'd say, I'm fair to middlin'."

Mr. Dave tips his head empathetically as if he understands our dilemma. But I don't think he does—I had to play hopscotch over the pots and pans to get here.

His pen taps the note pad with annoyance at Mum's tittering.

"How'd you do on your assignment this week? Did you try speaking kindly to one another?"

By now the amusement tapers, and Pauline slants her head. Her lazy eye wobbles before it comes into focus.

"Dunno', don't care," is all she says.

"I see," Mr. Dave says.

Dad wears his checkered dress shirt with rhinestone cowboy buttons. He crosses one dungaree leg over the other, massages his mustache in silence, and stares blankly at Mr. Dave.

"I see," Mr. Dave says again when he gets no response from us.

"Did you at least try the exercise I gave you?"

"Ayuh," I say, sliding both hands under my thighs to warm them.

"Would you like to share?" he asks, locking eyes with mine.

Not really.

I squirm.

"Well, since you insist," I say, "I told Pauline 'thank you' yesterday."

"I see. And does that qualify as vulnerability?"

"For our family, hell yeah, big time," Pauline chimes in.

Pauline's thighs hang over the sides of the metal chair, and her belly spills out of the plastic poncho like a waterfall.

"Oh, and I said, 'God b-b-bless you' once when Francine sneezed," Charlene adds.

"Did you know 'God bless you' was believed to keep evil spirits away?" Pauline asks. "Believe me," she nods, "Francine needs all the God bless you's she can get."

Pauline laughs along with the rest of them. But not Mr. Dave or me.

The skin between my eye's wrinkles. I stare past them to the poster of the happy family and ignore them.

"Francine, tell me, how did Pauline react when you said, 'thank you'?"

"How do you think?" Pauline interrupts. "I said, 'Who are you and what'd you do with my sister?'"

A throaty chuckle follows.

"Are you always this sarcastic?" Mr. Dave asks Pauline.

She grins mischievously and looks at him out of the corner of her eye.

"Hell naw," she responds, "worse. This is my good side." The gaps in her teeth spread apart like cotton balls stuffed between toes.

"I got one," Charlene says, raising her hand as if in school. "Mum and Dad both said 'please' this week. They never say please."

Mr. Dave's brow lifts. "Never?"

"Never, not ever," she answers, putting her hand down.

"They don't say, 'thank you', either," I add.

"Not to change the subject," Mum says, with her index finger in her ear hole shaking it fitfully to scratch an itch.

"Francine goes to court next week. She meets with the lawyer. Saturday mornin' at the courthouse to be exact."

The mood in the room shifts.

"Uncle Jerry's a big fat liar! I hate him!" I say, throwing my arms around myself and choking back emotion.

"Cheaters never win," Charlene says.

I hope she's right.

"The lawyer tells us that the burden of proof is on Francine. What if that monster gets off scot-free?" Mum asks with a voice full of concern.

I turn my head away to face the happy family on the wall and wipe my eyes.

"I see," Mr. Dave says, shaking his head.

"It makes me mad," Mum says hoarsely, "that he's puttin' her through this. Most of the family treats her like the black sheep."

Mr. Dave looks over at me.

"Francine, how does it make you feel to hear your mother say that?"

"Mum's right," I sniffle. "The whole family blames me. Aunt Mable said I seduced him, and they believe her."

Mr. Dave shakes his head again.

Mum's face turns deep red and she lets out an agonizing moan. Dad's hand moves from his mustache to her knee.

Mum's body convulses.

Tears sneak down my cheeks as sniffles fill the room.

None of this would be happening right now if I would have kept my mouth shut.

This is all my fault!

I clench my teeth, ball my fist at my sides, and will myself not to punch my legs, pinch my skin, pull my hair, or flip over a chair to relieve the pain I'm feeling inside.

Mum clears her throat. Her voice shakes.

"Mable's a monster too! Did I tell you she's phoned the whole family?"

Mr. Dave leans forward in his chair, and almost touches Mum's knee, but right before he does, he draws his hand back slowly.

"How does that make you feel?"

"Like I can't protect her. Look, I know I'm a shitty parent," Mum sobs. "And I know I haven't done everythin' right," she adds, "but this, this one thing I can do—I can be in her corner. I can stand up for her. I can do what no one did for me growin' up."

"It's not just Mable," I say. "You all can barely stomach me. So, if I don't belong in my immediate family, and I don't belong in my extended family, then where do I belong?"

"You can't mean that," Dad says, wiping his nose with his handkerchief.

"Nobody loves me. Everyone hates me," I sputter between sobs.

"You know we love you, hun," Dad says, adding with a chuckle, "even though you are a royal pain in the ass."

I flash Dad a smile.

"You still wanna know why I kicked Grammy?"

Dad gives a hard nod.

"It's because when I was at The House...I know I wasn't supposed to be...Aunt Mable said, 'Why don'tcha ask your grandmother if she wants you here.' So, I did, and Grammy looked at me without sayin' a word for a wicked long time before respondin'. The silence told me she didn't want me around. The silence told me she didn't love me."

"You kicked your grandmother?" Mr. Dave says with a look of surprise.

"I didn't mean to."

"So," Mr. Dave says, "in your eleven year old mind, your grandmother rejected you. Is that right?"

"Yes, I guess."

"How did you feel after kicking her?"

"Terrible. I wish I could take it back. Grammy will never forgive me. She'll never love me again. I don't blame her."

❧

THAT EVENING, WHEN WE GET HOME, WE PICK UP THE POTS and pans from the floor and toss the rainwater out the door. Afterward, Dad hooks up the Atari and challenges me to a game of Pac-Man. We sit in front of the television on two kitchen chairs with joysticks in our hand playing long past bedtime. Two hours into the game, my hands cramp and fingers stiffen. I massage them in between turns.

When Dad's turn ends, he watches me as I steer Pac-Man through the maze, eating all the pellets, and avoiding Inky, Blinky, Pinky, and Clyde. I advance through the levels in the attempt to beat my high score, while Dad and my sisters root me on. Three hours in, after surpassing my high score by 600,000 points, cheers erupt when I hit one million points, and the game starts counting back over at zero.

"You're the champion," Dad says with a smile as rare as the sighting of an ivory billed woodpecker.

Champion. I like it.

Mum closes her book.

"Now turn the news on, and go to bed. You have school in the mornin'."

"Don't remind me," I say, head low.

We girls line up for our nightly bedtime ritual—Charlene, Pauline, and then me.

When it's my turn, I lean down to kiss Mum on the forehead, and then take two steps to the left to kiss Dad on his forehead.

"Goodnight! Love you!" I say.

"Goodnight! Love you, too," they say back, never the other way around.

The hallway opens up like a whale's mouth into pitch blackness and I make my way down its hatch to my bed. Fear and doubt swirl in my head like a storm, tossing me back and forth in its belly.

What if he wins? What if Aunt Mable never stops? What if Grammy never speaks to me again?

The darkness within the darkness swallows me up. Inside my house, inside my bedroom, inside my sleeping bag, inside my head, I want the darkness to end. All the nightmares. All the humiliations. All the disappointments. All the rejections. All the shunning. All the blame. All the self-hate. All the pain. I want it to cease.

Where is the light at the end of the tunnel? Where is the justice I pledge my allegiance to every morning in school with my hand over my heart while staring at the flag?

When I can no longer fight sleep, lying on the top bunk with

Patches our family cat at my feet and Buster my stuffed dog under my arm, I close my eyes and yield myself to the giants—the six-legged octopus and the werewolf which visit me in my sleep. In the far corner of my mind, I see the little girl, the one with chestnut curls and bright blue eyes, huddled on a bed with black smoke and flames surrounding her. She pleads for help.

In the living room, her family watches reruns of M*A*S*H.

Why aren't they helping her? Don't they hear her?

Hey, I shout, jumping up and down on the property line of my mind, waving my arms frantically.

Go help her.

They can't hear me. No one can.

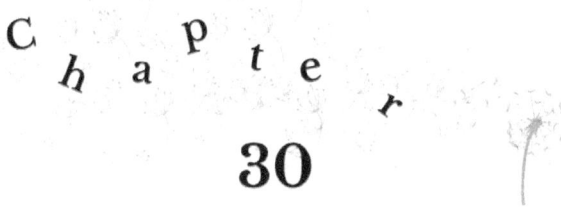

30

THE COURTHOUSE

On Saturday morning, we arrive at the courthouse in Skowhegan to prep for the upcoming trial. The courthouse is on the rotary above the drug store, overlooking the sixty-two-foot Indian statue, just a few doors down from Mr. Dave.

Charlene is with me. She holds my clammy hand. We stand at the bottom of the staircase and look up, way up. Then we climb each stair, one terrifying step at a time.

"You're shakin'," Charlene whispers halfway to the top.

I can't breathe, I want to tell her, but the words won't come out.

My body shakes from my toenails to my ponytail, and I will my legs to not buckle beneath me. I swat at my chest with my free hand, trying to swat away whatever the invisible thing is that squeezes the breath out of me.

Still holding hands, Charlene and I reach the top landing. Mum comes up the steps behind us with her frizzy ponytail and wool-lined moccasins on. The cream purse strap hangs over her shoulder and her burgundy cigarette pouch sticks out of her pocketbook.

I hear the words, "Miss Dodge" and look up to see my lawyer. She smiles and walks toward us.

"Ready?" she asks, looking down at me while swinging open the courtroom door.

Still holding Charlene's hand, I shake my head no and inch my way to the threshold, pulling Charlene with me. I peek my eyes around the doorjamb and take a small step inside. The lawyer holds out her hand to stop Mum and Charlene from entering.

"I'm going to need you two to wait outside. You can sit on the bench," she says, pointing to the wall.

I look back at Mum and over to Charlene, who's hand I squeeze.

The face Mum makes is the one she makes when she's doing crossword puzzles and the word she is trying to think of is on the tip of her tongue but she can't quite think of it.

I gulp and release Charlene's hand.

"Just me and you," the lawyer says.

The door closes but not all the way. Charlene hangs her head inside the doorjamb to observe.

The lawyer and I stand at the back of the courtroom and stare straight ahead at the wall with big bold words hanging over the judge's raised seat.

"This is the plaintiff's side and that is the defendant's side," she says, pointing with her right hand, then with her left as if curtseying.

My brow lifts.

What's a plaintiff and what's a defendant?

She sees the look I make and clears her throat.

"What I mean to say is, this is your side and that is his side."

"Oh," I say. My voice trembles.

The lawyer takes my hand and walks me down the middle aisle to the front of the room.

"I'll be sitting here at this table. Your uncle will be sitting there at that table with his lawyer. You," she says, taking ten steps forward with me in tow to the platform with rails and two raised seats, "will be sitting here in the lower box, beside the judge."

She guides me up into the box where I will testify.

"The first thing that will happen is the bailiff will swear you in. You will put your left hand on the Bible, raise your right hand, and swear to tell the whole truth and nothing but the truth."

"Will Uncle Jerry haveta' put his hand on the Bible and swear to tell the truth, too?"

"Yes, he will."

"Won't he get in trouble for lyin'?"

"It's going to depend greatly on your testimony," she says. "Let's practice. Okay? Sit up here." She pats the chair in the box.

I sit down.

She bends the silver neck that holds the microphone until the bulb on the end is close to my lips. I draw my neck back, moving my face away from it.

"Lean forward. You need to answer my questions and speak directly into the microphone. We want the judge and everyone else to hear your answers. Can you do that for me?"

"I think so," I say.

My lawyer takes ten steps backward and stands between the two tables.

"State your full name, please."

"Francine M—"

"Into the microphone, please," she interrupts.

"Francine Marie Dodge," I say, leaning forward in the chair and looking past her at Charlene who's head still hangs in the doorway.

"How old are you?"

"Ele—"

"Into the microphone," she interrupts again.

"Eleven years old," I say.

"Do you know Jerry Dodge?"

"Ayuh," I say with my lips pressed against the black cushion covering the bulb on the microphone.

"Do you see him here today?"

"Ayuh."

"And by ayuh, you mean?"

"Yes," I say.

"Can you point to him?"

I raise my finger and point at the table where she said he would be sitting.

"And how do you know him?"

"He's my uncle."

"Did your uncle do something that made you uncomfortable?"

"Yes."

"What did he do?" She pauses a moment, and then adds, "This is where you use the term we discussed last week, okay?"

I nod.

"He sexually abused me," I whisper.

"I'm sorry. Can you repeat that? I can't hear you."

"He sexually abused me," I say, leaning forward and talking louder.

"And by sexual abuse you mean, he penetrated you with his penis?"

"Yes," I say. My face feels as hot as a chimney stack.

"Very good, Francine. Do you think you can do this next week on the stand for me?"

"Yes," I say, even though my stomach says otherwise.

"There's going to be much harder questions asked of you by your uncle's lawyer. Are you sure you can do it?"

"Yes," I repeat.

❧

IN 1985, ON THE DAY OF THE TRIAL, I SIT OUTSIDE THE courtroom in a red checkered dress with a white scalloped collar.

My chestnut curls hang loosely over my shoulders. Brown clunky shoes tear at the blisters on my heels and a pair of red tights stretch over my knobby knees.

The bench is cold and hard. Sandwiched between Mum, who fiddles with the gold clasp on her cigarette pouch, and Dad, who rubs his mustache in silence, I wait to testify.

While I wait, I imagine the judge entering the courtroom with his long black robe on and the bailiff saying, "All rise," like on *The People's Court*. I'm nervous and lightheaded and think I might throw up, so I hold my stomach.

I tap my clunky shoe on the floor.

Mum touches my leg with her hand.

"Stop fidgetin'," she says.

"I can't help it," I whisper.

The courtroom door opens. I take a deep breath, squeeze my eyes shut, and wait for the bailiff to call my name.

There's a commotion to the left of me and when I don't hear my name being called, I open my eyes and look past Dad in his baby blue suit to see Aunt Mable and Grammy exiting the courtroom with Uncle Jerry's lawyer. Grammy clutches her sweater and without so much as a sideways glance, she disappears down the steep stairwell with Aunt Mable.

My lawyer exits next. A smile lights her face.

"Good news. It's over! You don't haveta' testify."

Mum's head swivels from the lawyer to Dad to me as if on a lazy Suzan.

"She don't?" Mum asks with surprise.

"Jerry Dodge threw himself at the mercy of the court and changed his plea to guilty. This is his first offense. Given that he was showing remorse and all, his sentence will be time served plus twenty days. That means in total, he will have served three months," my lawyer explains.

Mum hisses.

"Wait! You mean to tell me he'll get out in twenty days? That's not even a slap on the wrist."

My lawyer looks down at me then back up at Mum.

"He can never come in contact with Francine again. It's the best I could do, given his age at the time. There's no concrete evidence that he was over eighteen when the sexual abuse ended."

"Poppycock!" Mum says. "He was and everyone knows it! She's eleven years old and he's twenty."

"He wasn't at the time, at least, not that we could prove," my lawyer reminds her.

Mum slides the cigarette pouch into her pocketbook. She wears a black dress with flowers on it and red lipstick. Her hair is sprawled across her shoulders the way I like it.

Mum releases a choppy sigh.

"He's a monster! He'll be out doin' this to some other little girl before you know it."

"Well, we can't say for certain he will reoffend," the lawyer responds.

"Does a bear shit in the woods?" Mum asks, her voice laced with sarcasm.

There's a short pause before the lawyer nods the answer.

"There you have it. It's not a question of if but when. When he does this again, don't say I didn't tell you so."

Mum grabs my hand and pulls me down the courthouse staircase to the main street level where the drug store is. Once outside, she lights two cigarettes, one for her and one for Dad. Then she grabs my hand again, crosses the street, and continues through the parking to the Titanic parked at the base of the statue.

The door opens, and I melt into the back seat.

"Grammy hates me! She wouldn't even make eye contact with me."

"Look at me, Francine," Mum says as she whirls her head around. A stream of smoke billows over the headrest.

"It's not your fault. None of it is. You did the right thing."

"It doesn't feel like the right thing."

"Maybe it doesn't feel like it right now, but you are brave. I wish I had your courage when I was your age. The good thing is, he can never hurt you again. He can never have contact with you again," Mum says with a crooked smile from the cigarette that hangs out of the corner of her mouth.

I think about her words. The thought of Uncle Jerry never living next door to me again and never having access to me and my sisters warms my heart.

As we drive along Route 2 toward Canaan, I realize three things for sure: Giants do exist. I know because I just faced mine. My family isn't like everyone else's. But whose is? And unlike Canaan in the Bible, milk and honey doesn't flow here. It's purchased at the local Shop 'N Save. That is okay because I never much liked the taste of honey or the powdered milk.

I roll the window down and stick my arm out. The wind pushes it backward. I bring it forward, backward, then forward again, like an oar in the water. The breeze funnels through my curls and whips my hair around.

With a smile on my face, I think about the four ghosts on Pac-Man—Inky, Blinky, Pinky, and Clyde—the ones I beat to turn the game over, who in my mind, look like Jerry, Roger, Aunt Mable, and Grammy.

It's just like on Pac-Man when I reached one million points and the game started counting over at one. But this time, it's a reset for my sisters and me. We are starting over—without Uncle Jerry and Roger.

Sunlight breaks through the trees and crowns my head. The darkness spits me out.

I am free! I mouth into the wind.

My name is Francine, not girl, pissant, or poor abused baby. Free one—that's what my name means—like the prize inside a Cracker Jack box.

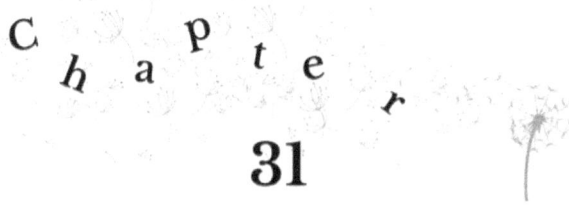

31

UNTRIMMED WICKS

Lynchburg, Virginia, Spring, 2000

That evening, I toss and turn in my bed and can't get Rita off my mind. I want her to tell the truth. I want the pastor to know I'm a good person. I want my brother in-law to know I didn't make it up. I want our stuff back and the twelve hundred dollars we gave Brother Clay and Brother Aaron to replace their things.

It's not fair!

I make two fists beneath the blankets and my entire body tenses up like a baby with colic. I haven't felt this kind of anger and injustice since I was a little girl, when all I wanted was for my uncle to tell the truth and for my aunt to believe me.

My eyes water again as I stare at my husband's V-shaped back and wonder how he does it.

How can he sleep at a time like this?

The pastor's words, the white car, and Rita's suspicious behavior pile up in my thoughts and in my fists only to empty out with my tears.

I roll over the other way, taking the blankets with me. Snot mixes with tears and I clench my teeth.

I hate her!

Suddenly, the sound of metal-on-metal sends shivers through my spine and up into my hairline. Red brake lights flash, then stop, flash, then stop.

They're back!

My heart pounds. I try to roll over, to sit up, to move, to call my husband's name—but nothing works, except for my eyeballs. They rotate in their sockets like when I was a little girl, when night terrors weren't quarantined to sleep, and when monsters—both real and imagined—chased me.

As soon as I am able, I throw the blankets off and zip through the darkness, like a field mouse, checking the locks on the windows and doors. When I don't see anything but an old green taxi in the street, I sigh with relief.

I'm not a little girl anymore! I'm a wife! A mom! I encourage myself, but this reminder comes too little, too late.

Pandora's box is open. I can't close it, and from it comes all the things I wish to forget.

Back in bed, I pull the blankets around me in hopes that when I wake up all the fear and anger and injustices will be back in the box where they belong.

I breathe deep and exhale. Breathe deep again, and exhale.

I'm fine.

But...am I really? I don't feel fine. I feel like *that* little girl.

My head sinks into the pillow. When I can no longer fight sleep, it yanks me from my bed in Virginia back to the little brown house with the mustard-trimmed door at night, lying on the top bunk with Patches, our family cat, at my feet and Buster, my stuffed dog, under my arm. It's the place where fear, anger, and injustice stems. Back to where it all began—back to the land of Canaan, Maine.

MARCH MARKS FIVE MONTHS SINCE MY HOUSE WAS ROBBED. It's been five sleepless months of obsessing over and wishing for Rita to confess—five months of wanting justice and giving each other the cold shoulder at church—five months of not going down to the basement to wash clothes, because I'm terrified a hand will grab me, pull me down the steps, and rape me—five months of checking the locks on the doors and windows multiple times a night while the family sleeps. *I know what I need to do to move past the past.*

On Sunday night, the sun splays through the stained-glass window like fingers on God's outstretched hand reaching for me. The small of my back presses into the hard pew.

Rita and Wayne arrive late to church. The only seats left are the ones in front of me. As the worship leader sings, I stare at Rita's raven-colored hair hanging over the back of the pew and wait for the right moment to do what God has been prodding me to do. The drummer drums loudly, and the saints stand, clap their hands, and sway. Before I can talk myself out of it, I lean forward and tap her on the shoulder. Rita's head rotates around and with a sharp piercing glance, she flicks her hair with her fingertips then turns back around to face the pulpit.

Knowing she never admitted to robbing my house, I knew I was taking a risk. But I trust the still small voice that tells me to forgive. Trusting my gut, I lean forward and tap her again.

Her head rotates around a second time.

"Wh—at?" she mouths.

Before she can turn back around, I quickly motion for her to come sit with me.

She rolls her eyes and sighs but then stands.

I take a deep breath and watch as she makes her way to me and sinks down in the pew beside me.

"What do you want?" she says with downcast eyes.

"I need to tell you something..." I say with a pause.

She tilts her head, her brow makes a question mark, and she peers up at me over her wire frames.

Without warning, I throw my arms around her, pull her close in a warm embrace, and with tears streaming down my face, I whisper in her ear the nine words God gave me.

"I forgive you! I release you of your burden." The *r*'s even after years of living in Virginia still sounding like *h*'s.

Rita breaks like a communion wafer and sobs in my arms.

"I don't understand. Why would you forgive me? I'm the one who did you wrong," she cries with choppy breaths.

I can taste the salt at the back of my throat.

"It's okay," I say as tears run down my face. "I forgive you!"

Right there in the middle of the song service, we stand, and for the first time since Halloween we worship together.

As I lift my eyes and hands toward heaven and sing, something happens. I see the spirit of unforgiveness as it leaves.

A strange barely visible shadow floats upward from where I stand, like the black smoke from an untrimmed wick, and when it reaches the ceiling, it disappears leaving me with an overwhelming sense of peace, joy, and love.

I am free!

FIDDLEHEADS
A Memoir
—*Excerpt*—

"The first sign of spring is not a day on the calendar.
The first sign of spring is the fiddlehead fern."

It's Mum. I can tell by her cough. Even over the phone, I hear the distinct sound of the flick of the Bic and wonder what number she's on for the day. She smokes and not in a charming Hollywood kind of way but more like a guppy sucking air way. First the unfiltered, then the filtered, before switching to the Lite, the phlegmy cough—not the cigarettes fault. *Never is.* Allergies or pollen or something like that.

Mum clears her throat.

"Hope you're sittin' down." Her words, coupled with her thick Maine accent, send shivers up my spine and into my hair.

My heart pounds.

Is Dad all right?

"Your uncle's had a massive heart attack. The doctors don't expect him to make it. Serves him right. Hope he dies. He'd be doing us all a favor then."

Uncle Jerry?

Memories flood my head and my heart. Unpleasant memories. Memories of pain and rejection. But something surges past the memories.

Regret.

"He can't die! I haven't told him I forgive him yet. Ever since March, when I forgave Rita for robbing my house, God has been dealing with me to tell him the same nine words I told her—I forgive you. I release you of your burden."

A series of loud hisses snake through the phone from Mum's lips to my ears. "That man's a monster! I thought you'd be happy! Your sisters sure the hell were. Why Pauline even said that she'd go to his funeral just to spit on his grave."

Mum's answer doesn't surprise me. A lot of people would tell me that my uncle did the unforgivable. Yet, my eyes well.

"Do you know which hospital?"

Mum talks fast and angry. "After all he did to you girls. After all he put our family through. You're gonna forgive him? He's never so much as said he was sorry. You're a fool Francine...a goddamn fool."

"I forgave him a long time ago, Mum, but now I need to tell him."

"Go ahead...Call him! He's at the Portland hospital. Do whatcha' want, but don't say I didn't tell you so."

The call ends, and a lump invades my throat. I think of the other guys who took what wasn't theirs and Aunt Mable who was pure evil. I might not be able to make it right with them right now, but this, this thing I could.

Before talking myself out of it, I force my fingers to dial 4-1-1. The silence stretches, and I wait for the operator to connect me.

My hands tremble without permission and butterflies freestyle in my stomach. Voices, so many voices, entangle my thoughts.

Should I be doing this? What if he doesn't recall or worse, what if he denies it all?

I listen for him to say 'hello' and gaze out the kitchen window at my three boys, Myles, Seth, and Ethan, playing baseball with their dad and tagging bases marked with shoes. I smile at how fortunate I am, and my eyes well at the memories that pop up.

I remember when I was eleven and the doctor saying, "The damage is too great. I don't know if she can have children."

I remember Mum crying.

I remember, in detail, the little brown house with the mustard-trimmed door that was tucked between Grammy Dodge's farmhouse and Aunt Mable's trailer in Canaan, Maine. The backsides of our properties were fenced in by Grandpa's junkyard with a thin stretch of pines separating the garbled metal from our view and cornfields bordered both sides—one to the left of Grammy's house and the other to the right of Mable's.

But the giggling from outside brings me back. My hands shake, and I press the receiver against my ear and stare out the kitchen window.

"Hello," a weak and gravelly voice says.

It's him!

A sinking feeling comes over me as I remember the two dimes and a nickel he always gave me, the mafia-styled car, the six-legged octopus, the green school bus, and the spring of '87 when warm chocolate chip cookies exchanged hands—I was thirteen.

The sound of his voice makes me feel small as if it's me *David*, and him, *Goliath,* again. Fear pumps through my veins like it did when I was small, and I push the button to end the call.

Despite the sweaty palms and knot in my throat, I summon the courage to dial him back. When I hear his voice the second time, I breathe deep.

"This is Francine! Please don't hang up," I say in one breath.

I pause and listen. No dial tone. So, I keep going.

"I forgive you! I release you of your burden."

Once the words are out, I feel my heart thud against my chest. These are the words I've wanted to say for some time. These are the words that I needed to say to be totally free.

I press the phone against my ear and wait for a dial tone.

When there is none, I quickly say, "We both know it hasn't done your heart any good carrying this burden around. Do you know what burden I'm referring to?"

There's a long pause.

I add, "I know you're not alone, because I can hear others in your room, so if 'ayuh' is the only answer you can give, then 'ayuh' is fine with me."

His breathing is labored, and I count in my head: one Mississippi, two Mississippi, three Mississippi, four Mississippi.

"Ayuh," he responds.

I squeeze the receiver in my hand and push back the urge to weep out loud.

"I know the doctors don't expect you to make it through the night, so I want you to know I'm praying for you."

"Thanks, I need all the prayer I can get right now," he says.

I gaze at the plush green fern growing on the porch and am drawn back to the relentless winters in Maine, where the true sign of spring was not a day indicated on the calendar but by the sighting of the emerald-green fiddlehead. All ferns start with the fiddlehead. The fiddlehead is a fern before it unfolds.

"Goodbye," I say as I pick up the pen and begin to write, glad that this season of my life has finally drawn to a close.

About the Author

Francine Westgate is the author of *The Forgiveness Effect* and the corresponding *10-Week Bible Study Companion Guide*. Francine is an inspirational speaker and teacher. She holds her minister's license through One Way Churches International under the leadership of Bishop Lorenzo Hall and Bishop S.Y. Younger. She is the wife of Pastor William Westgate, Associate Pastor of The Ramp Church International. Together they have three sons and one granddaughter.

In the Land of Canaan is Francine's first memoir, and she has a second memoir in the works, *Fiddleheads*. Francine also shares her wisdom and knowledge as she leads The Refreshed Women's Group at The Ramp Church International in Lynchburg, VA.

Francine continues to travel and teach workshops on forgiveness, where she shares her story to empower the hurting and to help them view their wounds as a means to help others. Francine loves to study and teach the Word of God and is the director of the Christian Education Department for One Way Churches International.

To purchase *The Forgiveness Effect* and/or the interactive *10-Week Bible Study Companion Guide*, go to: www.francinewestgate.com or wherever books are sold. Please go to Amazon and/or Goodreads to leave a review for *In the Land of Canaan*.

facebook.com/francine.westgate

instagram.com/francinewestgate

youtube.com/@Francinewestgate

www.ingramcontent.com/pod-product-compliance
Lightning Source LLC
Chambersburg PA
CBHW020434130626
46549CB00001B/132